Reviews by Scholars

I congratulate Jagannathesvari prabhu on her outstanding achievement in presenting to the world a comprehensive guide to family life, based on the inspired teachings of the Vaishnava tradition. Importantly, she emphasizes the need for mutual respect between husband and wife, consistent with the example found in Vaishnava scriptures. As my friend Burke Rochford mentions, good families are the essential basis of a good society, and so this intelligent, devoted guide to family life is an invaluable service in the great attempt to save planet Earth. I wish her, and her book, all success.
Howard J. Resnick PhD (Harvard) Sanskrit and Indian Studies. Former Professor, Graduate Theological Union, Berkeley, and University of Florida.

Rich with authentic quotes from the scriptures and thoroughly researched with commitment and passion, this book is meant for the reader who is looking for the eternal truths about marriage and family life. It is a must-read for any serious couple who are looking for a spiritually-based family life of togetherness. I highly recommend this book, not just to couples, but to pastors, priests, teachers, family therapists, marriage counselors and congregational leaders of any denomination or religious belief, but especially to those of us in ISKCON, as a guiding light for marriages in

this time of darkness. I thank Her Grace Jagannathesvari devi dasi for doing the painstaking work of putting this book together as a service to humanity. It will be a beacon of hope to generations to come and will serve as a shining instructive example of how to be blissful and happy in marriage, keeping God-Krishna in the center.
Dr. Lakshmi Dajak, MD, PhD (Louisiana) Marriage and Family Therapy.

Written largely for married devotees or for devotees requiring guidance about the purposes, duties and responsibilities of householders in the Krishna consciousness movement, *The Four Goals of Family Life* will undoubtedly be received as a welcome resource, one that presents detailed theological instruction as well as helpful commentary on key Vaishnava scriptures and texts pertaining to marriage and family life. For students and scholars of this *bhakti* movement, as well as for academics concerned with how writers within ISKCON seek both to nurture and to minister to its expanding householder community, the book will equally be a major focus of interest.
Graham Dwyer, Honorary Research Fellow,
Theology and Religious Studies, University of Winchester, UK.
Co-editor of *The Hare Krishna Movement: Forty Years of Chant and Change.*

Jagannathesvari Devi has dedicated several years to careful investigation and exploration of the teachings of Swami Prabhupada on marriage. Her new publication includes sections on sacred marriage, dharma, the life of the householder, the duties of married men and women, economic development, sense gratification and liberation. Jagannesthesvari Devi sets out to inspire readers with the spiritual vision of Vedic marriage infused with a sense of divine, sacramental purpose. It will therefore be of great value to married couples seeking guidance and to devotees seeking to nurture the next generation in the values of Vedic culture. However, scholars and students of religions will also be grateful to Jagannathesvari Devi for gathering together dispersed material from Swami Prabhupada's various translations and purports. She gives valuable and illuminating insights into Prabhupada's understanding of the ideals and role models that should regulate the grhastha ashram, and correspondingly his often critical attitudes to the changes in marriage that have taken place in the modern world.

Dr Anna S King, University Reader,
Theology and Religious Studies, University of Winchester.
Convenor: Spalding Symposium on Indian Religions.
Editor: *Religions of South Asia (ROSA)*.

Jagannathesvari Devi's excellent book is based mainly upon the teachings of A.C. Bhaktivedanta Swami Prabhupada (1896-1977) who was the Founding Acarya of the International Society for Krishna Consciousness. Bhaktivedanta Swami had a deep interest in social ethics and this book offers an extensive collection of his quotes supporting the dharma of marriage. However, this book aims to reach an audience beyond practitioners of Hindu dharma and as such is non-sectarian, as it aspires to further the practice and culture of Hindu marriage in the contemporary world; as such, it may be considered within the realm of 'Humanistic Hinduism'. In other words, it offers the Hindu tradition a vital and broad interpretation as a contribution to contemporary global values and culture.

Dr. Ithamar Theodor,
The Professorship in Indian Religions and Culture,
The Chinese University of Hong Kong.

The Four Goals of Family Life is a superb, useful application of Vedic philosophy and Vaisnava culture to marriage and family. With thorough research and practical organization, guided by knowledge handed down by her spiritual teacher, A.C. Bhaktivedanta Swami Prabhupada, Jagannathesvari Dasi leads us through the challenges and intricacies of *grhastha-asrama*. Her experience and insights help us reach a deeper and more comprehensive understanding of Swami Prabhupada's teachings and how we may actually live them. This is an invaluable book for readers interested in Vedic knowledge and for anyone committed to imbuing family life with spiritual value.

Carl Herzig PhD,
Professor of English,
St. Ambrose University, Iowa, USA.

The FOUR GOALS *of* FAMILY LIFE

The Ancient Fourfold Path of
Happiness in Marriage Relationships

JAGANNATHESVARI DEVIDASI

GAYATRI BOOKS

GAYATRI BOOKS

Published by Gayatri Books, Highway Cottage,
Berrygrove Lane, Aldenham, Herts, WD25 8AE, UK
www.krishnamarriage.com

ISBN 978-0-9566888-0-4

First printing, 2011: 5,000 copies

Cover design by Matthew Whitlock, Purelands Media
Book design and page layout by Sākṣi Gopāla dāsa
Typeset in ScaGoudy

Paintings reproduced by
Gopikanta Debnath and Suman Paul
Plate 1 photo courtesy of Bhaktivedanta Book Trust Inc.,
used with permission

Printed by Thomson Press (India) Ltd.

To Śrīla Bhaktivinoda Ṭhākura
(1838-1914)
jewel among householders

To Śrīla AC Bhaktivedanta Swami Prabhupāda
(1896-1977)
my eternal spiritual master

To Śrīla Tamāla Kṛṣṇa Goswami
(1946-2002)
who encouraged me to write this book

"Unless there is sufficient
education on these principles
—*dharma, artha, kāma, mokṣa*—
you cannot have peaceful life
in human society."

Bhaktivedanta lecture
Śrīmad Bhāgavatam 1.16.25
Hawaii 21/1/1974

Contents

Acknowledgements

This book could not have been produced without the desires, well wishes, help and support of my family and friends, as well as the guidance and blessings of my mentors. I owe a huge debt of gratitude to all of them. I would like to offer special thanks to the following:

His Holiness Girirāj Swami for his support, encouragement, and advice. His Holiness Indradyumna Swami for his ongoing encouragement, support, and feedback. His Holiness Hṛidayānanda Goswami (Dr Howard J. Resnick) for his detailed feedback on the first chapter, helpful comments, and endorsement. His Holiness Nirañjana Swami for his interest and encouragement and for reviewing the manuscript. Professor Burke Rochford for endorsing the book and writing the foreword. Professor Carl Herzig for his feedback, encouragement, and editing advice. Her Grace Śrīdevī dasī (Dr Lakshmi Dajak) for endorsing the book on behalf of the Grihastha Vision Team of North America. His Grace Rūpa-vilāsa dāsa adhikārī for editing the manuscript and for his helpful feedback (despite the fact that our views diverged in some areas). His Grace Sākṣi Gopāla dāsa for the page design and layout. Bhaktin Devina Moteelall for proofreading the text. Mr Graham Dwyer for his technical help and advice. His Grace Gaurī dāsa adhikārī for his support and referrals. His Grace Kṛṣṇa-dharma dāsa adhikārī for furnishing a pertinent letter from Śrīla

Prabhupāda. His Grace Śaunaka Ṛṣi dāsa adhikārī for helpful referrals. His Grace Śrī Rādhā-ramaṇa dāsa adhikārī for verse references from the *Sāma Veda*. Her Grace Uttama devī dāsī for her support and referrals. Her Grace Vrajasundari devī dāsī for her friendly feedback. Her Grace Kulāṇganā devī dāsī for her unending support and encouragement.

Also, for endorsing the book before publication: His Holiness Bhaktirasāmṛta Swami, His Grace Śeṣa dāsa adhikārī, His Grace Praghoṣa dāsa adhikārī, His Grace Kṛpāmoya dāsa adhikārī, His Grace Śruti-dharma dāsa adhikārī, Dr Anna King, Dr Ithamar Theodor.

And for undertaking to review the manuscript: His Holiness Rādhānātha Swami, His Holiness Bhaktividyā Pūrṇa Swami, Her Grace Praharaṇa devī dāsī, Her Grace Viśākhā devī dāsī, Her Grace Urmilā devī dāsī (Dr Edith Best), Professor Eleanor Nesbitt.

Finally, for their encouragement, support, and tolerance, my beloved sons, Daujī and Gaurāṅga Kṛpa. And my greatest debt of gratitude goes to my beloved husband, His Grace Viśvambhara dāsa adhikārī, for his unending support, guidance, tolerance, and patience, as well as for commissioning the artwork, touching up the paintings, overseeing every stage of the production of the book, and making it all possible.

Preface

This book has been produced to respond to a general shortage of available reading matter on marriage and relationships from ancient classical sources. In the present climate of high divorce rates, leading to a sad increase in broken families, there are lessons to be learnt from ancient societies that flourished and prospered on the basis of stable marriages and united families. For householders of today it can be a tough challenge to simply maintain a family and keep it together in harmony. Both husbands and wives could sometimes benefit from some divine inspiration and guidance.

This book focusses specifically on the Āryan civilisation of ancient India, which was prominent on the world stage until it began to decline approximately five thousand years ago. The leaders of that society were guided by *brāhmaṇa* priests who were well-versed in the *Vedas* and other corollary works, collectively known as the 'Vedic literatures'. The most important of these texts have been preserved to this day in their original Sanskrit versions, and many of them are now available in English and other modern languages.

The Vedic literatures cover a vast array of topics, including theology, philosophy, grammar, logic, mathematics, astronomy, astrology, medicine, architecture, politics, and sociology, to name but a few. The Āryan civilisation that was built around these teachings became culturally advanced and globally influential. The Vedic society was organised in pursuance of the *varṇāśrama* system of social and spiritual co-operation, with specific guidelines and directives for people according to their occupation and stage of life.

The Four Goals of Family Life is based on the most essential of Vedic teachings for householders, translated into modern terms. The main principles of these teachings are relevant and valuable, not only for people of a particular time in history or of a particular geographical location, but for all householders and families, beyond the limits of time and space. *The Four Goals of Family Life* explains how married couples can build strong and lasting relationships by following classical guidelines and co-operating together to balance out their material and spiritual goals. In today's world, where Vedic culture and *varṇāśrama* have been replaced by moral decline and social chaos, the main principles of Vedic spiritual and social teachings are as relevant and urgent as ever before.

The Four Goals of Family Life is mainly based on the translations and commentaries of His Divine Grace A.C. Bhaktivedanta Swami Prabhupāda, together with works of some of his predecessors in the line of spiritual masters descending from Śrīla Madhvācārya and Śrī Caitanya Mahāprabhu. The Vedic scriptures contain vast and detailed spiritual knowledge, most of which I have touched upon only briefly, due to the constraints of the subject matter at hand. For further study I recommend the books of His Divine Grace A.C. Bhaktivedanta Swami Prabhupāda from the Bhaktivedanta Book Trust.

His Divine Grace A.C. Bhaktivedanta Swami Prabhupāda

Śrīla A. C. Bhaktivedanta Swami Prabhupāda, Founder-*ācārya* of ISKCON, descends from the ancient line of spiritual masters known as the Brahma-Madhva-Gauḍīya-*sampradāya*. He is the author of more than eighty books, including English translations and summary studies of classical Vedic scriptures, together with detailed purports and commentaries.

Lord Śiva and Pārvatī-devī

Lord Śiva is the topmost Vaiṣṇava husband, and is traditionally worshipped in India by unmarried girls who are seeking a good husband. His devoted wife is the goddess Pārvatī, daughter of the Himalayas. Lord Śiva lives as an ascetic, absorbed in meditation on the Supreme Personality of Godhead.
[Ch 1 p 18]

Lakṣmī-devī (the goddess of fortune) and Lord Nārāyaṇa

"A man should be an ideal servant of the Lord, and a woman should be an ideal wife like the goddess of fortune. Then both husband and wife will be so faithful and strong that by acting together they will return home, back to Godhead, without a doubt."
(ŚB 7.11.29 purport) [Ch 4 p 124]

SĪTĀ-DEVĪ REUNITED WITH LORD RĀMACANDRA

"Lord Rāmacandra could have produced hundreds and thousands of Sītās from His pleasure energy, but just to show the duty of a faithful husband, He not only rescued Sītā from the hands of Rāvaṇa but also killed Rāvaṇa and all the members of his family." (ŚB 5.19.5 purport) [Ch 5 p 154]

THE DISROBING OF PRINCESS DRAUPADĪ

The five Pāṇḍava brothers waged war against their cousins and defeated them to restore the honour of their chaste wife Draupadī, who had been dishonoured in the court of Hastināpura. "Once Draupadī was dragged out, and attempts were made to insult her by stripping her naked in the vicious assembly of the Kurus. The Lord saved Draupadī by supplying an immeasurable length of cloth." (ŚB 1.8.24 purport) [Ch 5 p 154-5]

Śrī-Śrī Rādhā-Kṛṣṇa in the Rainy Season

The conjugal pastimes of Śrī Kṛṣṇa with Śrīmatī Rādhārāṇī and the other *gopīs* can never be gross or mundane. Their mutual dealings are supremely cultured and refined, never tinged by selfishness or material lust, but constantly driven by their unending emotions of sublime love for one another.
[Ch 7 p 296]

SUDĀMĀ BRĀHMAṆA EMBRACED BY LORD KṚṢṆA

Sudāmā's wife, being concerned for his welfare, requested him to approach Lord Kṛṣṇa in Dvārakā for help... The Lord was so moved by Sudāmā's love for Him and by his renunciation, that He bestowed great wealth on the poor *brāhmaṇa*.
[Ch 8 p 318]

Śrī Caitanya Mahāprabhu distributed Kṛṣṇa-*prema* by introducing the congregational chanting of the *mahā-mantra* (Hare Kṛṣṇa, Hare Kṛṣṇa, Kṛṣṇa Kṛṣṇa, Hare Hare; Hare Rāma, Hare Rāma, Rāma Rāma, Hare Hare) throughout the sub-continent of India. He was accompanied by His four principal associates, and together they are known as Pañca-tattva (the Absolute Truth in five features). [Ch 8 p 336]

Foreword

"...wherever there aren't householders, a religion can't live. [Religion] needs to have a matrix in which it is embedded."
—Rabbi Zalman Schachter-Shalomi 2003, 88

Historically religion and the family have existed in close relationship. Religion legitimates family patterns and relationships while the family promotes religious values that shape how each generation interprets and acts in the world. Owing to its importance, churches, temples, synagogues and mosques have historically legitimated the family by providing rituals that celebrate family unity and by providing normative guidelines and teachings expressly meant to protect the family and its members. As the noted sociologist of religion Robert Wuthnow (1999, 69) reminds us, "the most memorable aspects of growing up religious occur within families, especially through the daily routines and sacred objects, the holidays, and the intimate relationships of which families are composed."

Perhaps no development has been more consequential for the development of the International Society for Krishna Consciousness (ISKCON) than the growth and expansion of marriage and family life. By 1980, there were about an equal number of married and unmarried members residing within ISKCON's North American communities. By the early 1990s, less than one in five had never been married (Rochford 2007). Although appearing somewhat later in time, a similar pattern emerged in Western Europe and Australia and then in South America and Eastern Europe, as ISKCON became a global movement over the course of the 1980s and 1990s. Not surprisingly, the increase in marriage was accompanied by a growing number of children, many of whom were educated during their younger years within ISKCON schools. As this suggests, by the mid-1990s ISKCON had become a householder's movement.

Although householder life prevailed, numerous misconceptions served to undermine the legitimacy of marriage and family life within ISKCON (see Rochford 2007). Moreover, because the movement's leadership favored preaching and missionary work, little emphasis was placed on building and sustaining a domestic culture supportive of families. Without a religious culture inclusive of families, householders and their children found it difficult to live securely and peacefully in spiritual life. Yet, as Prabhupada emphasized, married couples can attain *moksa* or spiritual liberation by living in accordance with religious principles. *Artha* (economic development) and *kama* (sense gratification) only become spiritualized when a religious culture honors and supports married people and their children.

I give brief attention to ISKCON's history to underscore how crucial family life is to the development of religious communities and organizations. In light of this history, Jagannathesvari devi dasi's The *Four Goals of Family Life* is an especially welcome contribution. In reading the text, I found myself repeating over and over how I wished it had been available to the devotee community 30 or more years ago. While it is true that Prabhupada made a number of controversial statements relating to women's roles and polygamy, the fact is that few devotees had more than a partial grasp of his scriptural commentaries and spoken words on marriage and family life. What we learn in this thoroughly researched, comprehensive and thoughtfully organized book is that marriage and family are at the very center of Vedic culture. Like all societies and cultures, Vedic culture rests upon the many and varied contributions of husbands, wives, and children.

The Four Goals of Family Life is essential reading for any devotee considering marriage and starting a family. Many long married devotees will also benefit from reading this text, as it presents the recipe for success in marriage and family life, recognizing the need for balancing the demands of material life with the pursuit of spiritual growth and realization. I offer my thanks to Jagannathesvari devi dasi for dispelling the myths and reclaiming the spiritual basis of marriage and family life. She brings honor and respect to the many devotees committed to the wellbeing of their families in the service of Krishna. This in itself is an impressive achievement.

E. Burke Rochford, Jr.
Professor of Sociology and Religion
Middlebury College, USA
Author of *Hare Krishna Transformed* and *Hare Krishna in America*

References

Rochford, E. Burke, Jr. 2007. *Hare Krishna Transformed*. New York: New York University Press.

Schachter-Shalomi, Zalman. 2003. "Interview, April 25, 2001." In Harold Kasimow, John P. Keenan and Linda Klepinger Keenan (eds.), *Beside Still Water: Jews, Christians, and the Way of the Buddha*, pp. 85-97. Boston: Wisdom Publications.

Wuthnow, Robert. 1999. *Growing Up Religious: Christians and Jews and Their Journeys of Faith*. Boston: Beacon.

Introduction

The Four Goals of Family Life is a guide book for married or betrothed couples who are interested in pursuing harmony, ethical living, and spiritual culture. While the reference material is drawn from the Vedic tradition, the book is non-sectarian in as much as it is not limited in relevance to any particular ethnic group or religious denomination. Vedic knowledge is meant to be applicable to everyone and is not limited by time or space.

The four goals of family life are identified in Vedic philosophy as *dharma* (religious principles, or righteous action), *artha* (economic development), *kāma* (gratification of the senses), and *mokṣa* (spiritual liberation). To pursue the four goals is to lead a balanced life in which material and spiritual progress are both valued.

Religious principles, or codes of righteous action, known as *dharma*, are prescribed in ancient scriptures and taught by saints and sages. According to Vedic literatures, those who follow their prescribed *dharma*, or religious duties, and regulate their *artha* (economic development) and *kāma* (sense gratification) according to *dharma*, can ultimately attain *mokṣa* (spiritual liberation). *The Four Goals of Family Life* describes how, by pursuing these four goals according to scriptural directives, married couples can live happily and peacefully together and at the same time make spiritual advancement. While our lifestyles and thought patterns are influenced by the time, place and society in which we live, at the same time, because the basic characteristics of human nature do not change, the most fundamental secrets of happiness and progress in human life remain always the same. These secrets can be found in the teachings of enlightened sages from the past and present.

Vedic teachings explain that there are three modes of material nature, known as goodness, passion and ignorance, which constantly influence our desires and activities. The mode of goodness, which is cultivated by pursuing *dharma*, is conducive to knowledge and happiness. Conflict and suffering are products of the modes of passion and ignorance, which take over when *dharma* is neglected. By learning how to recognise these modes and deal with them, we can cultivate lasting peace and harmony in our lives and relationships.

Modern society has become ravaged by the internal destructive forces of marital conflict and divorce. In ancient Vedic society, marriages and families were stable and enduring. While making leaps and bounds in material advancement, Western society has become culturally and spiritually deficient, with the tragic consequence that marriages and families are breaking apart daily. The Vedic paradigm reveals how marriages that are focussed solely on material goals, such as economic development and sense gratification, are vulnerable. When material desires are unfulfilled, relationships can be affected, and marriages are put at risk. Marriages that foster the pursuance of all four goals, balancing both material and spiritual aspirations, are more likely to endure. A marriage relationship that enters the spiritual dimension becomes deep and everlasting.

The teachings that are presented in this book are not a new invention, but are eternal and time-tested. While some of the rules of *dharma* may appear daunting to us from a modern perspective, the principles are more important than the details. If we struggle with some of the details, that should not deter us from learning to understand the main principles of *dharma*. The most basic principles of the spiritual and moral teachings of Vedic scriptures are non-different from those of any other religious scripture. For those who understand and observe the main principles of these teachings, the further details gradually begin to make sense. Since none of us are perfect, we all need instructions, ideals, and role models to follow in order to gradually elevate ourselves. If we perceive a large gap between our present position and those ideals and role models, there is no need to become discouraged. The Vedic scriptures and spiritual masters present the highest standards of human conduct to give everyone the opportunity to realise his/her full potential and attain complete freedom from suffering. As far as we are concerned, we can choose our own pace, since we are each handicapped to some degree by our own variety of *karma* and material conditioning. Simply by respecting and appreciating the teachings and examples given in the Vedic literatures, while gradually learning to follow them according to our capacity, we can ultimately attain the highest goal.

The real credit for this work belongs not to me but to my merciful spiritual master, His Divine Grace A.C. Bhaktivedanta Swami Prabhupāda, who sacrificed everything he possessed to share his knowledge with the world and deliver people from suffering.

Jagannātheśvarī devī dāsī

"Our Kṛṣṇa consciousness movement is not one-sided. People should not think that our members are sentimentalists, simply chanting and dancing. No. There are volumes of philosophy of life, from all angles of vision. *Dharma, artha, kāma, mokṣa*: from the point of view of religion, from the point of view of economic development, from the point of view of sense gratification, and from the point of view of ultimate liberation, how to go back home, back to Godhead... It is a most scientific, authorised movement, which explains how to make people happy in this world and in the next."

—Bhaktivedanta lecture, *Śrīmad Bhāgavatam* 1.1.2
London 15/8/1971

Note about referencing
Book references without an author's name refer to either ancient Vedic classics, compilations, standard Vaiṣṇava guidebooks, or summary studies or commentaries by Śrīla Bhaktivedanta Swami Prabhupāda.

Chapter One

Vivāha
Sacred Marriage

Vedic Society—Astrology—Character and Taste
Varṇa—Nature—Culture—God's Grace
Karma—Loyalty

CHAPTER ONE

VIVĀHA

—SACRED MARRIAGE—

yad etad hṛdayaṁ tava
tad astu hṛdayaṁ mama
tad idaṁ hṛdayaṁ mama
tad astu hṛdayaṁ tava

"What is your heart, let that be my heart.
What is my heart, let that be yours."
—*Sāma Veda, Brāhmaṇa* 1.3.9

MOST OF US WILL BE MARRIED, ARE married or have been married for some part of our lives. The institution of marriage is as old as human civilisation itself. It is a tradition that is honoured by every race, religion and culture throughout the world. Stable marriages produce stable families, which are the building blocks of peaceful communities and societies. The most enduring and prosperous of ancient civilisations were constructed from the strong building blocks of traditional marriage and family life. A classic example, and the one on which we will be mainly focussing for the purposes of this book, is the ancient Āryan civilisation of India. According to the records of ancient Sanskrit manuscripts, the Āryan civilisation was the most advanced human culture in ancient history, both materially and spiritually, as well as the most enduring and globally influential.

> "India was the motherland of our race, and Sanskrit, the mother of European languages. She was the mother of our philosophy... of our mathematics... of the ideals embodied in Christianity..."
>
> —William Durant, *The Story of Civilization*

Vedic Society

The principles and tenets on which the Āryan society was ordered can be found in the vast library of literatures it left behind, known as the 'Vedic literatures'. The word *veda* in Sanskrit means 'knowledge'. The *Vedas* and other supplementary literatures, known as Vedic literatures, are sacred books of knowledge that have been preserved in India for approximately 5,000 years in their original Sanskrit verses. The *Vedas* are believed to have originally emanated from the breathing of God.

> "The four *Vedas*—namely the *Ṛg Veda, Yajur Veda, Sāma Veda,* and *Atharva Veda*—are all emanations from the breathing of the great Personality of Godhead."
>
> —*Bṛhad-āraṇyaka Upaniṣad* 4.5.11

Formerly the Vedic teachings were transmitted aurally, from spiritual master to disciple, in an unbroken chain. The same teachings were later composed into the Vedic literatures by the great sage Śrīla Vyāsadeva for the modern age of Kali in which memory capacity has diminished. In recent times, His Divine Grace A.C. Bhaktivedanta Swami Prabhupāda, who is connected with Śrīla Vyāsadeva through the illustrious line of the ancient Brahma-Madhva-Gauḍīya-*sampradāya* of Vaiṣṇava spiritual masters, has translated some of the principal Vedic literatures into English and written scholarly purports to explain them. The largest one of these is the *Bhāgavata Purāṇa*, otherwise known as *Śrīmad Bhāgavatam*, which is considered to be the ripened fruit of the tree of Vedic knowledge.

> "There are different branches of knowledge in the Vedic writings, including sociology, politics, medicine and military art... As far as spiritual knowledge is concerned, that is also perfectly described there, and *Śrīmad-Bhāgavatam* is considered to be the ripened fruit of this desire-fulfilling tree of the *Vedas*."
>
> —*The Nectar of Devotion* 12

The society that was based on the teachings of the *Vedas* is generally referred to as 'Vedic society'. Within this Vedic society, marriage was considered to be a sacred pact, never to be broken, and family members would support and care for each other until death. Children were traditionally educated from a young age to eventually become responsible and religious householders. Girls were carefully protected by their fathers until marriage and, by the time they reached puberty, they would be already betrothed. The psychology behind this system was that a girl who was married from a young age would become faithfully devoted to her husband and vice versa, since neither of them had known another partner.

> "So this was the training. And the psychology is that if a woman is married to the first man she meets and if she is kept carefully, she becomes a staunch lover. This is the psychology. This is a good psychology for maintaining the society. Therefore, a woman, especially in India, and especially in Bengal, before attaining puberty, was married. She did not meet the husband until she attained puberty. She remained at the father's house, but she would know that: 'I am married. I have got a husband.' This is the psychology. She became very chaste, because she thought of her husband, and became more and more devoted."
>
> —Bhaktivedanta lecture, *Bhagavad-gītā* 1.40
> London 28/7/1973

In Vedic society marriages would be carefully arranged by parents for their children, in consultation with qualified astrologers to ensure good compatibility. Rooted in these cultural traditions, marriages were stable and secure, and the concept of divorce was non-existent.

> "In Vedic civilization the husband and wife were not separated by such man-made laws as divorce."
>
> —*Śrīmad Bhāgavatam* 4.23.25 Bhaktivedanta purport

Today most marriages are not as carefully arranged as they used to be, and the institution of marriage has become further weakened by the introduction of the divorce law. It has become easy for couples to secure a divorce, with the result that families are often torn apart and children suffer.

> "Because care is no longer taken in marriage, we now find many divorces. Indeed, divorce has now become a common affair, although formerly one's marriage would continue lifelong, and the affection between husband and wife was so great that the wife would voluntarily die when her husband died or would remain a faithful widow throughout her entire life... Marriage now takes place simply by agreement... If the boy and girl simply agree to marry, the marriage takes place. But when the Vedic system is not rigidly observed, marriage frequently ends in divorce."
>
> —*Śrīmad Bhāgavatam* 9.18.23 Bhaktivedanta purport

While the Vedic system of arranging marriages is no longer rigidly observed in society in general, it is nevertheless possible for any sincere couple to build a stable and lasting marriage by learning from the examples and teachings given in the Vedic literatures.

> "We should understand the necessity for maintaining family life in human society... The husband and wife should live in Kṛṣṇa consciousness and follow in the footsteps of Lakṣmī-Nārāyaṇa or Kṛṣṇa-Rukmiṇī. In this way peace and harmony can be possible within this world."
>
> —*Śrīmad Bhāgavatam* 4.23.25 Bhaktivedanta purport

Lakṣmī-Nārāyaṇa and Kṛṣṇa-Rukmiṇī are two different manifestations of the Supreme Lord together with His eternal consort. Kṛṣṇa is the original Personality of Godhead.

ete cāṁśa-kalāḥ puṁsaḥ
kṛṣṇas tu bhagavān svayam
indrāri-vyākulaṁ lokaṁ
mṛḍayanti yuge yuge

> "All of the above-mentioned incarnations are either plenary portions or portions of the plenary portions of the Lord, but Lord Śrī Kṛṣṇa is the original Personality of Godhead. All of them appear on planets whenever there is a disturbance created by the atheists. The Lord incarnates to protect the theists."
>
> —*Śrīmad Bhāgavatam* 1.3.28

The Vedic culture, of which there are presently some remnants left in India, was previously influential throughout the world.

> "The whole of Bhārata-varṣa (the Vedic empire) has been partitioned. This portion is called America, this portion is called Europe, and this portion is called Asia. These are the modern names. Actually, the whole planet was Bhārata-varṣa, and the whole planet was being controlled by Vedic culture."
>
> —Bhaktivedanta lecture, *Bhagavad-gītā* 2.1
> Ahmedabad 6/12/1972

Today's increasingly widespread interest in Vedic philosophical principles, such as *karma*, *dharma*, *yoga*, and *mantra* meditation, is indicative of a gradual reintegration of Vedic culture into modern world thought. This phenomenon is consistent with the historical account that cites Vedic culture as being the predominant culture of the ancient world.

> "The researcher and scholar L. A. Waddell states in his book, *The Indo Sumerian Seals Deciphered*, that the discovery and translation of the Sumerian seals along the Indus Valley give evidence that the Aryan society existed there from as long ago as 3100 B.C... He believes that the decipherment of these seals from the Indus Valley confirms that the Sumerians were actually the early Aryans and authors of Indian civilization... Thus, he concludes that it was the Aryans who were the bearers of high civilization and who spread throughout the Mediterranean, Northwest Europe, and Britain, as well as India."
>
> —Stephen Knapp, *Death of the Aryan Invasion Theory*

Astrology

The ancient science of astrology originates from the *Vedas*.

> "There are different branches of knowledge in the *Vedas*, of which astrology and pathology are two important branches necessary for the common man. So the intelligent men, generally known as the *brāhmaṇas*, took up all the different branches of Vedic knowledge to guide society."
>
> —*Śrīmad Bhāgavatam* 1.12.29 Bhaktivedanta purport

As soon as a child was born in Vedic society, a *brāhmaṇa* would draw up a horoscope to identify the nature and qualities of the child and predict significant future events in that person's life.

> "Amongst the *karma-kāṇḍa* experts, the *jātaka* expert *vipras* were good astrologers who could tell all the future history of a born child simply by the astral calculations of the time (*lagna*)."
>
> —*Śrīmad Bhāgavatam* 1.12.29 Bhaktivedanta purport

Similarly, before accepting a marriage, a family would consult with a qualified astrologer to find out if the boy and girl were compatible.

> "According to the Vedic system, the parents would consider the horoscopes of the boy and girl who were to be married. If according to astrological calculations the boy and girl were compatible in every respect, the match was called *yotaka* and the marriage would be accepted... Regardless of the affluence of the boy or the personal beauty of the girl, without this astrological compatibility the marriage would not take place."
>
> —*Srīmad Bhāgavatam* 9.18.23 Bhaktivedanta purport

Still today there are practitioners of Vedic astrology, and it is growing in popularity. Some of the factors that are taken into account by Vedic astrologers for assessing compatibility are character, taste, *varṇa*, and *gaṇa* (nature). These factors can also be studied and understood to some extent by direct perception and by hearing from close friends and acquaintances.

Character and Taste

According to Vedic knowledge, every soul is an eternally individual personality.

na tv evāhaṁ jātu nāsaṁ
na tvaṁ neme janādhipāḥ
na caiva na bhaviṣyāmaḥ
sarve vayam ataḥ param

> "Never was there a time when I did not exist, nor you, nor all these kings; nor in the future shall any of us cease to be."
>
> —*Bhagavad-gītā As It Is* 2.12

When the soul enters a material body, this individuality is reflected in the unique karmic mixture of qualities that each person carries around. According to *karma* built up from previous lives, a person takes birth at a destined time and place, and under a specific configuration of planets. These are the signposts given by nature that help astrologers to read people's characters. When two people have enough in common to connect with and understand each other, and enough that is different to attract and complement each other, they are said to be compatible. Lord Brahmā, who is the demigod in charge of creation, instructed his son, Kardama Muni, to select husbands for his daughters according to their temperaments and likings.

atas tvam ṛṣi-mukhyebhyo
yathā-śīlaṁ yathā-ruci
ātmajāḥ paridehy adya
vistṛṇīhi yaśo bhuvi

"Therefore, today please give away your daughters to these foremost sages, with due regard for the girls' temperaments and likings, and thereby spread your fame all over the universe."

—*Śrīmad Bhāgavatam* 3.24.15

Two key words of this verse in Sanskrit are *śīlam* (temperament or character) and *ruci* (liking or taste). If a man and woman are to stay together happily, they need to be compatible in terms of character and they need to like each other. Within the Vedic social tradition, when loving parents would arrange marriages for their children, they would naturally make sure that the boy and girl were happy to accept the union. The system of *svayaṁvara*, by which princesses would choose their own husbands, literally means 'personal choice'. Both character and taste can also be read by astrology.

"The nine principal *ṛṣis*, or sages, are Marīci, Atri, Aṅgirā, Pulastya, Pulaha, Kratu, Bhṛgu, Vasiṣṭha and Atharvā. All these *ṛṣis* are most important, and Brahmā desired that the nine daughters already born of Kardama Muni be handed over to them. Here two words are used very significantly—*yathā-śīlam* and *yathā-ruci*. The daughters should be handed over to the respective *ṛṣis*, not blindly, but according to the combination of character and taste. That is the art of combining a man and woman. Man and woman should not be united simply on the consideration of sex life. There are many other considerations, especially character and taste. If the taste and character differ between the man and woman, their combination will be unhappy. Even about forty years ago, in Indian marriages, the taste and character of the boy and girl were first of all matched, and then they were allowed to marry. This was done under the direction of the respective parents. The parents used to astrologically determine the character and tastes of the boy and girl, and when they corresponded, the match was selected: 'This girl and this boy are just suitable, and they should be married.' Other considerations were less important. The same system was also advised in the beginning of the creation by Brahmā: 'Your daughters should be handed over to the *ṛṣis* according to taste and character.'"

—*Śrīmad Bhāgavatam* 3.24.15 Bhaktivedanta purport

Vedic astrology can help to indicate whether feelings of attraction between a man and a woman are signs of genuine compatibility or symptoms of a temporary infatuation.

"Before marrying, one should select a wife of like disposition and not be enamored by so-called beauty or other attractive features for sense gratification."

—*Śrīmad Bhāgavatam* 3.21.15 Bhaktivedanta purport

Varṇa

Within the ancient Vedic *varṇāśrama* system of society there are four social categories, known as *varṇas*. A person's *varṇa* is recognised by his/her innate qualities and natural talents.

cātur-varṇyaṁ mayā sṛṣṭaṁ
guṇa-karma-vibhāgaśaḥ

> "According to the three modes of material nature and the work associated with them, the four divisions of human society are created by Me."
>
> —Lord Kṛṣṇa, *Bhagavad-gītā As It Is* 4.13

The modern caste system of India, according to which a person's social status is determined by the caste of the family into which he or she is born, is a perversion of the Vedic social model. The original *varṇāśrama* system recognises *varṇa* by personal qualities and activities according to the influence of the three modes of material nature: goodness, passion, and ignorance.

sattvaṁ rajas tama iti
guṇāḥ prakṛti-sambhavāḥ
nibadhnanti mahā-bāho
dehe dehinam avyayam

> "Material nature consists of three modes—goodness, passion and ignorance. When the eternal living entity comes in contact with nature, O mighty-armed Arjuna, he becomes conditioned by these modes."
>
> —*Bhagavad-gītā As It Is* 14.5

While every conditioned soul is influenced to some extent by each of the three modes, it is the predominant mode that indicates his or her natural *varṇa.* Those who are mainly in the mode of goodness are potential *brāhmaṇas* (priests or teachers); those who are more in the mode of passion are potential *kṣatriyas* (leaders or warriors); those who are in passion and ignorance combined can become *vaiśyas* (farmers or merchants); and those who are mainly in the mode of ignorance are known as *śūdras* (artisans or labourers). A man and woman who are influenced by the same modes will share similar qualities and thus relate well together.

> "Vedic astrology reveals whether one has been born in the *vipra-varṇa, kṣatriya-varṇa, vaiśya-varṇa* or *śūdra-varṇa,* according to the three qualities of material nature. This must be examined because a marriage between a boy of the *vipra-varṇa* and a girl of the *śūdra-varṇa* is incompatible; married life would be miserable for both husband and wife. Consequently a boy should marry a girl of the same category."
>
> —*Śrīmad Bhāgavatam* 6.2.26 Bhaktivedanta purport

For those who are advanced in spiritual knowledge, which transcends the three modes of material nature, considerations of *varṇa* are less important.

> "Of course, this is *trai-guṇya,* a material calculation according to the *Vedas,* but if the boy and girl are devotees there need be no such considerations. A

devotee is transcendental, and therefore in a marriage between devotees, the boy and girl form a very happy combination."

—*Śrīmad Bhāgavatam* 6.2.26 Bhaktivedanta purport

trai-guṇya-viṣayā vedā
nistrai-guṇyo bhavārjuna
nirdvandvo nitya-sattva-stho
niryoga-kṣema ātmavān

"The *Vedas* deal mainly with the subject of the three modes of material nature. O Arjuna, become transcendental to these three modes. Be free from all dualities and from all anxieties for gain and safety, and be established in the self."

—*Bhagavad-gītā As It Is* 2.45

Nature

According to Vedic vision, there are three different categories of human beings.

"A person is born in one of three categories, known as *deva-gaṇa*, *manuṣya-gaṇa* and *rakṣasa-gaṇa*."

—*Śrīmad Bhāgavatam* 9.18.23 Bhaktivedanta purport

Pious human beings who are advancing spiritually belong to *deva-gaṇa*, the divine nature; those who are on the opposite side of the spectrum fall under *rakṣasa-gaṇa*, the demoniac nature; and those who are in between the two belong to *manuṣya-gaṇa*, the human nature. Vedic literatures describe heavenly planets in the upper portion of the universe where demigods reside, and hellish planets in the lower part of the universe where demons reside. On planet Earth, which is in the middle region of the universe, there is a mixture of godly, human and demoniac natures.

> "In different parts of the universe there are demigods and demons, and in human society also some people resemble demigods whereas others resemble demons."
> —*Śrīmad Bhāgavatam* 9.18.23 Bhaktivedanta purport

While these differences in earthly humans are not as noticeable externally as the differences between heavenly demigods and demons from lower planets, they are nevertheless significant. Divine and demoniac natures do not mix together well in marriage.

> "If according to astrological calculations there was conflict between a godly and a demoniac nature, the marriage would not take place."
> —*Śrīmad Bhāgavatam* 9.18.23 Bhaktivedanta purport

Those who are born with a divine nature are interested in spiritual knowledge and are willing to respect the laws of God.

> "Those who are born with divine qualities follow a regulated life; that is to say they abide by the injunctions in scriptures and by the authorities."
> —*Bhagavad-gītā As It Is* 16.6 purport

Those who are born with a demoniac nature, on the other hand, prefer to act independently or whimsically.

> "One who does not follow the regulative principles as they are laid down in the scriptures and who acts according to his whims is called demoniac or asuric."
>
> —*Bhagavad-gītā As It Is* 16.6 purport

A person of divine nature is happy when combined together with another of the same nature, while a person of demoniac nature would be happier together with someone of that same nature.

> "According to astrological calculation, a person is classified according to whether he belongs to the godly or demoniac quality. In that way the spouse was selected. A girl of godly quality should be handed over to a boy of godly quality. A girl of demoniac quality should be handed over to a boy of demoniac quality. Then they will be happy. But if the girl is demoniac and the boy is godly, then the combination is incompatible; they cannot be happy in such a marriage. At the present moment, because boys and girls are not married according to quality and character, most marriages are unhappy, and there is divorce."
>
> —*Śrīmad Bhāgavatam* 3.24.15 Bhaktivedanta purport

Culture

For those who are interested in spiritual advancement, culture plays an important part in the selection of a compatible partner.

> "Svayambhuva Manu was the emperor, but he went to offer his qualified daughter to a poor *brāhmaṇa*. Kardama Muni had no worldly possessions—he was a hermit living in the forest—but he was advanced in culture. Therefore, in offering one's daughter to a person, the culture and quality are counted as prominent, not wealth or any other material consideration."
> —*Śrīmad Bhāgavatam* 3.22.13 Bhaktivedanta purport

Kardama Muni was a poor *brāhmaṇa*, while Devahuti was the daughter of a great emperor, Svayambhuva Manu. Because she was interested in spiritual culture, she renounced her riches and accepted poverty to become the wife of the sage Kardama. Similarly, Lord Śiva is the topmost Vaiṣṇava husband, and is traditionally worshipped in India by unmarried girls who are seeking a good husband. His devoted wife is the goddess Pārvatī, daughter of the Himalayas. Lord Śiva lives as an ascetic, absorbed in meditation on the Supreme Personality of Godhead. While it is not necessary for householders to try to imitate Lord Śiva or Kardama Muni by renouncing all their possessions and moving into a cave or a hut with their wives and children, at the same time we can learn from the examples of these elevated souls that spiritual culture is more important than wealth. Wealth, fame and position are temporary attributes that come and go according to past *karma*, while spiritual advancement is never lost.

nehābhikrama-nāśo 'sti
pratyavāyo na vidyate
sv-alpam apy asya dharmasya
trāyate mahato bhayāt

"In this endeavor there is no loss or diminution, and a little advancement on this path can protect one from the most dangerous type of fear."

—*Bhagavad-gītā As It Is* 2.40

God's Grace

Ultimately it is by the will of Providence that two individuals are brought together.

"Only by God's grace can one get a nice wife just as he desires. Similarly, it is only by God's grace that a girl gets a husband suitable to her heart."

—*Śrīmad Bhāgavatam* 3.21.28 Bhaktivedanta purport

The soul requires the sanction of God in order to find his or her destined life partner.

"Without the sanction of the Supreme Soul, the individual soul cannot do anything."

—*Bhagavad-gītā As It Is* 13.23 purport

Thus, the prayer factor plays an essential part in the search for the right partner.

"Thus it is said that if we pray to the Supreme Lord in every transaction of our material existence, everything will be done nicely and just suitable to our heart's desire. In other words, in all circumstances we must take shelter of the Supreme Personality of Godhead and depend completely on His decision. Man proposes, God disposes. The fulfilment of desires, therefore, should be entrusted to the Supreme Personality of Godhead; that is the nicest solution... If we depend on the choice of the Supreme Personality of Godhead, we will receive benedictions in greater opulence than we desire."

—*Śrīmad Bhāgavatam* 3.21.28 Bhaktivedanta purport

Karma

Married couples may be brought together either by the direct grace of God or indirectly by His laws of *karma*. In many cases there is an element of both. For those who take shelter of the Lord, He reduces to a great extent the burden of their *karma*. While the grace of God is invoked by prayer, *karma* is set into motion as a result of our past activities, from this life and from previous lives.

aniṣṭam iṣṭaṁ miśraṁ ca
tri-vidhaṁ karmaṇaḥ phalam
bhavaty atyāgināṁ pretya
na tu sannyāsināṁ kvacit

"For one who is not renounced, the threefold fruits of action—desirable, undesirable and mixed—accrue after death."

—*Bhagavad-gītā As It Is* 18.12

Consequent to our desires and previous activities, we are brought together with others who share a similar *karma*. Once a marriage has been entered into, knowledge of the principle of *karma* also helps to protect the marital relationship. According to our *karma*, each one of us is allotted a certain amount of happiness and a certain amount of distress in a lifetime.

> "Every living entity has a predestined happiness and distress in his present body; this is called the law of *karma*."
>
> —*Śrīmad Bhāgavatam* 3.27.8 Bhaktivedanta purport

By understanding how *karma* works, and by accepting responsibility for our own *karma*, we can avoid the common mistake of blaming our husband, wife, other people or external circumstances when we face difficulties in life. This knowledge thus helps us to avoid criticising others and to remember to first examine our own shortcomings.

> "One mistake of judgment often made by the neophyte devotees is that any time there is some disturbance or some difficulty they are considering that the conditions or the external circumstances under which the difficulty took place are the cause of the difficulty itself. That is not the fact. In this material world there is always some difficulty, no matter whether in this situation or that situation. Therefore, simply by changing my status of occupation or my status of life, that will not help anything. Because the real fact is that if there is any difficulty with others, that is my lack of Kṛṣṇa consciousness, not theirs."
>
> —*Letters from Śrīla Prabhupāda* 4/1/1973

Peace and happiness in marriage are found by those who avoid imposing inflated expectations on their partners and learn to accept them as they are, appreciating their good qualities and overlooking their faults. Those who understand the principle of *karma* and develop a philosophical outlook towards the ups and downs of life, while at the same time being kind and caring in their relationships, can attain peace, and are very dear to God.

> "He for whom no one is put into difficulty and who is not disturbed by anxiety, who is steady in happiness and distress, is very dear to Me."
>
> —*Bhagavad-gītā As It Is* 12.15

Those souls who surrender to the Supreme Lord, accepting both the good and bad results of their *karma* without protesting, earn the right to ultimately enter His kingdom.

tat te 'nukampāṁ susamīkṣamāṇo
bhuñjāna evātma-kṛtaṁ vipākam
hṛd-vāg-vapurbhir vidadhan namas te
jīveta yo mukti-pade sa dāya-bhāk

> "My dear Lord, one who earnestly waits for You to bestow Your causeless mercy upon him, all the while patiently suffering the reactions of his past misdeeds and offering You respectful obeisances with his heart, words and body, is surely eligible for liberation, for it has become his rightful claim."
>
> —*Śrīmad Bhāgavatam* 10.14.8

There is only one person in existence who is not subject to the laws of *karma* and that is the Supreme Personality of Godhead. He alone can modify or eradicate karmic reactions for those who devote themselves to Him.

yas tv indra-gopam atha vendram aho sva-karma-
bandhānurūpa-phala-bhājanam ātanoti
karmāṇi nirdahati kintu ca bhakti-bhājāṁ
govindam ādi-puruṣaṁ tam ahaṁ bhajāmi

"I adore the primeval Lord Govinda, who burns up to their roots all fruitive activities of those who are imbued with devotion and impartially ordains for each the due enjoyment of the fruits of one's activities, of all those who walk in the path of work, in accordance with the chain of their previously performed works, no less in the case of the tiny insect that bears the name of *indragopa* than in that of Indra, king of the *devas*."

—*Śrī Brahma-saṁhitā* 5.54

Loyalty

Those who see the hand of the Lord behind everything, including their marriages, learn to value their partners as God-given companions and accept them as they are. This understanding helps them to stick together with their spouses, through thick and thin, and remain always loyal.

"You must accept whomever God has given you as husband or wife..."

—*Conversations with Śrīla Prabhupāda*, Baltimore 7/7/1976

Every conditioned soul in the material world is subject to the influence of false ego, which is manifest in the desire to be number one.

> "In fact, the pure soul is entangled in the material world because the mind is involved with the false ego, which desires to lord it over material nature."
>
> —*Bhagavad-gītā As It Is* 6.5 purport

Therefore, there are naturally sometimes disagreements between husband and wife. By understanding what is false ego and recognising how it influences our behaviour, we can learn how to detach ourselves from it and become more humble. Instead of becoming discouraged by conflict, if we accept it as a challenge and a test, then by facing it and overcoming it, we strengthen our relationships. Couples argue and get upset, and afterwards they calm down, apologise, and make up. This is a common scenario of the early years of a marriage and is part of the process of building a strong, close relationship. By passing through conflict, we reveal our flaws to each other, and build an honest partnership. As a relationship becomes closer and stronger, based on a secure foundation of love and trust, differences are more easily resolved. Misunderstandings are quickly overcome for those who avoid taking them seriously. A sense of humour is a vital ingredient for defusing tension and pre-empting conflict in a healthy marital relationship.

> "In this material world we have to pass through many circumstances, but sometimes, even if it is intolerable, we have to tolerate. According to the Hindu conception of life, even if there is some misunderstanding between the husband and wife, it is not taken very seriously... Mahātmā Gandhi was

> married when he was a student, sixteen years old, and his wife was also of the same age. Later on, Mahātmā Gandhi became a very famous man. One day there was a quarrel between the husband and the wife. Mahātmā Gandhi has written in his own biography that he drove away his wife: 'You get out of my house.' So the wife left the house and was crying in the street, 'Where shall I go?' Mahātmā Gandhi went there, and said, 'Come on.' Even between Mahātmā Gandhi and his wife there was a quarrel. However, this quarrel of husband and wife is not a very serious thing. I'll request you, even there is some misunderstanding, forget it. Don't take it seriously. Simply you concentrate on the business of Kṛṣṇa consciousness."
>
> Bhaktivedanta lecture, wedding, Los Angeles 25/12/1968

While a high compatibility rating is favourable for a potentially happy marriage, it does not offer an unconditional guarantee. Strong and healthy relationships take time to cultivate, and they require regular nourishment in the form of service, respect, appreciation, kindness, patience and affection. Even where there are factors of incompatibility between two horoscopes, a strong marriage can be built and maintained by the above forms of nourishment, and by mutual co-operation in the service of God. A husband and wife who constantly nourish their mutual relationship by expressing care and affection for each other, through word and action, become happy together, and all their other relationships also benefit as a result. Religious marriage is a sacred pact.

> "You should always remember that marriage means no separation, no divorce, lifetime."
>
> —Bhaktivedanta lecture, wedding, West Virginia 4/6/1969

Those who keep God in the centre of their marriage by serving Him together, with love and devotion, can achieve peace and harmony.

bhoktāraṁ yajña-tapasāṁ
sarva-loka-maheśvaram
suhṛdaṁ sarva-bhūtānāṁ
jñātvā māṁ śāntim ṛcchati

> "A person in full consciousness of Me, knowing Me to be the ultimate beneficiary of all sacrifices and austerities, the Supreme Lord of all planets and demigods, and the benefactor and well-wisher of all living entities, attains peace from the pangs of material miseries."
>
> —Lord Kṛṣṇa, *Bhagavad-gītā As It Is* 5.29

By remaining loyal to God and to each other, a husband and wife can build an unbreakable partnership. Between devotees of the Lord, spiritual relationships are eternal.

> "Our relationship is eternal. There is no separation. And this marriage is primarily for advancing Kṛṣṇa consciousness. Bodily relationship is secondary. That is not a very important thing. Our first engagement is Kṛṣṇa consciousness."
>
> —Bhaktivedanta lecture, wedding, Los Angeles 25/12/1968

CHAPTER TWO

Gṛhastha-āśrama
SPIRITUAL HOUSEHOLD LIFE

Spiritual Culture—The Safe Side
The Normal Condition—The Fortress
The Four Goals

Chapter Two

Gṛhastha-Āśrama

—Spiritual Household Life—

mānasa, deha, geha, yo kichu mora
arpiluṅ tuyā pade nanda-kiśora!

"Mind, body, home and family, whatever may be mine, I have offered at your lotus feet, O youthful son of Nanda!"

—Bhaktivinoda Ṭhākura, *Śaraṇāgati*

According to Vedic culture, human society is traditionally arranged into four *varṇas* (occupational divisions) and four *āśramas* (spiritual life stages), collectively known as the *varṇāśrama* system. The purpose of this system is to provide every member of society with an occupational and social identity, based on individual nature and qualities, and to accordingly define the duties and activities that will be most beneficial for each person's progress, both materially and spiritually. The ancient Āryan civilisation was organised according to this system.

> "*Āryan* means those who follow the *varṇāśrama-dharma*. They are Āryans. In India they were following strictly this *varṇāśrama-dharma*; therefore they were Āryans. Not now, but formerly they were."
>
> —Bhaktivedanta lecture, *Śrīmad Bhāgavatam* 6.2.2
> Vṛndāvana 6/9/1975

In present-day India there can be found superficial remnants of the *varṇāśrama* system, but the original core principles of *varṇāśrama* have been forgotten. *Varṇa* is now known as 'caste' and is identified by birth alone, instead of by *guṇa* and *karma* (nature and activity), and *āśrama* training has been superseded by a westernised system of education. Within the original *varṇāśrama* system, spiritual culture was prioritised throughout human life, from childhood to old age.

> "The whole *varṇāśrama* system is so designed that each and every status of life is called an *āśrama*. This means that spiritual culture is the common factor for all."
>
> —*Śrīmad Bhāgavatam* 1.7.2 Bhaktivedanta purport

Not only the hermitage but also the household was considered to be an *āśrama*, or a place for cultivating spiritual knowledge.

> "Śrīla Vyāsadeva was a householder, yet his residential place is called an *āśrama*. An *āśrama* is a place where spiritual culture is always foremost. It does not matter whether the place belongs to a householder or a mendicant."
>
> —*Śrīmad Bhāgavatam* 1.7.2 Bhaktivedanta purport

The four stages of life are known as *brahmacārī-āśrama* (student life), *gṛhastha-āśrama* (household life), *vānaprastha-āśrama* (retirement), and *sannyāsa-āśrama* (renunciation).

> "The *brahmacārīs*, the *gṛhasthas*, the *vānaprasthas* and the *sannyāsīs* all belong to the same mission of life, namely, realization of the Supreme. Therefore none of them are less important as far as spiritual culture is concerned. The difference is a matter of formality on the strength of renunciation. The *sannyāsīs* are held in high estimation on the strength of practical renunciation."
>
> —*Śrīmad Bhāgavatam* 1.7.2 Bhaktivedanta purport

According to Vedic culture, householders who are striving for spiritual advancement are known as *gṛhasthas*, and those who are dedicated to material advancement are known as *gṛhamedhīs*.

> "In the revealed scriptures there are two nomenclatures for the householder's life. One is *gṛhastha*, and the other is *gṛhamedhī*. The *gṛhasthas* are those who live together with wife and children but live transcendentally for realizing the ultimate truth. The *gṛhamedhīs*, however, are those who live only for the benefit of the family members, extended or centralized, and thus are envious of others. The word *medhī* indicates jealousy of others."
>
> —*Śrīmad Bhāgavatam* 2.1.2 Bhaktivedanta purport

Spiritual Culture

Spiritual culture begins with knowledge, by learning to understand the difference between matter and spirit.

nāsato vidyate bhāvo
nābhāvo vidyate sataḥ
ubhayor api dṛṣṭo 'ntas
tv anayos tattva-darśibhiḥ

"Those who are seers of the truth have concluded that of the non-existent (the material body) there is no endurance and of the eternal (the soul) there is no change. This they have concluded by studying the nature of both."

—*Bhagavad-gītā* As It Is 2.16

The position of the eternal spirit soul, which resides within the material body, is described as follows.

na jāyate mriyate vā kadācin
nāyaṁ bhūtvā bhavitā vā na bhūyaḥ
ajo nityaḥ śāśvato 'yaṁ purāṇo
na hanyate hanyamāne śarīre

"For the soul there is neither birth nor death at any time. He has not come into being, does not come into being, and will not come into being. He is unborn, eternal, ever-existing and primeval. He is not slain when the body is slain."

—*Bhagavad-gītā* As It Is 2.20

Vedic literatures describe how, when the material body perishes, the eternal soul transmigrates to another temporary material body.

dehino 'smin yathā dehe
kaumāraṁ yauvanaṁ jarā
tathā dehāntara-prāptir
dhīras tatra na muhyati

> "As the embodied soul continuously passes, in this body, from boyhood to youth to old age, the soul similarly passes into another body at death. A sober person is not bewildered by such a change."
>
> —*Bhagavad-gītā As It Is* 2.13

According to Vedic teachings, human life is meant for cultivating spiritual knowledge. Those who learn to understand the difference between matter and spirit can gradually learn to see others in terms of their eternal identities as spirit souls, rather than misidentifying them with their material bodies. This knowledge helps married couples to overcome conflicts of interest by relating with each other on a higher level. When they learn to see each other, beyond the body, mind, false ego, and social conditioning, as eternal spirit souls, they become deeply connected on that level. According to Vedic scriptures, all spirit souls are part and parcel of God, and their eternal constitutional position is to be engaged in His service.

jīvera 'svarūpa' haya—kṛṣṇera 'nitya-dāsa'
kṛṣṇera 'taṭasthā-śakti' 'bhedābheda-prakāśa'

sūryāṁśa-kiraṇa, yaiche agni-jvālā-caya
svābhāvika kṛṣṇera tina-prakāra 'śakti' haya

> "It is the living entity's constitutional position to be an eternal servant of Kṛṣṇa because he is the marginal energy of Kṛṣṇa and a manifestation simultaneously one with and different from the Lord, like a molecular particle of sunshine or fire. Kṛṣṇa has three varieties of energy."
>
> —*Śrī Caitanya-caritāmṛta, Madhya-līlā* 20.108-9

By serving the Supreme Personality of Godhead, under the guidance of a bona fide spiritual master, one can gradually reawaken his/her eternal love for the Lord.

abhidheya-nāma 'bhakti', 'prema'—prayojana
puruṣārtha-śiromaṇi prema mahā-dhana

> "Devotional service, or sense activity for the satisfaction of the Lord, is called *abhidheya* because it can develop one's original love of Godhead, which is the goal of life. This goal is the living entity's topmost interest and greatest wealth. Thus one attains the platform of transcendental loving service unto the Lord."
>
> —*Śrī Caitanya-caritāmṛta, Madhya-līlā* 20.125

By reviving their original love for God, devotees simultaneously develop love for all living entities, since they are all part and parcel of the Supreme Lord.

> "When love of Godhead is attained, love for all other beings automatically follows because the Lord is the sum total of all living beings."
>
> —Bhaktivedanta introduction to *Śrīmad Bhāgavatam*

Those who extend their love to all living entities will certainly include in that love their spouses and families, who naturally occupy a special place in their hearts. According to *Śrī Upadeśāmṛta* by Rūpa Gosvāmī, there are six varieties of affectionate exchanges through which devotees demonstrate their spiritual love for one another.

dadāti pratigṛhṇāti
guhyam ākhyāti pṛcchati
bhuṅkte bhojayate caiva
ṣaḍ-vidhaṁ prīti-lakṣaṇam

> "Offering gifts in charity, accepting charitable gifts, revealing one's mind in confidence, inquiring confidentially, accepting *prasāda* and offering *prasāda* are the six symptoms of love shared by one devotee and another."
>
> —*The Nectar of Instruction* 4

Couples can strengthen and sweeten their relationships by engaging in these six loving exchanges – sharing together whatever they possess, revealing their minds in confidence to one another, and feeding each other with *prasāda* (food that has been offered to God).

> "Even in ordinary social activities, these six types of dealings between two loving friends are absolutely necessary... Thus whenever there is a dealing of *priti*, or love in intimate dealings, these six activities are executed."
>
> —*The Nectar of Instruction* 4 purport

The secret formula for building a harmonious relationship is to keep service to God at the centre of the equation.

> "If everyone is dedicated to glorifying the Personality of Godhead, Kṛṣṇa, there will not be any impediment in mutual association. However, in a place where people have many different purposes besides the pleasure of the Supreme Lord, social dealings will certainly be disrupted."
>
> —*Śrīmad Bhāgavatam* 11.9.10 Bhaktivedanta purport

Where people are willing to leave aside their separate interests for the sake of a higher common interest, i.e. service to God, there is no scope for conflict.

The Safe Side

Since all of the four *āśramas* are meant for spiritual culture, three of them are celibate orders. The practice of celibacy is highly conducive for spiritual advancement. However, those who can observe lifelong celibacy are rare in this world, especially in the present age of Kali. Systematic progression through the four *āśramas* is therefore recommended for most people.

> "For example, those who are affected by sexual desire are ordered to accept the *vivāha-yajña*, or religious marriage ceremony. We often see that because of false pride a so-called *brahmacārī*, or celibate student of Vedic knowledge, rejects the marriage ceremony as *māyā*, or material illusion. But if such a celibate student is unable to control his senses he will undoubtedly degrade himself by eventually engaging in illicit sex, which has no connection to Vedic culture."
>
> —*Śrīmad Bhāgavatam* 11.3.45 purport by Hṛidayānanda Goswami

For most men, *gṛhastha-āśrama* is recommended to be accepted for some portion of their lives.

> "*Vivāha-yajña*, the marriage ceremony, is meant to regulate the human mind so that it may become peaceful for spiritual advancement. For most men, this *vivāha-yajña* should be encouraged even by persons in the renounced order of life."
>
> —*Bhagavad-gītā As It Is* 18.5 purport

Marriage is also recommended for all women, for their ongoing protection.

> "In childhood a woman must be subject to her father, in youth to her husband, when her lord is dead to her sons; a woman must never be independent."
>
> —*Manu-saṁhitā* 5.148

The protection of women is given high priority in Vedic culture. Women are advised to remain always dependent, under the care of either the father, husband, or grown-up sons, to protect them from the potential risk of abuse or exploitation by other men. Marriage is on the safe side for women because it protects them from the danger of being exploited by irresponsible men. And marriage is on the safe side for men because it provides some allowance for sense enjoyment without incurring the severe karmic reactions that would follow from engaging in illicit sex with unmarried girls or with other men's wives.

> "Kaśyapa meant that householders living with wives enjoy the heavenly blessings of sense enjoyment and at the same time have no fear of going down to hell."
>
> —*Śrīmad Bhāgavatam* 3.14.21 Bhaktivedanta purport

According to religious principles, anyone who is not married is supposed to observe celibacy. It is therefore safer for a married man to remain in *gṛhastha-āśrama* as long as necessary than to try to become artificially renounced by taking *sannyāsa* prematurely, and thereby incur the risk of becoming degraded.

> "The man in the renounced order of life has no wife and may be driven by sex desire to seek another woman or another's wife and thus go to hell. In other words, the so-called man of the renounced order, who has left his house and wife, goes to hell if he again desires sexual pleasure, knowingly or unknowingly. In that way the householders are on the side of safety."
>
> —*Śrīmad Bhāgavatam* 3.14.21 Bhaktivedanta purport

The Normal Condition

The *varṇāśrama* system facilitates the spiritual progress of the human being towards liberation from all material desires. Only by becoming free from sex desire can one become liberated from the cycle of birth and death in the material world.

puṁsaḥ striyā mithunī-bhāvam etaṁ
tayor mitho hṛdaya-granthim āhuḥ
ato gṛha-kṣetra-sutāpta-vittair
janasya moho 'yam ahaṁ mameti

yadā mano-hṛdaya-granthir asya
karmānubaddho dṛḍha āślatheta
tadā janaḥ samparivartate 'smād
muktaḥ paraṁ yāty atihāya hetum

"The attraction between male and female is the basic principle of material existence. On the basis of this misconception, which ties together the hearts of the male and female, one becomes attracted to his body, home, property, children, relatives and wealth. In this way one increases life's illusions and thinks in terms of 'I and mine'. When the strong knot in the heart of a person implicated in material life due to the results of past action is slackened, one turns away from his attachment to home, wife and children. In this way, one gives up the basic principle of illusion (I and mine) and becomes liberated. Thus one goes to the transcendental world."

—*Śrīmad Bhāgavatam* 5.5.8-9

To make spiritual progress towards liberation, a person must first be honest about his present condition.

> "There are four *āśramas: brahmacārī, gṛhastha, vānaprastha, sannyāsa.* Whichever *āśrama* is suitable for you, you accept it, but be sincere. Don't be a hypocrite. If you think that you want sex, all right. You marry and remain like a gentleman."
>
> —Bhaktivedanta lecture, *Śrīmad Bhāgavatam* 6.1.23
> Honolulu 23/5/1976

The importance of accepting the most suitable *āśrama* is beautifully illustrated in the story of Gajendra, the king of the elephants. One day Gajendra was enjoying a bath in a beautiful lake, surrounded by female elephants, when suddenly he was attacked by a huge crocodile who had become disturbed by their splashing. The powerful crocodile closed his jaws around Gajendra's leg and kept it tightly in his grip. The ensuing struggle lasted for a very long time. As time went on, the elephant became weaker, and the crocodile became stronger.

> "Thereafter, because of being pulled into the water and fighting for many long years, the elephant became diminished in his mental, physical and sensual strength. The crocodile, on the contrary, being an animal of the water, increased in enthusiasm, physical strength and sensual power."
>
> —*Śrīmad Bhāgavatam* 8.2.30

While the elephant was larger and more powerful than the crocodile, he was becoming weaker in the water because he was by nature a land animal; while the crocodile, who was naturally an animal of the water, was becoming stronger.

> "In the fighting between the elephant and the crocodile, the difference was that although the elephant was extremely powerful, he was in a foreign place, in the water. During one thousand years of fighting, he could not get any food, and under the circumstances his bodily strength diminished, and because his bodily strength diminished, his mind also became weak and his senses less powerful. The crocodile, however, being an animal of the water, had no difficulties. He was getting food and was therefore getting mental strength and sensual encouragement. Thus while the elephant became reduced in strength, the crocodile became more and more powerful."
>
> —*Śrīmad Bhāgavatam* 8.2.30 Bhaktivedanta purport

Drawing on this example, Bhaktivedanta Swami Prabhupāda explains the importance for us of accepting the *āśrama* for which we are most naturally suited so that we may become strong enough to fight against the attacks of the material energy. The material energy of the Lord is known as *māyā*, or 'that which is not'. The task of *māyā* is to keep rebellious souls imprisoned in the material world by the illusion of sensual enjoyment. One who tries to become freed from this prison by taking shelter of God is literally declaring war against *māyā*, who is a formidable opponent. To fight a war requires strength and enthusiasm.

"Now from this we may take the lesson that in our fight with *māyā* we should not be in a position in which our strength, enthusiasm and senses will be unable to fight vigorously... The soldiers in this Kṛṣṇa consciousness movement must always possess physical strength, enthusiasm and sensual power. To keep themselves fit, they must therefore place themselves in a normal condition of life. What constitutes a normal condition will not be the same for everyone, and therefore there are divisions of *varṇāśrama—brāhmaṇa, kṣatriya, vaiśya, śūdra, brahmacarya, gṛhastha, vānaprastha* and *sannyāsa*... One may stay in whichever *āśrama* is suitable for him; it is not essential that one take *sannyāsa*. If one is sexually agitated, he can enter the *gṛhastha-āśrama*. But one must continue fighting. For one who is not in a transcendental position, to take *sannyāsa* artificially is not a very great credit. If *sannyāsa* is not suitable, one may enter the *gṛhastha-āśrama* and fight *māyā* with great strength. But one should not give up the fighting and go away."

—*Śrīmad Bhāgavatam* 8.2.30 Bhaktivedanta purport

The Fortress

In the Fifth Canto of *Śrīmad Bhāgavatam*, the *gṛhastha-āśrama* is compared to a fortress. The embodied soul is continually under attack from the mind and senses, which pull him in various directions to engage in material enjoyment, and thus hamper his spiritual advancement. The fortress of *gṛhastha-āśrama* provides a safe position from which the soul can systematically defuse the attacks of these enemies without becoming smashed, by regulating his sense gratification according to religious principles and gradually learning to conquer his senses. Once his victory is complete, he can leave the shelter of the fortress and move around without fear.

> "One who is situated in household life and who systematically conquers his mind and five sense organs is like a king in his fortress who conquers his powerful enemies. After one has been trained in household life and his lusty desires have decreased, he can move anywhere without danger."
>
> —*Śrīmad Bhāgavatam* 5.1.18

The purpose of the *varṇāśrama* system is to help people to gradually learn to control the senses, to the point that they can eventually become free from material bondage.

> "The Vedic system of four *varṇas* and four *āśramas* is very scientific, and its entire purpose is to enable one to control the senses."
>
> —*Śrīmad Bhāgavatam* 5.1.18 Bhaktivedanta purport

For this reason, in *brahmacārī-āśrama*, boys and young men are traditionally taught by a *guru* to observe vows of poverty and celibacy.

> "Before entering household life (*gṛhastha-āśrama*), a student is fully trained to become *jitendriya*, a conqueror of the senses."
>
> —*Śrīmad Bhāgavatam* 5.1.18 Bhaktivedanta purport

Householders who have previously received *brahmacārī* training are equipped to make the next transition, to *vānaprastha-āśrama*, when the time is right.

> "Such a mature student is allowed to become a householder, and because he was first trained in conquering his senses, he retires from household life and becomes *vānaprastha* as soon as the strong waves of youthful life are past and he reaches the verge of old age at fifty years or slightly more."
>
> —*Śrīmad Bhāgavatam* 5.1.18 Bhaktivedanta purport

Vānaprastha-āśrama is the retired stage of life at which a husband and wife may begin to travel away from the comforts of household life and become more focussed on spiritual pursuits. The final stage of life, for those who succeed in attaining a mature level of genuine renunciation, is the *sannyāsa-āśrama*, which requires a man to leave his wife in the care of her grown-up sons and leave home, to travel and preach for the rest of his life.

> "Then, after being further trained, he accepts *sannyāsa*. He is then a fully learned and renounced person who can move anywhere and everywhere without fear of being captivated by material desires."
>
> —*Śrīmad Bhāgavatam* 5.1.18 Bhaktivedanta purport

Household life is the fortress that protects people when they are vulnerable.

> "The senses are considered very powerful enemies. As a king in a strong fortress can conquer powerful enemies, so a householder in *gṛhastha-āśrama*, household life, can conquer the lusty desires of youth and be very secure when he takes *vānaprastha* and *sannyāsa*."
>
> —*Śrīmad Bhāgavatam* 5.1.18 Bhaktivedanta purport

The senses are powerful enemies and the battle to conquer them continues from childhood to old age. The Vedic system of *brahmacārī-āśrama* before household life helps to prepare men for moving on to *vānaprastha* and *sannyāsa* in later life. Those who have not received the benefit of such training in their youth can nevertheless take shelter of a bona fide spiritual master at any stage of life and begin the process of learning to control the senses by following religious principles and engaging the senses in serving the Supreme Personality of Godhead.

> "The whole material disease is based on the process of sense gratification, and liberation from the diseased condition is re-engagement of the senses to see the beauty of the Lord, hear His glories, and act on His account"
>
> —*Śrīmad Bhāgavatam* 2.9.39 Bhaktivedanta purport

The Four Goals

Vedic scriptures delineate four goals that are recommended to be pursued by all married couples. These are called the four *puruṣārthas*, or human goals of life, and are known as *dharma* (religion), *artha* (economic development), *kāma* (sense gratification) and *mokṣa* (liberation). According to Vedic wisdom, the secret of happiness in household life is to balance and regulate the pursuance of these four goals.

> "Without discipline, without proper understanding of the four principles of life, *dharma, artha, kāma, mokṣa*, nobody can become happy."
>
> —Bhaktivedanta lecture, *Śrīmad Bhāgavatam* 1.16.25
> Hawaii 21/1/1974

Happiness and distress are experienced by all of us as a result of our interaction with the forces of nature, which influence us in different ways according to the three modes known as goodness, passion and ignorance.

> "Material nature consists of three modes—goodness, passion and ignorance. When the eternal living entity comes in contact with nature, O mighty-armed Arjuna, he becomes conditioned by these modes."
>
> —*Bhagavad-gītā As It Is* 14.5

The pursuit of religious principles (*dharma*) elevates the soul to the mode of goodness, the symptoms of which are happiness and knowledge.

> "O sinless one, the mode of goodness, being purer than the others, is illuminating, and it frees one from all sinful reactions. Those situated in that mode become conditioned by a sense of happiness and knowledge."
>
> —*Bhagavad-gītā As It Is* 14.6

Unrestricted economic development is driven by the mode of passion, which induces us to work hard to try to fulfil our material desires.

rajo rāgātmakaṁ viddhi
tṛṣṇā-saṅga-samudbhavam
tan nibadhnāti kaunteya
karma-saṅgena dehinam

> "The mode of passion is born of unlimited desires and longings, O son of Kuntī, and because of this the embodied living entity is bound to material fruitive actions."
>
> —*Bhagavad-gītā As It Is* 14.7

Overindulgence in sense gratification, in the mode of passion, can lead to the mode of ignorance, which makes us lazy, dull and mentally disturbed.

tamas tv ajñāna-jaṁ viddhi
mohanaṁ sarva-dehinām
pramādālasya-nidrābhis
tan nibadhnāti bhārata

> "O son of Bharata, know that the mode of darkness, born of ignorance, is the delusion of all embodied living entities. The results of this mode are madness, indolence and sleep, which bind the conditioned soul."
>
> —*Bhagavad-gītā As It Is* 14.8

Indulgence in hedonism, in the mode of ignorance, degrades the soul and obstructs spiritual advancement.

> "Those who strongly desire to cross the ocean of nescience must not associate with the modes of ignorance, for hedonistic activities are the greatest obstructions to realization of religious principles, economic development, regulated sense gratification and, at last, liberation."
>
> —*Śrīmad Bhāgavatam* 4.22.34

Householders can elevate themselves from the modes of ignorance and passion to the mode of goodness, and thus become happy and peaceful, by regulating their *artha* (economic development) and *kāma* (sense gratification) according to *dharma* (religious principles).

> "Actually, life, perfection of life, begins with religion, *dharma*. Then *artha*. Following religious principles, you acquire money, *artha*. *Artha* is required, not sinfully, but properly. *Dharma artha kāma*. Since you have senses, you require to satisfy the senses. *Artha* is required for sense gratification, but that *artha* must be based on religion. This is called *dharma, artha* and *kāma*. *Dharma-artha-kāma-mokṣa*. Then, when one actually becomes wise, he is no longer attracted by sense gratification."
>
> —Bhaktivedanta lecture, *Bhagavad-gītā* 7.7, Mumbai 22/2/1974

Tension and conflict in marital relationships arise from the influence of false ego in the mode of passion. By following *dharma*, or religious principles, we cultivate the mode of goodness and become more tranquil. *Gṛhastha-āśrama* is family life that is focussed, not just on *artha* and *kāma*, but on *dharma, artha, kāma* and *mokṣa*.

> "The four principles of life allow one to live according to religious principles, to earn money according to one's position in society, to allow the senses to enjoy the sense objects according to regulations, and to progress along the path of liberation from this material attachment. As long as the body is there, it is not possible to become completely free from all these material interests. It is not, however, recommended that one act only for sense gratification and earn money for that purpose only, sacrificing all religious principles."
>
> —*Śrīmad Bhāgavatam* 4.22.34 Bhaktivedanta purport

The fourth goal, liberation, is attained by transcending the three modes of material nature and coming to the platform of *śuddha-sattva*, or pure goodness. While the material mode of goodness tends to become tainted by passion and ignorance, pure goodness is completely untinged by the lower modes. This is the state of pure spiritual happiness, which is eternal and unlimited.

guṇān etān atītya trīn
dehī deha-samudbhavān
janma-mṛtyu-jarā-duḥkhair
vimukto 'mṛtam aśnute

> "When the embodied being is able to transcend these three modes associated with the material body, he can become free from birth, death, old age and their distresses and can enjoy nectar even in this life."
> —*Bhagavad-gītā As It Is* 14.20

The material mode of goodness is the springboard from which one can rise towards *śuddha-sattva* (pure goodness) and *mokṣa* (liberation). Thus it can be understood that, by regulating *artha* and *kāma* according to *dharma*, in the mode of goodness, one can progress towards *mokṣa*.

> "The Vedic process of sense gratification is therefore planned in such a way that one can economically develop and enjoy sense gratification and yet ultimately obtain liberation. Vedic civilization offers us all knowledge in the *śāstras*, and if we live a regulated life under the direction of *śāstras* and *guru*, all our material desires will be fulfilled; at the same time we will be able to go forward to liberation."
> —*Śrīmad Bhāgavatam* 4.22.34 Bhaktivedanta purport

Householders who balance these four goals, according to the directions of the revealed scriptures, can live peacefully together and at the same time make spiritual progress.

> "Therefore, to attain the mercy of the Lord, a *gṛhastha* Vaiṣṇava should accept the divisions of *varṇāśrama* and along with his wife practice *dharma, artha, kāma,* and *mokṣa* in order to maintain his life... Thus by

> properly performing the activities of *trivarga*, the *gṛhastha* Vaiṣṇava's character becomes pure. With such pure characteristics, he should hear, chant, and remember the names, forms, qualities, and pastimes of the Lord with full surrender. The wife should also always endeavor for spiritual perfection..."
>
> —Bhaktivinoda Ṭhākura, *Śrī Bhaktyāloka* 11

Ultimately, by pursuing *dharma, artha, kāma* and *mokṣa* according to Vedic directives, one can attain the perfection of human life and go back home, back to Godhead.

> "Human society is actually meant for realization of perfection in Kṛṣṇa consciousness. There is no restriction against living with a wife and children, but life should be so conducted that one may not go against the principles of religion, economic development, regulated sense enjoyment and, ultimately, liberation from material existence. The Vedic principles are designed in such a way that the conditioned souls who have come to this material existence may be guided in fulfilling their material desires and at the same time be liberated and go back to Godhead, back home."
>
> —*Śrīmad Bhāgavatam* 3.22.33 Bhaktivedanta purport

Chapter Three

Dharma

Religious Principles

Varṇāśrama-dharma—*Varṇa-dharma*—*Āśrama-dharma*
Gṛhastha-dharma—*Sanātana-dharma*
Devotional Service for *Gṛhasthas*
Śravaṇaṁ kīrtanaṁ (Hearing & Chanting)
Bhakti-yoga (The Path of Devotion)

Chapter Three

Dharma

—Religious Principles—

"*Dharma* (righteousness) is the pivot on which the universe balances. The man of righteousness is accessible to all. Righteousness wipes out all sins. In righteousness alone all things are found to exist."
—*Taittirīya-āraṇyaka* 10.78

OF THE FOUR *PURUṢĀRTHAS* (HUMAN GOALS) of household life, *dharma* appears first on the list as the embodiment of ethical codes that govern human action, and *mokṣa* (liberation), being the final goal, comes last.

"Regulated human civilization promotes *dharma, artha, kāma* and *mokṣa.*"
—*Śrīmad Bhāgavatam* 4.22.36 Bhaktivedanta purport

When activities of *artha* (economic development) and *kāma* (sense gratification) are based on and regulated by *dharma*, the end result is *mokṣa.*

> "In human society there must be religion. Without religion, human society is only animal society. Economic development and sense gratification must be based on religious principles. When religion, economic development and sense gratification are adjusted, liberation from this material birth, death, old age and disease is assured."
>
> —*Śrīmad Bhāgavatam* 4.22.36 Bhaktivedanta purport

The eternal principles of religion for all human beings are given by God.

dharmaṁ tu sākṣād bhagavat-praṇītaṁ

> "Real religious principles are enacted by the Supreme Personality of Godhead."
>
> —*Śrīmad Bhāgavatam* 6.3.19

As God is one, similarly *dharma* is one and the same for everyone.

> "When we create different *dharmas*, that is due to ignorance: Hindu *dharma*, Muslim *dharma*, Christian *dharma* or this *dharma*, that *dharma*... No. Gold is gold."
>
> —Bhaktivedanta lecture, *Śrīmad Bhāgavatam* 3.25.1
> Mumbai 1/11/1974

The laws of God are revealed through sacred literatures and confirmed by His representatives in the form of bona fide spiritual masters and saintly people.

> "Narottama dāsa Ṭhākura says, *sādhu-śāstra-guru-vākya, cittete kariyā aikya*: 'One should accept as one's guide the words of the *sādhus*, the *śāstra* and the *guru*.'"
>
> —*Śrī Caitanya-caritāmṛta, Madhya-līlā* 17.185
> Bhaktivedanta purport

While there are different scriptures for different 'religions', the same basic spiritual truths and similar moral codes can be seen to be propounded by all of them. Where differences can be found to exist between them, they are generally confined to external details, such as geographic, linguistic or cultural.

> "When we speak of *Veda*, *Veda* means knowledge. So knowledge means knowledge of God. Any scripture that gives knowledge of God is *Veda*. Don't think that the *Vedas* mean only the *Sāma*, *Yajuḥ*, *Atharva*. Those scriptures that are following the principle of giving knowledge about God, they are *Vedas*."
>
> —*Conversations with Śrīla Prabhupāda*
> Conversation with Sir Alistair Hardy, London 21/7/1973

Of all these religious scriptures, or *Vedas*, the ancient Vedic literatures of India are not only the oldest but also the most voluminous, detailed and consistent. They explain that religious principles are given by God for the benefit of all living entities, to facilitate their ultimate liberation from the material world of birth and death.

dharmasya hy āpavargyasya
nārtho 'rthāyopakalpate

nārthasya dharmaikāntasya
kāmo lābhāya hi smṛtaḥ

"All occupational engagements are certainly meant for ultimate liberation. They should never be performed for material gain. Furthermore, according to sages, one who is engaged in the ultimate occupational service should never use material gain to cultivate sense gratification."

—*Śrīmad Bhāgavatam* 1.2.9

Varṇāśrama-dharma

Vedic religious principles that govern codes of human behaviour are prescribed differently for different people according to age, gender, nature, activities, and spiritual advancement.

"By *dharma* is meant the allotted functions of *varṇa* and *āśrama* manifested by the twenty *dharma-śāstras* on the authority of the *Vedas*. Of these two divisions, *varṇa-dharma* is that function which is the outcome of the distinctive natures of the four *varṇas*, viz., *brāhmaṇa*, *kṣatriya*, *vaiśya* and *śūdra*, and *āśrama-dharma* is that function which is appropriate to the respective *āśramas* or stations of those who belong to the four stages, viz., *brahmacarya*, *gṛhastha*, *vānaprastha* and *sannyāsa*."

—*Śrī Brahma-saṁhitā* 5.53 Bhaktisiddhānta purport

According to the Vedic *varṇāśrama* culture, every human being falls into one of four *varṇas* (occupational groups) and one of four *āśramas* (spiritual life stages). Duties that are defined according to the *varṇa* and *āśrama* in which a person is situated are known as *varṇāśrama-dharma*. The *varṇāśrama* system and the duties that are awarded within it are governed by the Supreme Personality of Godhead.

yena sva-dhāmny amī bhāvā
rajaḥ-sattva-tamomayāḥ
guṇa-nāma-kriyā-rūpair
vibhāvyante yathā-tatham

> "The supreme cause of all causes, Nārāyaṇa, is situated in His own abode in the spiritual world, but nevertheless He controls the entire cosmic manifestation according to the three modes of material nature—*sattva-guṇa*, *rajo-guṇa* and *tamo-guṇa*. In this way all living entities are awarded different qualities, different names (such as *brāhmaṇa*, *kṣatriya* and *vaiśya*), different duties according to the *varṇāśrama* institution, and different forms. Thus Nārāyaṇa is the cause of the entire cosmic manifestation."
>
> —*Śrīmad Bhāgavatam* 6.1.41

A person's *varṇa* is determined by his/her relationship with the three modes of material nature, goodness (*sattva-guṇa*), passion (*rajo-guṇa*), and ignorance (*tamo-guṇa*). A *brāhmaṇa* (priest or teacher) is mainly situated in the mode of goodness; a *kṣatriya* (leader or warrior) is mainly in passion; a *vaiśyā* (farmer or businessman) is influenced by a mixture of passion and ignorance; and a *śūdrā* (labourer or artisan) is mainly in ignorance.

> "According to the three modes of material nature and the work associated with them, the four divisions of human society are created by Me."
>
> —Lord Kṛṣṇa, *Bhagavad-gītā* As It Is 4.13

Āśrama is determined by stage of life and spiritual development. The four *āśramas* are known as *brahmacarya* (student life), *gṛhastha* (household life), *vānaprastha* (retirement), and *sannyāsa* (renunciation). By executing prescribed duties according to *varṇāśrama-dharma*, a person can gradually advance from the bodily platform to the spiritual platform.

> "As long as one is not liberated, one has to perform the duties of his particular body in accordance with religious principles in order to achieve liberation… On the bodily plane *sva-dharma* is called *varṇāśrama-dharma*, or man's steppingstone for spiritual understanding."
>
> —*Bhagavad-gītā* As It Is 2.31 purport

And by advancing from bodily consciousness to spiritual consciousness, a person can reawaken his/her consciousness of God.

dharmaḥ svanuṣṭhitaḥ puṁsāṁ
viṣvaksena-kathāsu yaḥ
notpādayed yadi ratiṁ
śrama eva hi kevalam

> "The occupational activities a man performs according to his own position are only so much useless labor if they do not provoke attraction for the message of the Personality of Godhead."
>
> —*Śrīmad Bhāgavatam* 1.2.8

According to the teachings of *Śrīmad Bhāgavatam*, the perfection of *varṇāśrama-dharma* is to perform one's prescribed duties for the pleasure of the Supreme Lord.

ataḥ pumbhir dvija-śreṣṭhā
varṇāśrama-vibhāgaśaḥ
svanuṣṭhitasya dharmasya
saṁsiddhir hari-toṣaṇam

> "O best among the twice-born, it is therefore concluded that the highest perfection one can achieve by discharging the duties prescribed for one's own occupation according to caste divisions and orders of life is to please the Personality of Godhead."
>
> —*Śrīmad Bhāgavatam* 1.2.13

The original purpose of *varṇāśrama-dharma* is to help anyone, from any position, to gradually advance to the highest stage of God consciousness.

> "Everyone has to cleanse his heart by a gradual process, not abruptly. However, when one transcends the modes of material nature and is fully situated in Kṛṣṇa consciousness, he can perform anything and everything under the direction of a bona fide spiritual

master. ...But as long as one is on the material platform, he must perform his duties according to the modes of material nature. At the same time, he must have a full sense of Kṛṣṇa consciousness."

—*Bhagavad-gītā As It Is* 3.35 purport

One who is honest about his/her own nature, rather than trying to repress it, can make tangible spiritual advancement by following *varṇāśrama-dharma.*

sadṛśaṁ ceṣṭate svasyāḥ
prakṛter jñānavān api
prakṛtiṁ yānti bhūtāni
nigrahaḥ kiṁ kariṣyati

"Even a man of knowledge acts according to his own nature, for everyone follows the nature he has acquired from the three modes. What can repression accomplish?"

—*Bhagavad-gītā As It Is* 3.33

The *ācāryas* (spiritual authorities) advise that, until one is liberated from material desires, he/she should continue to perform his/her prescribed duties according to *varṇa* and *āśrama*, while at the same time following the instructions of the spiritual master for making further advancement in God consciousness.

"Kṛṣṇa consciousness helps one to get out of the material entanglement, even though one may be engaged in his prescribed duties in terms of material existence. Therefore, without being fully in Kṛṣṇa consciousness, one should not give up his occupational duties. No one should suddenly give up his prescribed duties and become a so-called *yogī* or transcendentalist artificially. It is better to be situated in one's position and to try to attain Kṛṣṇa consciousness under superior training. Thus one may be freed from the clutches of Kṛṣṇa's *māyā*."

—*Bhagavad-gītā As It Is* 3.33 purport

A pure devotee of the Lord is not obliged to follow the rules and regulations of *varṇāśrama*. Nevertheless, out of humility, he/she respects the rules and never claims himself/herself to be pure or transcendental.

"Actually, a Vaiṣṇava is above this *varṇāśrama-dharma*. But we don't claim that we have become perfect Vaiṣṇavas. We are not so impudent."

—Bhaktivedanta lecture, *Śrīmad Bhāgavatam* 1.8.41
Māyāpura 21/10/1974

Varṇa-dharma

Every human being falls into one of the four *varṇas*, or occupational divisions of society, according to his/her inherent nature and activities.

"Even though the system of *varṇāśrama* is not clearly present in some countries, still it exists in a seedling form. According to one's nature, he develops his occupation and, accordingly, his means of livelihood."

—Bhaktivinoda Ṭhākura, *Śrī Bhaktyāloka* 12

While every conditioned soul is influenced to some extent by all the three modes, his/her *varṇa* is determined by whichever mode is prominent.

> "Where there is prominence of the quality of goodness, that is *brāhmaṇa*. When there is prominence of the quality of passion, that is *kṣatriya*. When there is prominence of the quality of mixture—there is mixture also—that is *vaiśya*. And when there is prominence of the quality of ignorance, that is *śūdra*."
>
> —Bhaktivedanta lecture, *Śrīmad Bhāgavatam* 1.7.2-4
> Durban 14/10/1975

The real *varṇa* of an individual cannot be determined simply by birth in a particular family.

yasya yal lakṣaṇaṁ proktaṁ
puṁso varṇābhivyañjakam
yad anyatrāpi dṛśyeta
tat tenaiva vinirdiśet

> "If one shows the symptoms of being a *brāhmaṇa*, *kṣatriya*, *vaiśya* or *śūdra*, as described above, even if he has appeared in a different class, he should be accepted according to those symptoms of classification."
>
> —*Śrīmad Bhāgavatam* 7.11.35

The caste system of India originates from the Vedic *varṇāśrama* system, but eventually it became corrupted by the misconception that *varṇa* should be determined by birth alone, instead of by qualities and activities.

> "These social orders, according to the different grades of work and qualification, are described in *Bhagavad-gītā*. Unfortunately, for want of proper protection by responsible kings, the system of social and spiritual orders has now become a hereditary caste system... Indian civilization on the basis of the four *varṇaṣ* and *āśramas* deteriorated because of her dependency on foreigners, or those who did not follow the civilization of *varṇāśrama*. Thus the *varṇāśrama* system has now been degraded into the caste system."
>
> —*Śrīmad Bhāgavatam* 3.21.52-4 Bhaktivedanta purport

The hereditary caste system, rather than facilitating the spiritual progress of society, as *varṇāśrama* is meant to do, has had the opposite effect.

> "The stereotyped, crippled idea that only a person born in a *brāhmaṇa* family can become a *brāhmaṇa* has killed Vedic civilization."
>
> —*Teachings of Queen Kuntī* 3

The duties of the four *varṇas* are prescribed according to the respective modes of nature that influence people's inherent skills and talents.

> "The duties of a *brāhmaṇa, kṣatriya, vaiśya* and *śūdra* are prescribed according to their particular modes of nature. One should not imitate another's duty. A man who is by nature attracted to the kind of work done by *śūdras* should not artificially claim to be a *brāhmaṇa*, although he may have been born into a

> *brāhmaṇa* family. In this way one should work according to his own nature; no work is abominable, if performed in the service of the Supreme Lord."
>
> —*Bhagavad-gītā As It Is* 18.47 purport

The four *varṇas* are compared to four parts of the human body: head, arms, belly, and legs. The *brāhmaṇas* are compared to the head because they provide knowledge and spiritual guidance to the rest of the society; the *kṣatriyas* are the arms, giving protection and defence; the *vaiśyas* are the belly, providers of food and commodities; and the *śūdras* are the legs, providing manual labour and service. As all four parts of a human body work together to keep the body functioning smoothly, similarly all four *varṇas* are considered to be essential contributors to the progress of human society.

> "In the human social body, the *brāhmaṇas* are considered the head, the *kṣatriyas* are the arms, the *vaiśyas* are the belly, and the *śūdras* are the legs. At the present moment the body has legs and a belly, but there are no arms or head, and therefore society is topsy-turvy. It is necessary to re-establish the brahminical qualifications in order to raise the fallen human society to the highest standard of spiritual consciousness."
>
> —*Śrīmad Bhāgavatam* 4.8.36 Bhaktivedanta purport

The symptoms of a genuine *brāhmaṇa* are described as follows.

samo damas tapaḥ śaucaṁ
santoṣaḥ kṣāntir ārjavam
jñānaṁ dayācyutātmatvaṁ
satyaṁ ca brahma-lakṣaṇam

"The symptoms of a *brāhmaṇa* are control of the mind, control of the senses, austerity and penance, cleanliness, satisfaction, forgiveness, simplicity, knowledge, mercy, truthfulness, and complete surrender to the Supreme Personality of Godhead."
—*Śrīmad Bhāgavatam* 7.11.21

The following are the symptoms of a true *kṣatriya*.

śauryaṁ vīryaṁ dhṛtis tejas
tyāgaś cātmajayaḥ kṣamā
brahmaṇyatā prasādaś ca
satyaṁ ca kṣatra-lakṣaṇam

"To be influential in battle, unconquerable, patient, challenging and charitable, to control the bodily necessities, to be forgiving, to be attached to the brahminical nature and to be always jolly and truthful—these are the symptoms of the *kṣatriya*."
—*Śrīmad Bhāgavatam* 7.11.22

The symptoms of a good *vaiśya* are described as follows.

deva-gurv-acyute bhaktis
tri-varga-paripoṣaṇam
āstikyam udyamo nityaṁ
naipuṇyaṁ vaiśya-lakṣaṇam

"Being always devoted to the demigods, the spiritual master and the Supreme Lord, Viṣṇu; endeavoring for advancement in religious principles, economic development and sense gratification (*dharma, artha* and *kāma*); believing in the words of the spiritual master and scripture; and always endeavoring with expertise in earning money—these are the symptoms of the *vaiśya*."

—*Śrīmad Bhāgavatam* 7.11.23

And these are the symptoms of an ideal *śūdra*.

śūdrasya sannatiḥ śaucaṁ
sevā svāminy amāyayā
amantra-yajño hy asteyaṁ
satyaṁ go-vipra-rakṣaṇam

"Offering obeisances to the higher sections of society (the *brāhmaṇas, kṣatriyas* and *vaiśyas*), being always very clean, being free from duplicity, serving one's master, performing sacrifices without uttering mantras, not stealing, always speaking the truth and giving all protection to the cows and *brāhmaṇas*—these are the symptoms of the *śūdra*."

—*Śrīmad Bhāgavatam* 7.11.24

Varṇa-dharma means to be true to one's own natural occupation and the prescribed duties pertaining to it.

śreyān sva-dharmo viguṇaḥ
para-dharmāt sv-anuṣṭhitāt

svabhāva-niyataṁ karma
kurvan nāpnoti kilbiṣam

> "It is better to engage in one's own occupation, even though one may perform it imperfectly, than to accept another's occupation and perform it perfectly. Duties prescribed according to one's nature are never affected by sinful reactions."
>
> —*Bhagavad-gītā As It Is* 18.47

To accept a different occupation, for which one is not suited, will bring neither happiness nor progress.

> "By accepting the livelihood and occupation of others, one meets with misfortune. What to speak of misfortune, it especially obstructs one's devotional service."
>
> —Bhaktivinoda Ṭhākura, *Śrī Bhaktyāloka* 12

A person who is honestly situated, according to his natural *varṇa*, can make spiritual progress.

sve sve karmaṇy abhirataḥ
saṁsiddhiṁ labhate naraḥ

> "By following his qualities of work, every man can become perfect."
>
> —*Bhagavad-gītā As It Is* 18.45

While rightly engaged in their natural occupations, members of all four *varṇas* are further advised to endeavour to cultivate the mode of goodness and to make spiritual progress towards the transcendental platform by engaging in devotional service under the guidance of the Lord's devotees.

> "Members of the four *varṇas* and the lower castes should be eager to develop their sattvic nature. Everyone should give prominence to devotional service and engage in the cultivation of goodness to the platform of *nirguṇa*, transcendence, by the mercy of the devotees."
>
> —Bhaktivinoda Ṭhākura, *Śrī Bhaktyāloka* 12

Furthermore, in the service of God and under the guidance of a bona fide spiritual master, any activity can be carried out by a devotee of the Lord.

> "A devotee is always a servant of God. Whatever service is required as a *brāhmaṇa*, *kṣatriya* or *vaiśya*, it doesn't matter. We are ready."
>
> —Bhaktivedanta lecture, *Śrīmad Bhāgavatam* 1.16.26-30
> Hawaii 23/1/1974

People of all four *varṇas* can develop their sattvic nature by gradually learning to observe the following principles, which are prescribed for all human beings.

> "These are the general principles to be followed by all human beings: truthfulness, mercy, austerity (observing fasts on certain days of the month), bathing twice a day, tolerance, discrimination between

right and wrong, control of the mind, control of the senses, nonviolence, celibacy, charity, reading of scripture, simplicity, satisfaction, rendering service to saintly persons, gradually taking leave of unnecessary engagements, observing the futility of the unnecessary activities of human society, remaining silent and grave and avoiding unnecessary talk, considering whether one is the body or the soul, distributing food equally to all living entities (both men and animals), seeing every soul (especially in the human form) as a part of the Supreme Lord, hearing about the activities and instructions given by the Supreme Personality of Godhead (who is the shelter of the saintly persons), chanting about these activities and instructions, always remembering these activities and instructions, trying to render service, performing worship, offering obeisances, becoming a servant, becoming a friend, and surrendering one's whole self. O King Yudhiṣṭhira, these thirty qualifications must be acquired in the human form of life. Simply by acquiring these qualifications, one can satisfy the Supreme Personality of Godhead."

—*Śrīmad Bhāgavatam* 7.11.8-12

One who follows his or her *varṇa-dharma*, according to the instructions of the Supreme Personality of Godhead, and who offers respect to every living entity, is considered to be an Āryan, a civilised and cultured person, whichever *varṇa* he/she belongs to.

"My dear Lord, one's occupational duty is instructed in *Śrīmad Bhāgavatam* and *Bhagavad-gītā* according to Your point of view, which never deviates from the highest goal of life. Those who follow their occupational duties under Your supervision, being equal to all living entities, moving and non-moving, and not considering high and low, are called Āryans. Such Āryans worship You, the Supreme Personality of Godhead."

—*Śrīmad Bhāgavatam* 6.16.43

Āśrama-dharma

The four *āśramas* apply to the four stages of human life. The first one is the *brahmacārī-āśrama* (celibate student life), the second is the *gṛhastha-āśrama* (regulated household life), the third is the *vānaprastha-āśrama* (retired life for performing austerities), and the fourth is the *sannyāsa-āśrama* (renounced life), when a man gives up the association of his wife and they both dedicate the rest of their lives to serving God. While the four *varṇas* are meant to situate people in the right occupational activities, the four *āśramas* are meant to facilitate their spiritual advancement. Especially for the *brāhmaṇas*, all the four *āśramas* are prescribed.

"The *brāhmaṇa* (one who is qualified as a *brāhmaṇa*) has to observe the four *āśramas*: the *brahmacārī-āśrama*, the *gṛhastha-āśrama*, the *vānaprastha-āśrama* and *sannyāsa-āśrama*. The *kṣatriya* will have to observe

> three *āśramas*: *brahmacārī*, *gṛhastha* and *vānaprastha*. The *vaiśya*, two *āśramas*: *brahmacārī* and *gṛhastha*. The *śūdra*, only one *āśrama*: *gṛhastha*."
>
> —Bhaktivedanta lecture, *Śrīmad Bhāgavatam* 1.8.4
> Māyāpura 21/10/1974

Just as there are prescribed duties for each *varṇa*, or occupational division of society, similarly there are prescribed duties for each *āśrama*, or order of life.

vidyā dānaṁ tapaḥ satyaṁ
dharmasyeti padāni ca
āśramāṁś ca yathā-saṅkhyam

> "Education, charity, penance and truth are said to be the four legs of religion, and to learn this there are four orders of life."
>
> —*Śrīmad Bhāgavatam* 3.12.41

The four *āśramas* – *brahmacarya, gṛhastha, vānaprastha and sannyāsa* – are meant to uphold the four legs of religion respectively, i.e. education, charity, penance and truth.

> "Student life is meant for acquiring the best education; household family life is meant for gratifying the senses, provided it is performed with a charitable disposition of mind; retirement from household life is meant for penance, for advancement in spiritual life; and renounced life is meant for preaching the Absolute Truth to the people in general."
>
> —*Śrīmad Bhāgavatam* 3.12.41 Bhaktivedanta purport

The main religious duties of the four *āśramas* are further described as follows.

bhikṣor dharmaḥ śamo 'hiṁsā
tapa īkṣā vanaukasaḥ
gṛhiṇo bhūta-rakṣejyā
dvijasyācārya-sevanam

"The main religious duties of a *sannyāsī* are equanimity and nonviolence, whereas for the *vānaprastha* austerity and philosophical understanding of the difference between the body and soul are prominent. The main duties of a householder are to give shelter to all living entities and perform sacrifices, and the *brahmacārī* is mainly engaged in serving the spiritual master."

—*Śrīmad Bhāgavatam* 11.18.42

Gṛhastha-dharma

There are three activities that are especially recommended for *gṛhasthas*, i.e. performance of sacrifices, distribution of charity, and execution of occupational duties (*varṇa-dharma*).

"For the *gṛhasthas*, or householders, performance of sacrifices, distribution of charity, and action according to prescribed duties are especially recommended."

—*Śrīmad Bhāgavatam* 3.32.34-6 Bhaktivedanta purport

Regarding charity, it is traditionally the *gṛhasthas* who support the other three *āśramas* by providing them with the basic necessities of life.

> "Except for the *gṛhasthas*, or the householders, everyone is supposed to engage in the spiritual advancement of life, and therefore the *brahmacārī*, the *vānaprastha* and the *sannyāsī* have very little time to earn a livelihood. They therefore collect alms from the *gṛhasthas*, and thus they secure the bare necessities of life and cultivate spiritual understanding. By helping the other three sections of society cultivate spiritual values, the householder also makes advancement in spiritual life. Ultimately every member of society automatically becomes spiritually advanced and easily crosses the ocean of nescience."
> —*Śrīmad Bhāgavatam* 3.14.18 Bhaktivedanta purport

As well as giving in charity, those *gṛhasthas* who are *brāhmaṇas* may also accept charity, while passing on to others whatever they receive that is above and beyond their needs.

> "A *gṛhastha* must be prepared or trained to give in charity. And who will accept the charity? The charity will be accepted by the *brahmacārī* and *sannyāsa*. Not the *vānaprastha*. A *brahmacārī* will accept charity on behalf of the spiritual master. And a *sannyāsī* will accept charity only for his maintenance. That's all. The *gṛhastha* cannot accept charity. But a *gṛhastha-brāhmaṇa*, he can accept charity, but he will not

accumulate money by taking charity. Whatever he gets, he must spend. Then *dāna-pratigraha. Pratigraha* means to accept. But he cannot maintain a bank balance. He must, whatever extra he has, immediately give in charity. Then a *gṛhastha-brāhmaṇa* can accept charity. There is a proverb in Bengali: 'A *brāhmaṇa*, even if he gets a lakh of rupees (one hundred thousand rupees) still remains a beggar.'"

—Bhaktivedanta lecture, *Bhagavad-gītā* 18.5, London 5/9/1973

(Here it is mentioned that a *vānaprastha* does not accept charity. According to the traditional system, *vānaprasthas* would sometimes accept alms in the form of food from *gṛhasthas*, but not money.) Together with the distribution of charity, the performance of sacrifices is also especially recommended for *gṛhasthas*. Traditional Vedic fire sacrifices are performed to satisfy the Supreme Personality of Godhead. Because they are costly affairs, they are usually performed by householders.

"Sacrifice is another item to be performed by the householders, because sacrifices require a large amount of money. Those in other orders of life, namely *brahmacarya, vānaprastha and sannyāsa,* have no money; they live by begging. So performance of different types of sacrifice is meant for the householders."

—*Bhagavad-gītā As It Is* 16.1-3 purport

For this age however, another type of sacrifice is recommended, which is free of charge.

"They should perform *agni-hotra* sacrifices as enjoined in the Vedic literature, but such sacrifices at the present moment are very expensive, and it is not possible for any householder to perform them. The best sacrifice recommended in this age is called *saṅkīrtana-yajña*. This *saṅkīrtana-yajña*, the chanting of Hare Kṛṣṇa, Hare Kṛṣṇa, Kṛṣṇa Kṛṣṇa, Hare Hare/ Hare Rāma, Hare Rāma, Rāma Rāma, Hare Hare, is the best and most inexpensive sacrifice. Everyone can adopt it and derive benefit."

—*Bhagavad-gītā As It Is* 16.1-3 purport

Sanātana-dharma

On the spiritual level, the word *dharma* signifies the original constitutional position of the soul, which is eternal service to God. This is called *sanātana* (eternal) *dharma*. Religious principles and prescribed duties (*varṇāśrama-dharma*) are stepping stones on the path towards eternal service to God (*sanātana-dharma*).

"Prescribed and prohibited rules are further divided into two categories – conditional and constitutional. The living entity is pure spirit. The prescriptions and prohibitions in the living entity's constitutional position are constitutional rules. But when the living entity is separated from his transcendental position, he accepts the designations given by the illusory energy and is entangled in this world – these are false designations. These designations are of many varieties, but the constitutional situation is one without second."

—Bhaktivinoda Ṭhākura, *Śrī Bhaktyāloka* 4

While *varṇāśrama-dharma* refers to specified occupational duties for different human beings, according to *varṇa* and *āśrama*, *sanātana-dharma* signifies the supreme occupational duty for all humanity, regardless of *varṇa* and *āśrama*.

sa vai puṁsāṁ paro dharmo
yato bhaktir adhokṣaje
ahaituky apratihatā
yayātmā suprasīdati

> "The supreme occupation (*dharma*) for all humanity is loving devotional service unto the transcendent Lord. Such devotional service must be unmotivated and uninterrupted to completely satisfy the self."
> —*Śrīmad Bhāgavatam* 1.2.6

The occupational duties of *varṇāśrama* are meant to pave the way for the development of *bhakti* or devotion to the Lord.

> "There is a need for *varṇāśrama-dharma* while a human remains in the stage of piety and impiety that are born of his nature. The main purpose of *varṇāśrama-dharma* is this: by gradually following *varṇāśrama-dharma* a human being will become eligible to perform devotional service... As long as one has a material body the system of *varṇāśrama-dharma* must be followed, but it should remain under the full control and domination of *bhakti*. *Varṇāśrama-dharma* is like the foundation of one's supreme occupational duty. When one's supreme occupational

> duty is matured and one achieves his goal, then the process is gradually neglected. Again, it is also abandoned at the time of death."
>
> —Bhaktivinoda Ṭhākura, *Śrī Bhaktyāloka* 12

Sanātana-dharma means 'eternal religion' or 'the eternal function of the soul'. Sometimes we identify with a particular faith or religion, which is changeable, but our eternal religion is that which remains integral to our real self.

> "The English word 'religion' is a little different from *sanātana-dharma*. Religion conveys the idea of faith, and faith may change. One may have faith in a particular process, and he may change this faith and adopt another, but *sanātana-dharma* refers to that activity which cannot be changed. For instance, liquidity cannot be taken from water, nor can heat be taken from fire. Similarly, the eternal function of the eternal living entity cannot be taken from the living entity. *Sanātana-dharma* is eternally integral to the living entity."
>
> —Introduction to *Bhagavad-gītā As It Is*

Sanātana-dharma is not limited to any religious denomination, but is meant for every living entity.

> "So far as Vedic religion is concerned, it is not for the Hindus. That is to be understood. The *sanātana-dharma*, it is for all living entities, all human beings...

The living entity is *sanātana*, God is *sanātana*, and there is *sanātana-dharma*... So actually, the Vedic system is called *sanātana-dharma*, not Hindu *dharma*. This is a wrong conception. The *sanātana-dharma* is meant for all living entities – not the so-called Hindus, Muslims, Christians – for everyone. That is *sanātana-dharma*. These are later misconceptions, 'Hinduism' and this 'ism', that 'ism'. Actually, it is called *sanātana-dharma*, or *varṇāśrama-dharma*. That is meant for everyone. But because it was being followed regularly in India and Indians were called 'Hindus' by the Muslims because they lived on the other side of the River Sind, or Sindu, and the Muslims pronounced Sind as 'Hind'. Therefore they called India as 'Hindustan', meaning on the other side of the Sindu, or 'Hindu' River. Otherwise, it has no Vedic reference. So this Hindu *dharma* has no Vedic reference. The real Vedic dharma is *sanātana-dharma*, *varṇāśrama-dharma*... Now that *sanātana-dharma*, or Vedic *dharma*, is being distorted, not being obeyed, not being carried out properly, it has come to be understood as Hinduism. That is a freak understanding. That is not the real understanding. We have to study *sanātana-dharma* or *varṇāśrama-dharma*. Then we'll understand what is Vedic religion."

—*Conversations with Śrīla Prabhupāda*
Answers to a Questionnaire from *Bhavan's Journal*, 28/6/1976

By definition, God is one. While He possesses unlimited names and forms, there can only be one God.

> "Every one of us may possess some riches, may be a little wise or a little strong. But when you find that person who possesses more opulences than anyone else, that is God. The Sanskrit word for this is '*asamordhva*'. *Sama* means 'equal', and *asama* means 'not equal'. And *ūrdhva* means 'above'. No one is equal to or greater than God. That is the definition of God. 'God is great' means that nobody is equal to Him and nobody is above Him in any kind of opulence. That is called *bhagavān*."
>
> —*The Quest for Enlightenment* 4

In the same way, eternal religion, or devotional service to God, is also one and the same for every living entity.

> "Kṛṣṇa is eternal, we are eternal, and the place we live, exchanging our feelings, that is eternal. And the system that teaches this eternal system of reciprocation, that is called *sanātana-dharma.* That is meant for everyone."
>
> —*Conversations with Śrīla Prabhupāda*
> Answers to a Questionnaire from *Bhavan's Journal*, 28/6/1976

Sanātana-dharma refers to activities that pertain to the soul, and are not subject to material designations. Spiritual culture is meant for anyone and everyone, whether in the body of a man or a woman, young or old, married or unmarried. In any situation, the natural proclivity of the soul is to serve the Supersoul, the Supreme Personality of Godhead.

"It is not possible for the living entity to be happy without rendering transcendental loving service unto the Supreme Lord."

—Introduction to *Bhagavad-gītā As It Is*

There are nine processes of devotional service, described as follows.

śravaṇaṁ kīrtanaṁ viṣṇoḥ
smaraṇaṁ pāda-sevanam
arcanaṁ vandanaṁ dāsyaṁ
sakhyam ātma-nivedanam

iti puṁsārpitā viṣṇau
bhaktiś cen nava-lakṣaṇā
kriyeta bhagavaty addhā
tan manye 'dhītam uttamam

"Hearing and chanting about the transcendental holy name, form, qualities, paraphernalia and pastimes of Lord Viṣṇu, remembering them, serving the lotus feet of the Lord, offering the Lord respectful worship with sixteen types of paraphernalia, offering prayers to the Lord, becoming His servant, considering the Lord one's best friend, and surrendering everything unto Him (in other words, serving Him with the body, mind and words)—these nine processes are accepted as pure devotional service. One who has dedicated his life to the service of Kṛṣṇa through these nine methods should be understood to be the most learned person, for he has acquired complete knowledge."

—*Śrīmad Bhāgavatam* 7.5.23-4

Devotional service is a natural activity of the soul and, since each soul is a unique individual, there are different ways to serve the Lord, according to personal inclination.

> "According to the regulative principles, there are nine departmental activities, as described above, and one should specifically engage himself in the type of devotional service for which he has a natural aptitude. For example, one person may have a particular interest in hearing, another may have a particular interest in chanting, and another may have a particular interest in serving in the temple. So these, or any of the other six different types of devotional service (remembering, serving, praying, engaging in some particular service, being in a friendly relationship or offering everything in one's possession), should be executed in full earnestness. In this way, everyone should act according to his particular taste."
>
> —*The Nectar of Devotion* 16

There are also five specific activities of devotional service that are considered to be especially potent.

sādhu-saṅga, nāma-kīrtana, bhāgavata-śravaṇa
mathurā-vāsa, śrī-mūrtira śraddhāya sevana

sakala-sādhana-śreṣṭha ei pañca aṅga
kṛṣṇa-prema janmāya ei pāṅcera alpa saṅga

"One should associate with devotees, chant the holy name of the Lord, hear *Śrīmad-Bhāgavatam*, reside at Mathurā and worship the Deity with faith and veneration. These five limbs of devotional service are the best of all. Even a slight performance of these five awakens love for Kṛṣṇa."

—*Śrī Caitanya-caritāmṛta, Madhya-līlā* 22.128-9

Devotional Service for *Gṛhasthas*

Out of the five processes cited above, three of them have been specifically recommended for householders, i.e. to chant the holy name of the Lord, to worship the Deity and to serve the devotees.

gṛhastha viṣayī āmi, ki mora sādhane
śrī-mukhe ājñā kara prabhu—nivedi caraṇe

"Satyarāja Khān said, 'My dear Lord, being a householder and a materialistic man, I do not know the process of advancing in spiritual life. I therefore submit myself unto Your lotus feet and request You to give me orders.'"

prabhu kahena,—'kṛṣṇa-sevā', 'vaiṣṇava-sevana'
'nirantara kara kṛṣṇa-nāma-saṅkīrtana'

"Śrī Caitanya Mahāprabhu replied, 'Without cessation continue chanting the holy name of Lord Kṛṣṇa. Whenever possible, serve Him and His devotees, the Vaiṣṇavas.'"

—*Śrī Caitanya-caritāmṛta, Madhya-līlā* 15.103-4

Of these three activities, the chanting of the holy names is the first and foremost and is recommended by Lord Caitanya to be performed constantly.

> "It is the duty of a *gṛhastha* to constantly chant the holy names of the Lord and serve the Vaiṣṇavas and the Lord with the help of his relatives and by the wealth he has earned through his pious life."
> —Bhaktivinoda Ṭhākura, *Śrī Bhaktyāloka* 12

Śravaṇaṁ kīrtanaṁ (Hearing and Chanting)

There are four ages of mankind described in Vedic literatures, and each one has its own process of spiritual advancement that is specifically suited for the people of that age.

kṛte yad dhyāyato viṣṇuṁ
tretāyāṁ yajato makhaiḥ
dvāpare paricaryāyāṁ
kalau tad dhari-kīrtanāt

> "Whatever result one obtained in Satya-yuga by meditating on Viṣṇu, in Tretā-yuga by performing sacrifices, and in Dvāpara-yuga by serving the Lord's lotus feet, one can also obtain in Kali-yuga simply by chanting the Hare Kṛṣṇa *mahā-mantra*."
> —*Śrīmad Bhāgavatam* 12.3.52

For the age of Kali, otherwise known as 'the age of quarrel and hypocrisy', in which we are now living, the recommended process for spiritual advancement is the chanting of the holy names of the Lord.

harer nāma harer nāma
harer nāmaiva kevalam

kalau nāsty eva nāsty eva
nāsty eva gatir anyathā

"In this age of quarrel and hypocrisy the only means of deliverance is chanting the holy name of the Lord. There is no other way. There is no other way. There is no other way."

—*Bṛhan-nāradīya Purāṇa*

The holy name of the Lord can bestow love of God on the offenceless chanter.

tāra madhye sarva-śreṣṭha nāma-saṅkīrtana
niraparādhe nāma laile pāya prema-dhana

"Of the nine processes of devotional service, the most important is to always chant the holy name of the Lord. If one does so, avoiding the ten kinds of offences, one very easily obtains the most valuable love of Godhead."

—*Śrī Caitanya-caritāmṛta, Antya-līlā* 4.71

Husbands and wives can take shelter of the holy name of the Lord by chanting the Hare Kṛṣṇa *mahā-mantra* while carrying out their regular daily activities.

"Whatever social dealings a householder has to perform should be done while taking shelter of the holy name of Kṛṣṇa. Regarding the character of the *mahājana* Śrī Kalidāsa, the *Śrī Caitanya-caritāmṛta* (*Antya-līlā* 16.6-7) states:

> 'Kālidāsa was a very advanced devotee, yet he was simple and liberal. He would chant the holy name of Kṛṣṇa while performing all his ordinary dealings. When he used to throw dice in jest, he would chant 'Hare Kṛṣṇa' while throwing the dice.'"
>
> —Bhaktivinoda Ṭhākura, *Śrī Bhaktyāloka* 12

Householders can create a sublime atmosphere in the home by hearing and chanting the holy names and pastimes of the Lord, following the example of Svāyambhuva Manu, one of the ancient fathers of mankind.

> "Emperor Svāyambhuva Manu enjoyed life with his wife and subjects and fulfilled his desires without being disturbed by unwanted principles contrary to the process of religion. Celestial musicians and their wives sang in chorus about the pure reputation of the Emperor, and early in the morning, every day, he used to listen to the pastimes of the Supreme Personality of Godhead with a loving heart."
>
> —*Śrīmad Bhāgavatam* 3.22.33

The practice of Svāyambhuva Manu, to hear the singing of devotional songs in the early morning and at night, is still followed by some of the royal families in India.

> "This custom is still prevalent in India in some of the royal families and temples. Professional musicians sing with *śahnāīs*, and the sleeping members of the house gradually get up from their beds in a pleasing atmosphere. During bedtime also the singers sing songs

in relationship with the pastimes of the Lord, with *śahnāī* accompaniment, and the householders gradually fall asleep remembering the glories of the Lord."

—*Śrīmad Bhāgavatam* 3.22.33 Bhaktivedanta purport

The rest of us can take advantage of modern technology to hear spiritual sound vibrations in our own homes. The hearing or watching of mundane entertainment that is devoid of spiritual content are considered to be forms of *prajalpa* (talking unnecessarily about mundane subject matters).

"In the Western countries old men, retired from active life, play cards, fish, watch television and debate about useless socio-political schemes. All these and other frivolous activities are included in the *prajalpa* category. Intelligent persons interested in Kṛṣṇa consciousness should never take part in such activities."

—*The Nectar of Instruction* 2 purport

Prajalpa is one of the six activities that can spoil one's devotional service if one becomes too much entangled in them.

atyāhāraḥ prayāsaś ca
prajalpo niyamāgrahaḥ
jana-saṅgaś ca laulyaṁ ca
ṣaḍbhir bhaktir vinaśyati

"One's devotional service is spoiled when he becomes too entangled in the following six activities: (1) eating

> more than necessary or collecting more funds than required; (2) overendeavoring for mundane things that are very difficult to obtain; (3) talking unnecessarily about mundane subject matters; (4) practicing the scriptural rules and regulations only for the sake of following them and not for the sake of spiritual advancement, or rejecting the rules and regulations of the scriptures and working independently or whimsically; (5) associating with worldly-minded persons who are not interested in Kṛṣṇa consciousness; and (6) being greedy for mundane achievements."
>
> —*The Nectar of Instruction* 2

Mundane movies may attract the mind and senses, but, if they are devoid of God consciousness, they do not satisfy the self, the soul. Those who practise replacing these with more God conscious forms of recreation develop a higher taste for hearing the transcendental pastimes of the Supreme Lord and eventually lose their attraction for mundane entertainment.

> "Those words which do not describe the glories of the Lord, who alone can sanctify the atmosphere of the whole universe, are considered by saintly persons to be like a place of pilgrimage for crows. Since the all-perfect persons are inhabitants of the transcendental abode, they do not derive any pleasure there."
>
> —*Śrīmad Bhāgavatam* 1.5.10

Devotees of the Lord can experience the transcendental pleasure of remembering Him, while waking and sleeping, by hearing and chanting about Him.

> "In every house, in addition to the singing program, there is an arrangement for *Bhāgavatam* lectures in the evening; family members sit down, hold Hare Kṛṣṇa *kīrtana*, hear narrations from *Śrīmad-Bhāgavatam* and *Bhagavad-gītā*, and enjoy music before going to bed. The atmosphere created by this *saṅkīrtana* movement lives in their hearts, and while sleeping they also dream of the singing and glorification of the Lord. In such a way, perfection of Kṛṣṇa consciousness can be attained."
>
> —*Śrīmad Bhāgavatam* 3.22.33 Bhaktivedanta purport

A householder who is initiated by a *sannyāsī* can also invite others to his home and share his knowledge with them.

> "A person who is a householder but is initiated by a *sannyāsī* has the duty to spread Kṛṣṇa consciousness at home; as far as possible, he should call his friends and neighbors to his house and hold classes in Kṛṣṇa consciousness. Holding a class means chanting the holy name of Kṛṣṇa and speaking from *Bhagavad-gītā* or *Śrīmad-Bhāgavatam*. There are immense literatures for spreading Kṛṣṇa consciousness, and it is the duty of each and every householder to learn about Kṛṣṇa from his *sannyāsī* spiritual master."
>
> —*Śrīmad Bhāgavatam* 3.21.31 Bhaktivedanta purport

While preaching programmes are usually held in the evening, the most auspicious time of the day to begin hearing and chanting is early in the morning, especially before sunrise. This practice was demonstrated by the Supreme Personality of Godhead Himself during His earthly pastimes as the King of Dvārakā.

> "Lord Kṛṣṇa used to lie down with His sixteen thousand wives, but He would also rise from bed very early in the morning, three hours before sunrise. By nature's arrangement the crowing of the cocks warns of the *brāhma-muhūrta* hour. There is no need of alarm clocks: as soon as the cocks crow early in the morning, it is to be understood that it is time to rise from bed. Hearing that sound, Kṛṣṇa would get up from bed, but His rising early was not very much to the liking of His wives... An ideal householder should learn from the behavior of Lord Kṛṣṇa how to rise early in the morning, however comfortably he may be lying in bed embraced by his wife."
>
> —*Kṛṣṇa the Supreme Personality of Godhead* 70

While it is not possible for human beings to imitate the transcendental pastimes of the Supreme Personality of Godhead, some of His activities are meant to set an ideal example for others to follow.

> "We should clearly note this fact: the activities of the Lord should be followed, but they cannot be imitated. For example, Kṛṣṇa's ideal life as a householder can

be followed, but if one wants to imitate Kṛṣṇa by expanding into many forms, that is not possible."

—*Kṛṣṇa the Supreme Personality of Godhead* 70

The peaceful early morning hours are favourable for quality hearing and chanting of the holy names of the Lord. By rising early in the morning and chanting the Hare Kṛṣṇa *mahā-mantra*, devotees become peacefully situated in the mode of goodness, which is conducive for remembering Kṛṣṇa throughout the day.

"After rising from bed, Lord Kṛṣṇa would wash His mouth, hands and feet and would immediately sit down and meditate on Himself. This does not mean, however, that we should also sit down and meditate on ourselves. We have to meditate upon Kṛṣṇa, Rādhā-Kṛṣṇa. That is real meditation. Kṛṣṇa is Kṛṣṇa Himself; therefore He was teaching us that *brāhma-muhūrta* should be utilized for meditation on Rādhā-Kṛṣṇa. By such meditation Kṛṣṇa would feel very much satisfied, and similarly we will also feel transcendentally pleased and satisfied if we utilize the *brāhma-muhūrta* period to meditate on Rādhā and Kṛṣṇa and if we think of how Śrī Rukmiṇīdevī and Kṛṣṇa acted as ideal householders to teach the whole human society to rise early in the morning and immediately engage in Kṛṣṇa consciousness. There is no difference between meditating on the eternal forms of Rādhā-Kṛṣṇa and chanting the *mahā-mantra*, Hare Kṛṣṇa."

—*Kṛṣṇa the Supreme Personality of Godhead* 70

The Hare Kṛṣṇa *mahā-mantra* is composed as follows:

HARE KṚṢṆA, HARE KṚṢṆA, KṚṢṆA KṚṢṆA, HARE HARE;
HARE RĀMA, HARE RĀMA, RĀMA RĀMA, HARE HARE.

It is a prayer to the Supreme Lord Kṛṣṇa, 'the all-attractive', also known as Rāma, 'the reservoir of all pleasure', together with His eternal feminine consort, Rādhā, or Hara, the personification of love, devotion, and compassion. While early morning chanting is highly recommended, at the same time there are no hard and fast rules for chanting the *mahā-mantra*. It can be chanted at any time and in any place.

> "Kṛṣṇa has thousands and thousands of names, of which the name Kṛṣṇa is the chief, and there are no hard and fast rules for chanting. It is not that one must chant at a certain time. No. At any time one may chant."
>
> —*Teachings of Queen Kuntī* 8

The *mahā-mantra* is so powerful that it can be chanted by anyone, in any stage of life, and award the same spiritual benefit.

dharmas te gṛha-medhīyo
varṇitaḥ pāpa-nāśanaḥ
gṛhastho yena padavīm
añjasā nyāsinām iyāt

> "The process of chanting the holy name of the Lord is so powerful that by this chanting even householders

> (*gṛhasthas*) can very easily gain the ultimate result achieved by persons in the renounced order. Mahārāja Yudhiṣṭhira, I have now explained to you that process of religion."
>
> —*Śrīmad Bhāgavatam* 7.15.74

> Bhaktivedanta purport:
> "Mahārāja Yudhiṣṭhira thought that because he was a *gṛhastha* there was no hope of his being liberated, and therefore he asked Nārada Muni how he could get out of material entanglement. But Nārada Muni, citing a practical example from his own life, established that by associating with devotees and chanting the Hare Kṛṣṇa *mantra*, any man in any condition of life can achieve the highest perfection without a doubt."

Whether one remains at home as a householder, or away from home in the renounced order of life, either way one can become dear to God by chanting the Hare Kṛṣṇa *mantra*.

> "So the aim should be how to become a friend of God. It doesn't matter whether you remain at home or out of home. Narottama dāsa Ṭhākura says, *gṛhe bā vanete thāke, 'hā gaurāṅga' bale ḍāke*. Either you remain at home or outside of the home, but you chant *śrī kṛṣṇa caitanya prabhu nityānanda śrī-advaita gadādhara śrīvāsādi-gaura-bhakta-vṛnda*. This is the process, very simple process, and then Hare Kṛṣṇa. If you want knowledge, knowledge will of course come automatically. If your heart is purified by this

> *śravanaṁ kīrtanam* method, *ceto-darpaṇa-mārjanam*, then the heart will be purified, and God is situated within your heart. Then, as soon as your heart is purified, you'll be able to see God within yourself, within your heart. That is called meditation. You will see God within yourself constantly: 'Here is God. Here is Kṛṣṇa.' That is meditation."
>
> —Bhaktivedanta lecture, *Śrīmad Bhāgavatam* 5.5.2
> Johannesburg 22/10/1975

Wherever we fall short in following *varṇāśrama-dharma*, due to the chaotic influence of the age of Kali, we can achieve the same result of self-realisation simply by chanting the Hare Kṛṣṇa *mahā-mantra*.

> "Now everything is topsy-turvy. Therefore, by His grace, Caitanya Mahāprabhu has simply recommended... only chant... This will give the same result that is introduced by the Vedic culture and will purify the heart to be able to understand one's position. By the chanting of the Hare Kṛṣṇa *mantra*, the same result will come... Therefore, there is no question of being depressed that: 'We do not belong to this, do not belong to that.' Never mind. Whatever it is, simply chant and you'll become purified."
>
> —Bhaktivedanta lecture, *Bhagavad-gītā* 1.40
> London 28/7/1973

Bhakti-yoga (The Path of Devotion)

The supreme *dharma* for all human beings is to render pure devotional service to the Supreme Lord. Service that is rendered out of love, without any selfish motivation and consistently, is known as pure devotional service and is the source of unlimited spiritual happiness.

> "The supreme occupation for all humanity is that by which men can attain to loving devotional service unto the transcendent Lord. Such devotional service must be unmotivated and uninterrupted to completely satisfy the self."
>
> —*Śrīmad Bhāgavatam* 1.2.6

The four goals of family life are also easily fulfilled for those who engage in devotional service to the Supreme Personality of Godhead.

> "Any person who desires the fruits of the four principles religiosity, economic development, sense gratification and, at the end, liberation, should engage himself in the devotional service of the Supreme Personality of Godhead, for worship of His lotus feet yields the fulfilment of all of these."
>
> —*Śrīmad Bhāgavatam* 4.8.41

The ultimate religious principle is simply to surrender to the Supreme Lord. He assures us in the *Gita* that, if we do this, He will protect us from all karmic reactions.

sarva-dharmān parityajya
mām ekaṁ śaraṇaṁ vraja
ahaṁ tvāṁ sarva-pāpebhyo
mokṣayiṣyāmi mā śucaḥ

"Abandon all varieties of religion and just surrender unto Me. I shall deliver you from all sinful reactions. Do not fear."

—*Bhagavad-gītā As It Is* 18.66

Materially motivated religious activities become superfluous for those who are engaged in pure devotional service to the Supreme Personality of Godhead.

dharmaḥ projjhita-kaitavo 'tra paramo nirmatsarāṇāṁ satāṁ
vedyaṁ vāstavam atra vastu śivadaṁ tāpa-trayonmūlanam
śrīmad-bhāgavate mahā-muni-kṛte kiṁ vā parair īśvaraḥ
sadyo hṛdy avarudhyate 'tra kṛtibhiḥ śuśrūṣubhis tat-kṣaṇāt

"Completely rejecting all religious activities which are materially motivated, this *Bhāgavata Purāṇa* propounds the highest truth, which is understandable by those devotees who are fully pure in heart. The highest truth is reality distinguished from illusion for the welfare of all. Such truth uproots the threefold miseries. This beautiful *Bhāgavatam*, compiled by the great sage Vyāsadeva in his maturity, is sufficient in itself for God realization. What is the need of any other scripture? As soon as one attentively and submissively hears the message of *Bhāgavatam*, by this

> culture of knowledge the Supreme Lord is established within his heart."
>
> —*Śrīmad Bhāgavatam* 1.1.2

One who has attained pure devotional service is not required to fulfil the duties and obligations of *varṇāśrama-dharma.*

> "The beauty of Kṛṣṇa consciousness, however, is that by one stroke, by engaging in devotional service, one can surpass all the rituals of the different orders of life."
>
> —*Bhagavad-gītā As It Is* 8.28 purport

A pure devotee of the Lord, who is fully immersed in Kṛṣṇa consciousness, no longer identifies himself with *varṇāśrama* designations.

> *nāhaṁ vipro na ca nara-patir nāpi vaiśyo na śūdro*
> *nāhaṁ varṇī na ca gṛha-patir no vanastho yatir vā*
> *kintu prodyan-nikhila-paramānanda-pūrnāmṛtābdher*
> *gopī-bhartuḥ pada-kamalayor dāsa-dāsānudāsaḥ*

> "I am not a *brāhmaṇa*, I am not a *kṣatriya*, I am not a *vaiśya* or a *śūdra*. Nor am I a *brahmacārī*, a householder, a *vānaprastha* or a *sannyāsī*. I identify myself only as the servant of the servant of the servant of the lotus feet of Lord Śrī Kṛṣṇa, the maintainer of the *gopīs*. He is like an ocean of nectar, and He is the cause of universal transcendental bliss. He is always existing with brilliance."
>
> Śrī Caitanya Mahāprabhu (*Padyāvalī* 74)

At the same time, however, a liberated soul continues to observe the rules and regulations of *varṇāśrama* in order to set a good example for people in general. Śrī Caitanya Mahāprabhu, who was an incarnation of the Supreme Lord in the guise of a devotee, accepted the *sannyāsa* order and rigidly observed the rules and regulations of *sannyāsa-āśrama*. His austerities gave pain to the hearts of His devotees.

> "Being a *sannyāsī*, I have a duty to lie down on the ground and to take a bath three times a day, even during the winter. But Mukunda becomes very unhappy when he sees My severe austerities."
>
> *Śrī Caitanya-caritāmṛta, Madhya-līlā* 7.23

Caitanya Mahāprabhu performed His pastimes five hundred years ago in India, among people who carried some awareness of Vedic cultural traditions. To satisfy the general public, to protect them from making offences, and to teach them by His example how to follow the *varṇāśrama* system, He chose to strictly adhere to the rules and regulations of the *sannyāsa-āśrama*. According to time, place and circumstances, pure devotees of the Lord may also sometimes transcend certain details of the *varṇāśrama* system for the higher purpose of giving Kṛṣṇa consciousness to others.

> "An advanced devotee, who remains aloof from material sense gratification, is not bound by the Vedic social divisions; thus even a householder may live very austerely, travelling and preaching Kṛṣṇa consciousness

away from home, and even a *sannyāsī* may sometimes engage women in the devotional service of Lord Kṛṣṇa. The most advanced devotees cannot be restricted by the rituals and regulations of the *varṇāśrama* system, and they move freely around the world distributing love of Godhead. *Mat-para* indicates a pure devotee of the Lord who always keeps the Lord fixed in his heart and consciousness. One who falls down to become a victim of sense gratification is not fully established on the platform of *mat-para* and should rigidly observe the social divisions and regulations to remain steady on the platform of pious human life."
—*Śrīmad Bhāgavatam* 11.17.38 purport by Hṛdayānanda Goswami

Generally, however, we are advised to respect the rules and regulations of *varṇāśrama-dharma* and to follow them as far as possible. One who performs sinful activities on the plea of being transcendental to *varṇāśrama* only becomes degraded.

"If, however, one performs illicit activities on the strength of being transcendental to Vedic social divisions, one is revealed to be a materialistic neophyte and not an advanced devotee of the Lord."
—*Śrīmad Bhāgavatam* 11.17.38 purport by Hṛdayānanda Goswami

In this connection, the main pitfall to be avoided is known as *niyamāgraha*, which is one of the six faults that obstruct spiritual advancement in devotional service. The word *niyamāgraha* has two meanings. One is to reject scriptural rules and act independently, and the other is to follow the rules fanatically with some material motivation.

> "Accepting some of the scriptural rules and regulations for immediate benefit, as utilitarians advocate, is called *niyama-āgraha*, and neglecting the rules and regulations of the *śāstras*, which are meant for spiritual development, is called *niyama-agraha*. The word *āgraha* means 'eagerness to accept,' and *agraha* means 'failure to accept.' By the addition of either of these two words to the word *niyama* ('rules and regulations'), the word *niyamāgraha* is formed. Thus *niyamāgraha* has a twofold meaning that is understood according to the particular combination of words. Those interested in Kṛṣṇa consciousness should not be eager to accept rules and regulations for economic advancement, yet they should very faithfully accept scriptural rules and regulations for the advancement of Kṛṣṇa consciousness. They should strictly follow the regulative principles by avoiding illicit sex, meat-eating, gambling and intoxication."
>
> —*The Nectar of Instruction* 2 purport

As any machine is accompanied by an instruction manual, similarly the machine of this material world is accompanied by the instruction manual of ancient scriptures. Scriptural rules and regulations are provided by God to give people the opportunity to attain liberation and get out from this world. This goal cannot be attained either by those who totally neglect scriptural injunctions or by those who are over-eager to follow scriptural injunctions for the sake of achieving short-term material benefits. The ultimate purpose of following scriptural regulations is to advance in *bhakti*, devotional service to the Supreme Personality of Godhead, which is the path of eternal liberation. Rules and regulations are meant to be accepted to the extent that they are favourable for spiritual advancement in devotional service. Wherever it becomes impractical to observe all the details of Vedic injunctions, one can nevertheless remain faithful to their underlying principles. According to time, place, and circumstance, details may sometimes be adjusted; but the main principles of religion are universally applicable.

> "One religion is given in the *Bhagavad-gītā*: *sarva-dharmān parityajya mām ekaṁ śaraṇaṁ vraja*. To surrender to God, the Great, and to abide by His instruction, that is called religion. It may be that the Hindus are following the same principle in a different way or the Christian may be following the same principle in a different way. That is called *deśa-kāla-pātra*. According to time, atmosphere, and the performer, there may be little differences. But the real purpose of *dharma* is to surrender to God and try to love Him. That is religion."
>
> —Bhaktivedanta lecture, *Bhagavad-gītā* 7.1, Fiji 24/5/1975

The process of surrender to the Supreme Personality of Godhead has six characteristics.

> "In the process of surrender unto the Supreme Personality of Godhead there are six items: to accept everything favorable for devotional service, to reject everything unfavorable for devotional service, to believe that Kṛṣṇa will always give protection, to identify oneself with Kṛṣṇa's devotees, always to feel inability without the help of Kṛṣṇa and always to think oneself inferior to Kṛṣṇa, even though one may have full capacity to perform something on his own."
> —*The Nectar of Devotion* 39

The essence and purpose of all religious principles is to remember the Supreme Personality of Godhead always.

smartavyaḥ satataṁ viṣṇur
vismartavyo na jātucit
sarve vidhi-niṣedhāḥ syur
etayor eva kiṅkarāḥ

> "Kṛṣṇa is the origin of Lord Viṣṇu. He should always be remembered and never forgotten at any time. All the rules and prohibitions mentioned in the *śāstras* should be the servants of these two principles."
> —*Padma Purāṇa*

The main guiding principle of spiritual life is to mould one's activities in such a way that one can always remember the Supreme Personality of Godhead.

> "We should always try to mold the activities of our lives in such a way that we will constantly remember Viṣṇu, or Kṛṣṇa. That is Kṛṣṇa consciousness...

> Within this simple order and prohibition, all regulative principles are found complete. This regulative principle is applicable to all *varṇas* and *āśramas*, the castes and occupations of life. If this injunction is followed, then all other rules and regulations will automatically fall into line. All other rules and regulations should be treated as assistants or servants to this one basic principle."
>
> —*The Nectar of Devotion* 2

Whatever unintentional discrepancies may occur in one's attempts to follow the Vedic rules can be counteracted by the chanting of the Hare Kṛṣṇa *mahā-mantra*.

nāmno hi yāvatī śaktiḥ
pāpa-nirharaṇe hareḥ
tāvat kartuṁ na śaknoti
pātakaṁ pātakī naraḥ

> "Simply by chanting one holy name of Hari, a sinful man can counteract the reactions to more sins than he is able to commit."
>
> —*Bṛhad-viṣṇu Purāṇa*

The *Padma Purāna* specifies ten offences that need to be avoided for effective chanting of the holy names of the Lord.

> "(1) To blaspheme the devotees who have dedicated their lives for propagating the holy name of the Lord. (2) To consider the names of demigods like Lord Śiva or Lord Brahmā to be equal to, or independent of, the name of Lord Viṣṇu. (3) To disobey the orders of the

> spiritual master. (4) To blaspheme the Vedic literature or literature in pursuance of the Vedic version. (5) To consider the glories of chanting Hare Kṛṣṇa to be imagination. (6) To give some interpretation on the holy name of the Lord. (7) To commit sinful activities on the strength of the holy name of the Lord. (8) To consider the chanting of Hare Kṛṣṇa one of the auspicious ritualistic activities offered in the *Vedas* as fruitive activities (*karma-kāṇḍa*). (9) To instruct a faithless person about the glories of the holy name. (10) To not have complete faith in the chanting of the holy names and to maintain material attachments, even after understanding so many instructions on this matter."
>
> —*The Nectar of Devotion* 8

To disobey the orders of the spiritual master and to disrespect the revealed scriptures are two of the offences that hamper the effectiveness of chanting. Those who respect the Vedic scriptures and the instructions of the bona fide spiritual master and try to follow them, even though imperfectly, while also endeavouring to avoid the other offences, can make steady advancement in chanting the holy names of the Lord and become freed from all sinful reactions.

nāmābhāsa haite haya sarva-pāpa-kṣaya

> "If one offenselessly utters the holy name even imperfectly, one can be freed from all the results of sinful life."
>
> —*Śrī Caitanya-caritāmṛta, Antya-līlā* 3.61

Chapter Four

Patnī-dharma

Duties for Married Women

Satī (Chastity)—To Serve the Husband
To Favour the Husband
To Favour the Husband's Relatives & Friends
To Follow the Vows of the Husband

Chapter Four

Patnī-dharma

—Duties for Married Women—

dhruvā dyauḥ dhruvā pṛthivī
dhruvaṁ viśvaṁ idaṁ jagat
dhruvāsaḥ parvatā ime
dhruvā strī pati-kule

śrī-viṣṇu-vaiṣṇava-sevāsu iyaṁ

"Fixed is the sky, fixed is the earth. Fixed is the world, the universe. Fixed are these mountains, fixed is this wife, in her husband's house, in the service of Viṣṇu and His devotees."

—*Sāma Veda, Brāhmaṇa* 1.3.7

Satī (Chastity)

According to Vedic teachings, the foremost religious principle for a married woman is chastity to the husband. Women in Vedic culture are traditionally trained from childhood to become chaste wives.

> "If a woman is trained as a girl from the very beginning that: 'You should remain chaste,' that is *dharma*. It is called *satītā dharma*. *Satī* means chastity."
>
> —Bhaktivedanta lecture, *Bhagavad-gītā* 1.40
> London 28/7/1973

Women are soft-hearted by nature, and a woman who is well protected and taught to be chaste naturally becomes a faithful wife and an affectionate mother, the heart of a happy home.

> "These are very important things, that soft-hearted woman, *vāma-svabhāvā*, they should be given protection. They should be trained to become faithful wives, affectionate mothers. Then the home will be very happy, and without happiness we cannot make any spiritual progress. We must be peaceful. This is the preliminary condition."
>
> —Bhaktivedanta lecture, *Śrīmad Bhāgavatam* 1.7.43
> Vṛndāvana 3/11/1976

In modern societies where this type of basic training and protection for women have become neglected, the divorce rate has also increased. It is the chastity of women that upholds and protects the institution of marriage and produces good children who become assets to society.

> "Good population in human society is the basic principle for peace, prosperity and spiritual progress in life. The *varṇāśrama* religion's principles were so designed that good population would prevail in society

> for the general spiritual progress of state and community. Such population depends on the chastity and faithfulness of its womanhood."
>
> —*Bhagavad-gīta As It Is* 1.40 purport

By the help of a chaste wife, a man can attain the four goals of marriage along with her.

> "There is a verse: *svargāpta kāma mokṣāya dharā samprati hetutā. Dharā* means wife. A wife can help one to be elevated to the heavenly planets, and *dharma ārtha kāma*, to become helpful in the matter of advancement in religious and spiritual knowledge, *dharma*; *artha*, economic development; *kāma*, satisfying the husband for sense gratification; *dharma artha kāma*, and *mokṣa* also, also for salvation. The wife is so important. If there is a chaste wife, she can help the husband in these four principles of life, *dharma, artha, kāma, mokṣa... dharā samprati hetutā.* If the society can train girls to become nice wives, such wives become a great source of energy to their husbands."
>
> —Bhaktivedanta lecture, *Bhagavad-gītā* 1.41-2
> London 29/7/1973

There are four prescribed principles to be followed by a chaste wife.

strīṇāṁ ca pati-devānāṁ
tac-chuśrūṣānukūlatā
tad-bandhuṣv anuvṛttiś ca
nityaṁ tad-vrata-dhāraṇam

"To render service to the husband, to be always favorably disposed toward the husband, to be equally well disposed toward the husband's relatives and friends, and to follow the vows of the husband, these are the four principles to be followed by women described as chaste."

—*Śrīmad Bhāgavatam* 7.11.25

To Serve the Husband

"For a chaste woman, service to the husband without duplicity is the best religious principle."

—*Kṛṣṇa the Supreme Personality of Godhead* 29

Since the eternal constitutional position of the spirit soul is to be a servant of God, there is a natural pleasure to be derived from service to others, especially to those who are near and dear. Service to the devotees of the Lord is dearer to Him than direct service.

"My dear Pārtha, one who claims to be My devotee is not so. Only a person who claims to be the devotee of My devotee is actually My devotee."

—*Ādi Purāṇa*

According to Vedic teachings, the husband is said to be the supreme demigod for a woman. In other words, by serving her husband, she satisfies the Supreme Personality of Godhead and all the demigods.

> "A husband is the supreme demigod for a woman. The Supreme Personality of Godhead, Lord Vasudeva, the husband of the goddess of fortune, is situated in everyone's heart and is worshiped through the various names and forms of the demigods by fruitive workers. Similarly, a husband represents the Lord as the object of worship for a woman."
>
> —*Śrīmad Bhāgavatam* 6.18.33-4

Demigods are administrators of the various departments of universal affairs and they are servants of the Supreme Personality of Godhead, working under His direction. People who worship demigods are actually worshipping the Supreme Personality of Godhead through those demigods, though they may be unaware of it.

> "Endowed with such a faith, he endeavors to worship a particular demigod and obtains his desires. But in actuality these benefits are bestowed by Me alone."
>
> —Lord Kṛṣṇa, *Bhagavad-gītā As It Is* 7.22

Similarly, women who are engaged in serving their husbands can also worship the Supreme Lord through the media of their husbands.

> "If women, who are usually very much attached to their husbands, worship their husbands as representatives of Vāsudeva, the women benefit... In India a husband is still called *pati-guru*, the husband spiritual master. If husband and wife are attached to one another for

advancement in Kṛṣṇa consciousness, their relationship of co-operation is very effective for such advancement."

—*Śrīmad Bhāgavatam* 6.18.34 Bhaktivedanta purport

As well as the universal administrators, devotees of God are also sometimes referred to as demigods, or godly people.

"The devotees are all demigods... Anyone who is a devotee of Lord Kṛṣṇa is called a *deva*... Lord Kṛṣṇa is very much pleased with His devotees, even if they are not on the topmost stage of devotional service. Even on the lower stages of devotional service one is transcendental, and if one continues with devotional life, he continues to be a *deva* or *sura*. If one continues in this way, Kṛṣṇa will always be pleased with him and will give him all instructions so that he may very easily return home, back to Godhead."

—*Śrīmad Bhāgavatam* 8.5.24 Bhaktivedanta purport

According to Vedic culture, the husband is the supreme demigod for a woman; the *guru* is regarded by his disciple as God's representative; children are taught to respect their parents as *gurus*, or God's representatives; a righteous king is treated by his subjects as God's representative; *brāhmaṇas* and *sannyāsīs* are worshipped by all other members of society as agents of God; and a guest who arrives at the door of a householder is treated as a god. The culture of respect is applicable to all these relationships and fosters the divine quality of humility. The understanding behind this culture is that everyone is a servant of God, and that all worship and service are received on His behalf and returned to Him. While devotees are naturally humble and do not like to receive worship for themselves, they are actually worshipable as representatives of God.

ārādhanānāṁ sarveṣāṁ
viṣṇor ārādhanaṁ param
tasmāt parataraṁ devi
tadīyānāṁ samarcanam

> "Of all types of worship, worship of Lord Viṣṇu is best, and better than the worship of Lord Viṣṇu is the worship of His devotee, the Vaiṣṇava."
> —*Padma Purāṇa*

The method by which a wife is recommended to worship her husband is not elaborate or reverential, but simple and natural.

> "Accepting her husband as the representative of the Supreme Person, a wife should worship him with unalloyed devotion by offering him *prasāda*. The husband, being very pleased with his wife, should engage himself in the affairs of his family."
> —*Śrīmad Bhāgavatam* 6.19.17

For a woman to cook for her husband is nothing new or out of the ordinary. This is a normal daily ritual for millions of women throughout the world.

> "Women should be expert in cooking. That is their natural tendency. They should be educated how to cook nicely, how to please the husband, how to take care of the children. This is Vedic civilisation. In the beginning a woman, in childhood, is trained by her mother. As soon as she is married, formerly child marriage, she is transferred to the care of the mother-in-law. There she is further trained. She becomes a very good housewife, takes care of household affairs, husband, children, and the home becomes a happy place."
>
> —*Conversations with Śrīla Prabhupāda*, Baltimore 7/7/1976

Today a woman's life is not as simple as it used to be. There is no more child marriage, and girls are educated along the same lines as boys. Consequently the above scenario has changed. Nevertheless, natural tendencies towards cooking and household management usually manifest themselves in women in due course of time. Cooking and eating become spiritually beneficial for both husband and wife when they cook pure vegetarian food and offer it first to the Supreme Personality of Godhead. The food then becomes *prasāda* (God's mercy) and free from *karma.*

yajña-śiṣṭāśinaḥ santo
mucyante sarva-kilbiṣaiḥ
bhuñjate te tv aghaṁ pāpā
ye pacanty ātma-kāraṇāt

> "The devotees of the Lord are released from all kinds of sins because they eat food that is offered first for

> sacrifice. Others, who prepare food for personal sense enjoyment, verily eat only sin."
>
> —*Bhagavad-gītā As It Is* 3.13

The simple act whereby a wife serves *prasāda* to her husband with affection and he receives it with appreciation is a loving exchange that nourishes their spiritual relationship.

> "The family relationship of husband and wife should be established spiritually according the process mentioned above."
>
> —*Śrīmad Bhāgavatam* 6.19.17 Bhaktivedanta purport

A chaste wife can also please her husband by dressing and decorating herself nicely, and by keeping the house clean. Cleanliness is in the mode of goodness and is favourable for peace of mind.

> "A chaste woman must dress nicely and decorate herself with golden ornaments for the pleasure of her husband. Always wearing clean and attractive garments, she should sweep and clean the household with water and other liquids so that the entire house is always pure and clean. She should collect the household paraphernalia and keep the house always aromatic with incense and flowers."
>
> —*Śrīmad Bhāgavatam* 7.11.26

This description of the duties of a chaste wife is in keeping with the traditional roles of homemaker-wife and breadwinner-husband. A wife who remains at home is secure and peaceful, and can take good care of children and household affairs, such as cooking, cleaning, etc. When a wife is peacefully situated and takes care of household affairs, the husband is free to concentrate on his own occupational duties and maintaining the family. This is the most natural division of labour between husband and wife. Just as the *varṇa* duties of men are defined according to *guṇa* and *karma*, qualities and activities, similarly the duties of women are defined according to their *guṇa* and *karma*. Most women are naturally inclined to be expert in cooking, cleaning, managing household affairs, and taking care of children. Whatever other skills and talents a woman has been given by God can also be engaged in His service. At the same time, responsible husbands and wives are always ready to do the needful.

> "A devotee is always a servant of God. Whatever service is required, as a *brāhmaṇa*, *kṣatriya*, *vaiśya*, it doesn't matter. We are ready."
>
> —Bhaktivedanta lecture, *Śrīmad Bhāgavatam* 1.16.26-30
> Hawaii 23/1/1974

A caring husband and wife are willing to assist one another with their duties when the need arises. Nowadays women are often required to go out to work to help pay the bills, and men may be required to help out at home, since most people cannot afford to keep servants. While details of service may be adjusted according to time, place and circumstance, a wife can protect her harmonious relationship with her husband by continuing to serve and respect him. A Vedic marital relationship is not an artificial stereotype. The

Vedic psychology of marriage is based on the most natural social relationship between man and woman, which has been observed since time immemorial. A man becomes empowered to successfully fulfil his responsibilities when he is given a leadership role. Vedic teachings on marriage provide the social guidelines within which unique relationships between individual men and women can prosper and progress. The guidelines serve to protect these relationships and bring out the best in people by teaching couples how to stay on track and avoid offending each other. For example, a chaste wife is recommended to decorate herself attractively only for the pleasure of her husband, and not when he is away from home.

> "According to Yājñavalkya's religious instructions, a woman whose husband is away from home should not take part in any social functions, should not decorate her body, should not laugh and should not go to any relative's house in any circumstance. This is the vow of the ladies whose husbands are away from home. At the same time, it is also enjoined that a wife should never present herself before the husband in an unclean state. She must decorate herself with ornaments and good dress and should always be present before the husband in a happy and joyous mood."
>
> —*Śrīmad Bhāgavatam* 1.11.31 Bhaktivedanta purport

When her husband is away, a chaste wife keeps a low profile, avoids going out to socialise, dresses simply, and maintains a sober mood. These are natural patterns of behaviour for a woman who is loyal and affectionate to her husband. When her husband is at home, she feels happy and dresses nicely. A loving wife can make her husband happy by serving him in a happy mood. The duties of a chaste woman are further elaborated as follows.

> "A chaste woman should not be greedy, but satisfied in all circumstances. She must be very expert in handling household affairs and should be fully conversant with religious principles. She should speak pleasingly and truthfully and should be very careful and always clean and pure. Thus a chaste woman should engage with affection in the service of a husband who is not fallen."
>
> —*Śrīmad Bhāgavatam* 7.11.28

A husband who is not fallen is qualified to accept service from a chaste wife. A fallen husband is defined as follows.

> "A fallen husband is one who is addicted to the four principles of sinful activity—namely illicit sex, meat-eating, gambling and intoxication. Specifically, if one is not a soul surrendered to the Supreme Personality of Godhead, he is understood to be contaminated."
>
> —*Śrīmad Bhāgavatam* 7.11.28 Bhaktivedanta purport

A woman is not obliged to serve a husband who is addicted to the four sinful activities and is inimical towards God. Remarriage for women, however, is not endorsed by Vedic culture.

> "If her husband is fallen, it is recommended that she give up his association. Giving up the association of her husband does not mean however that a woman should marry again..."
>
> —*Śrīmad Bhāgavatam* 7.11.28 Bhaktivedanta purport

At the same time, women need to be always protected from those who would take advantage of them.

> "As children are very prone to be misled, women are similarly very prone to degradation. Therefore, both children and women require protection by the elder members of the family."
>
> —*Bhagavad-gītā As It Is* 1.40 purport

In Vedic society where girls and women were protected by their families, marriages were carefully arranged, and men were allowed to accept a second wife without abandoning the first one, the rule against remarriage for women could naturally be upheld. Today's situation is unfortunately different. A woman may be abandoned by her husband in favour of another woman and find herself bereft of proper protection. While remarriage should ideally be avoided, in such situations women sometimes choose remarriage as a safer option than remaining unprotected and vulnerable. Where girls are protected and marriages are carefully arranged, according to Vedic guidelines, there both divorce and remarriage can be avoided. By serving a husband who is a Vaiṣṇava (worshipper of God), a wife becomes a participant in his devotional service to the Lord and reaps the same spiritual benefit.

> "The wife is dependent on the husband and if the husband is a Vaiṣṇava, then naturally she shares the devotional service of the husband because she renders him service. This reciprocation of service and love between husband and wife is the ideal of a householder's life."
> —*Śrīmad Bhāgavatam* 3.23.1 Bhaktivedanta purport

As the Supreme Lord can become conquered by the love of His pure devotees, by the same principle a husband becomes conquered by the wife who serves him with love.

> "As chaste women bring their gentle husbands under control by service, the pure devotees, who are equal to everyone and completely attached to Me in the core of the heart, bring Me under their full control."
> —*Śrīmad Bhāgavatam* 9.4.66

In this connection, there is a conversation in the *Mahābhārata* between two great chaste wives, Queen Satyabhāmā (wife of Lord Kṛṣṇa) and Princess Draupadī (wife of the Pāṇḍavas), in which Satyabhāmā asks Draupadī what is the secret by which she is keeping her powerful husbands obedient to her. Since Queen Satyabhāmā is an eternal consort of the Supreme Lord, she already knows the answer, but she asks the question for our benefit and to glorify Draupadī.

> "By what behaviour is it, O daughter of Drupada, that you are able to rule the sons of Pāṇḍu – those heroes imbued with strength and beauty? Beautiful lady, how

> is it that they are so obedient to you and are never angry with you? Without doubt the sons of Pāṇḍu are ever submissive to you and watchful to do your bidding, you of lovely features!"
>
> —*Mahābhārata, Vana-parva* 15.231

While it is not generally recommended for a woman to marry more than one husband, Draupadī was married to the five Pāṇḍava brothers. This was a special case that cannot be imitated by others.

> "According to Vedic principles, a woman cannot have many husbands, although a husband can have many wives. In special instances, however, it is found that a woman has more than one husband. Draupadī, for instance, was married to all of the five Pāṇḍava brothers. Similarly, the Supreme Personality of Godhead ordered all the sons of Prācīnabarhiṣat to marry the one girl born of the great sage Kaṇḍu and Pramlocā. In special cases, a girl is allowed to marry more than one man, provided she is able to treat her husbands equally. This is not possible for an ordinary woman. Only one who is especially qualified can be allowed to marry more than one husband. In this age of Kali, to find such an equipoised woman is very difficult."
>
> —*Śrīmad Bhāgavatam* 4.30.16 Bhaktivedanta purport

Draupadī replied to Satyabhāmā's question that it was by her devoted service to her husbands that she was keeping them obedient to her.

"Keeping aside vanity, and controlling desire and wrath, I always serve with devotion the sons of Pāṇḍu along with their wives. Restraining jealousy, with deep devotion of heart, without a sense of degradation at the services I perform, I wait upon my husbands... I never bathe or eat or sleep until my husband has bathed or eaten or slept, until, in fact, our attendants have bathed, eaten, or slept. Whether he is returning from the field, the forest, or the town, hastily rising up I always salute my husband with water and a seat. I always keep the house and all household articles and the food that is to be taken well-ordered and clean. I carefully keep the rice, and serve the food at the proper time... I always refrain from laughing loudly and indulging in high passion, and from everything that may give offence. Indeed, O Satyabhāmā, I am always engaged in waiting upon my lords. A separation from my lords is never agreeable to me. When my husband leaves home for the sake of any relative, then renouncing flowers and fragrant paste of every kind, I begin to undergo penances. Whatever my husband does not drink, whatever my husband does not eat, whatever my husband does not enjoy, I always renounce. O beautiful lady, decked in ornaments and ever controlled by the instructions imparted to me, I always devotedly seek the good of my lord... I think that eternal virtue for women is that which is based upon a regard for the husband. The husband is the wife's god, and he is her refuge. Indeed, there is no other refuge for her. How then can the wife do the least injury to her lord? I never, in sleeping or eating or adorning myself, act against the

> wishes of my lord, and always guided by my husbands, I never speak ill of my mother-in-law. O blessed lady, my husbands have become obedient to me in consequence of my diligence, my alacrity, and the humility with which I serve superiors."
>
> —*Mahābhārata, Vana-parva* 15.231

By her devotion, self-control, and attentive service, Princess Draupadī was able to rule her five powerful warrior husbands, who were obedient to her every wish. Therefore, she is exalted among the ranks of the greatest chaste women of history. Formerly girls were trained in every detail by their mothers from a young age how to serve the future husband, whereas today there is not so much emphasis on such training. While standards of service have declined, there is still much that can be learnt from Draupadī's self-control and selfless service mood. The secret by which a woman can conquer the heart of her husband and become victorious is further explained in the story of Cyavana Muni and Sukanyā. By the will of Providence, the young princess Sukanyā was married to the old sage Cyavana who was invalid and irritable. Sukanyā carefully learnt the art of serving her husband in such a way as to pacify him and keep him happy.

> "Cyavana Muni was very irritable, but since Sukanyā had gotten him as her husband, she dealt with him carefully, according to his mood. Knowing his mind, she performed service to him without being bewildered."
>
> —*Śrīmad Bhāgavatam* 9.3.10

This is a classic example of a wife becoming happy with her husband by understanding his mind and learning how to make him happy.

> "This is an indication of the relationship between husband and wife. A great personality like Cyavana Muni has the temperament of always wanting to be in a superior position. Such a person cannot submit to anyone. Therefore, Cyavana Muni had an irritable temperament. His wife, Sukanyā, could understand his attitude, and under the circumstances she treated him accordingly. If any wife wants to be happy with her husband, she must try to understand her husband's temperament and please him. This is victory for a woman."
>
> —*Śrīmad Bhāgavatam* 9.3.10 Bhaktivedanta purport

Real heart victory for a married woman is achieved not by combat, but by humility and service.

> "However great a woman may be, she must place herself before her husband in this way; that is to say, she must be ready to carry out her husband's orders and please him in all circumstances. Then her life will be successful. When the wife becomes as irritable as the husband, their life at home is sure to be disturbed or ultimately completely broken. In the modern day, the wife is never submissive, and therefore home life is broken even by slight incidents. Either the wife or the husband may take advantage of the divorce laws.

> According to Vedic law, however, there is no such thing as divorce laws, and a woman must be trained to be submissive to the will of her husband. Westerners contend that this is a slave mentality for the wife, but factually it is not; it is the tactic by which a woman can conquer the heart of her husband, however irritable or cruel he may be."
>
> —*Śrīmad Bhāgavatam* 9.3.10 Bhaktivedanta purport

Humility is the shining ornament of devotees of the Lord and chaste wives. Pārvatī devī gave up all material possessions to engage in humble service to Lord Śiva.

> "Bhavānī, or Pārvatī, the daughter of the King of the Himalayas, selected Lord Śiva, who appears to be just like a beggar, as her husband. In spite of her being a princess, she undertook all kinds of tribulations to associate with Lord Śiva, who did not even have a house, but was sitting underneath the trees and passing his time in meditation. Although Bhavānī was the daughter of a very great king, she used to serve Lord Śiva just like a poor woman."
>
> —*Śrīmad Bhāgavatam* 3.23.1 Bhaktivedanta purport

Similarly Devahūti renounced her opulence to serve Kardama Muni.

> "Similarly, Devahūti was the daughter of an emperor, Svāyambhuva Manu, yet she preferred to accept Kardama Muni as her husband. She served him with great love and affection, and she knew how to please him. Therefore, she is designated here as *sādhvī*, which

> means 'a chaste, faithful wife.' Her rare example is the ideal of Vedic civilization. Every woman is expected to be as good and chaste as Devahūti or Bhavānī."
>
> —*Śrīmad Bhāgavatam* 3.23.1 Bhaktivedanta purport

If "every woman is expected to be as good and chaste as Devahūti or Bhavānī", this means that it is not only such exalted personalities as Lord Śiva or Kardama Muni who are qualified to accept the service of a chaste, devoted wife. Whoever the husband may be, as long as he is a good person and a servant of God, he deserves to be served with love and respect, as the protector, maintainer, friend and guide of his faithful wife. The topmost example of a chaste and faithful wife is the goddess of fortune, the wife of Lord Viṣṇu.

yā patiṁ hari-bhāvena
bhajet śrīr iva tat-parā
hary-ātmanā harer loke
patyā śrīr iva modate

> "The woman who engages in the service of her husband, following strictly in the footsteps of the goddess of fortune, surely returns home, back to Godhead, with her devotee husband, and lives very happily in the Vaikuṇṭha planets."
>
> —*Śrīmad-Bhāgavatam* 7.11.29

> Bhaktivedanta purport:
>
> "The faithfulness of the goddess of fortune is the ideal for a chaste woman. The *Brahma-saṁhitā* (5.29) says, *lakṣmī-sahasra-śata-sambhrama-sevyamānam*. In the

> Vaikuṇṭha planets, Lord Viṣṇu is worshiped by many, many thousands of goddesses of fortune, and in Goloka Vṛndāvana, Lord Kṛṣṇa is worshiped by many, many thousands of *gopīs*, all of whom are goddesses of fortune. A woman should serve her husband as faithfully as the goddess of fortune. A man should be an ideal servant of the Lord, and a woman should be an ideal wife like the goddess of fortune. Then both husband and wife will be so faithful and strong that by acting together they will return home, back to Godhead, without a doubt."

To follow in the footsteps does not mean to artificially imitate. The service mood is natural for the soul, not mechanical. Like the endeavour for spiritual advancement, a successful marriage requires patience with ourselves and with each other, as we strive to purify ourselves from countless lifetimes of material conditioning. Patience is one of the six most important principles in the execution of devotional service.

utsāhān niścayād dhairyāt
tat-tat-karma-pravartanāt
saṅga-tyāgāt sato vṛtteḥ
ṣaḍbhir bhaktiḥ prasidhyati

> "There are six principles favorable to the execution of pure devotional service: (1) being enthusiastic, (2) endeavoring with confidence, (3) being patient, (4) acting according to regulative principles [such as *śravaṇaṁ kīrtanaṁ viṣṇoḥ smaraṇam*—hearing,

> chanting and remembering Kṛṣṇa], (5) abandoning the association of nondevotees, and (6) following in the footsteps of the previous *ācāryas*. These six principles undoubtedly assure the complete success of pure devotional service."
>
> —*The Nectar of Instruction* 3

A wife's service to her husband is performed both out of love and as a duty. A successful marital relationship begins with acceptance of mutual responsibility and performance of prescribed duties.

> "...And you also must agree to serve him under all circumstances and assist him in every way so that he may make advancement in Kṛṣṇa consciousness. By his making advancement in Kṛṣṇa consciousness, automatically the wife will make advancement by following in the husband's footsteps. But if you do not assist him and are not very obedient to his welfare, then he may become disgusted and go away. So there must be mutual responsibility by both parties, and now that you are a married couple, there is no question of your separation, but you must both strive very hard to serve Kṛṣṇa together in harmony. What are these nonsense emotions that cause you to go this way and that way? The real thing is your duty. Now you are a married couple, and you know what your duty is, so the best thing is to perform your duty and always think of Kṛṣṇa. Never mind some temporary inconveniences, we must remain steady in our duty to Kṛṣṇa."
>
> —*Letters from Śrīla Prabhupāda* 15/9/1972

By performing prescribed duties in marriage and spiritual life, we advance in love and humility. A famous example of a humble woman is Kuntīdevī, the aunt of Lord Kṛṣṇa. Although she was a liberated soul and an eternal associate of the Supreme Lord, she humbly took the position of an ordinary woman.

> "Kuntīdevī humbly submits, 'You are meant for the *paramahaṁsas* and *munis*, those who are cleansed in heart and are engaged in *bhakti-yoga*. But what are we? We are simply women. We are in a lower class. How can we understand You?' Although she understands everything, she still takes the position of an ordinary woman and says, 'How can I understand You?' This is humility."
>
> —*Teachings of Queen Kuntī* 3

When the relationship between husband and wife becomes mature, mutual dealings become naturally and spontaneously loving, consistently, and services are rendered out of love more than duty. An affectionate wife, even if she is a great queen surrounded by servants, takes pleasure in serving her husband personally. Queen Arci, the wife of King Pṛthu, was glorified for serving her husband in the same way as the goddess of fortune serves Lord Viṣṇu.

> "The wives of the demigods said: All glories to Queen Arci! We can see that this queen of the great King Pṛthu, the emperor of all the kings of the world, has served her husband with mind, speech and body exactly

as the goddess of fortune serves the Supreme Personality of Godhead, Yajñeśa, or Viṣṇu."
—*Śrīmad Bhāgavatam* 4.23.25

Bhaktivedanta purport:
"In this verse the words *yajñeśaṁ śrīr vadhūr iva* indicate that Queen Arci served her husband just as the goddess of fortune serves the Supreme Personality of Godhead Viṣṇu. We can observe that even in the history of this world, when Lord Kṛṣṇa, the supreme Viṣṇu, was ruling over Dvārakā, Queen Rukmiṇī, who was the chief of all Kṛṣṇa's queens, used to serve Lord Kṛṣṇa personally in spite of having many hundreds of maidservants to assist her. Similarly, the goddess of fortune in the Vaikuṇṭha planets also serves Nārāyaṇa personally, although there are many thousands of devotees prepared to serve the Lord. This practice is also followed by the wives of the demigods, and in days past the wives of men also followed this same principle."

Cyavana Muni eventually found an opportunity to have his old, diseased body transformed into a beautiful young body for the pleasure of his young wife Sukanyā. While such a feat is not possible for ordinary people, this outcome provides a vivid illustration of how a man can become empowered by the faithful service of his wife to make her happy.

To Favour the Husband

"...To be always favorably disposed toward the husband..."
—*Śrīmad Bhāgavatam* 7.11.25

A chaste wife considers her husband's happiness before her own, and serves him with love and respect.

> "Being ready to execute the desires of her husband, being modest and truthful, controlling her senses, and speaking in sweet words, a chaste woman should engage in the service of her husband with love, according to time and circumstances."
> —*Śrīmad Bhāgavatam* 7.11.27

To be modest and truthful, to control the senses, and to speak in sweet words; these are all symptoms of the mode of goodness. The tendency of the false ego is to engage in conflict, in the mode of passion. This passion can be subdued by an increase in qualities of goodness, which can be gradually developed by observance of religious principles, avoidance of sinful activities, and regular engagement in devotional practices, such as hearing and chanting the holy names of the Lord.

yasyāsti bhaktir bhagavaty akiñcanā
sarvair guṇais tatra samāsate surāḥ

> "All the demigods and their exalted qualities, such as religion, knowledge and renunciation, become manifest in the body of one who has developed

unalloyed devotion for the Supreme Personality of Godhead, Vāsudeva."

—*Śrīmad Bhāgavatam* 5.18.12

Where a woman is always favourably disposed towards her husband and does not fight with him, there will be not only peace but also prosperity in that home.

"Where fools are never respected, grain is well stored and where the husband and wife do not quarrel, there of her own volition resides Lakṣmī, the goddess of wealth."

—*Śrī Cāṇakya Nīti-śāstra* 3.21

Naturally there are sometimes differences of opinion between two people, which are not taken seriously by a loving and committed couple. The word "quarrel" here can be understood to refer to conflict of a more serious and ongoing nature.

"As soon as there is no quarrel between the husband and wife, the home will be happy. And as soon as there is a misunderstanding between the husband and wife, it will be hell. So the principle is that the husband honestly tries to earn a livelihood, and at home the wife should be so intelligent that whatever money the husband has earned, she'll manage with that. She'll not demand, 'Bring money, bring money, bring money.'"

—*Conversations with Śrīla Prabhupāda*, Detroit 14/6/1976

A chaste wife never speaks ill of her husband to others, and she is prepared to sacrifice her own desires, when necessary, to follow her husband's directives. Any team, to be successful, requires a leader.

> "The best course for a woman is to abide by the orders of her husband. That makes family life very peaceful."
> —*Śrīmad Bhāgavatam* 4.4.3 Bhaktivedanta purport

A happy and peaceful relationship between husband and wife is comprised of a balanced mix of both intimacy and respect.

viśrambheṇātma-śaucena
gauraveṇa damena ca
śuśrūṣayā sauhṛdena
vācā madhurayā ca bhoḥ

> "O Vidura, Devahūti served her husband with intimacy and great respect, with control of the senses, with love and with sweet words."
> —*Śrīmad Bhāgavatam* 3.23.2

> Bhaktivedanta purport:
> "Here two words are very significant. Devahūti served her husband in two ways, *viśrambheṇa* and *gauraveṇa*. These are two important processes in serving the husband or the Supreme Personality of Godhead. *Viśrambheṇa* means 'with intimacy,' and *gauraveṇa* means 'with great reverence.' The husband is a very intimate friend; therefore, the wife must render service just like an intimate friend, and at the same time she

must understand that the husband is superior in position, and thus she must offer him all respect. A man's psychology and woman's psychology are different. As constituted by bodily frame, a man always wants to be superior to his wife, and a woman, as bodily constituted, is naturally inferior to her husband. Thus, the natural instinct is that the husband wants to post himself as superior to the wife, and this must be observed. Even if there is some wrong on the part of the husband, the wife must tolerate it, and thus there will be no misunderstanding between husband and wife. *Viśrambheṇa* means 'with intimacy,' but it must not be familiarity that breeds contempt. According to the Vedic civilization, a wife cannot call her husband by name. In the present civilization the wife calls her husband by name, but in Hindu civilization she does not. Thus the inferiority and superiority complexes are recognized."

The terms "superior" and "inferior" are used here with reference to the material body and social position, and bear no reflection on personal worth. While we are not these bodies, according to the bodies we have received as a result of our previous *karma*, there are certain rules of protocol that are designed to help us to live peacefully together and gradually elevate ourselves. A relationship where two people are competing with each other for control cannot be peaceful. A wife should not envy the position of her husband. With his authority comes also the weight of responsibility for the material and spiritual welfare of the family. According to Vedic culture, the respected position of the husband in a marital relationship is established from the time of betrothal.

> "The general procedure of Vedic marriage is that a father offers his daughter to a suitable boy. That is a very respectable marriage. A boy should not go to the girl's father and ask for the hand of his daughter in marriage. That is considered to be humbling one's respectable position."
>
> —*Śrīmad Bhāgavatam* 3.22.13 Bhaktivedanta purport

Where there are misunderstandings between husband and wife, a gentle wife can defuse conflict by pacifying her husband with sweet words, instead of arguing with him.

> "*Damena ca*: a wife has to learn to control herself even if there is a misunderstanding. *Sauhṛdena vācā madhurayā* means always desiring good for the husband and speaking to him with sweet words. A person becomes agitated by so many material contacts in the outside world; therefore, in his home life he must be treated by his wife with sweet words."
>
> —*Śrīmad Bhāgavatam* 3.23.2 Bhaktivedanta purport

As materially conditioned souls in this world, we are marred by the tendency to try to control and dominate others, but our real spiritual nature is to be eternal servants of God. By learning how to become selfless servants in this world, we prepare ourselves for a higher eternal life. From this perspective, birth as a woman can be seen as a great opportunity for spiritual advancement.

> "In everyday life, our relationships with one another are practice for the divine relationships we will eventually experience. The quality of our interactions indicates how well we are preparing ourselves for association with the Supreme Lord... The highest level of the spiritual world is a realm of eternal spiritual romance and of selfless, loving exchanges. To enter the realm of pure love, we must begin here and now in the material world to become pure, unmotivated servants. Any egocentric motivation disqualifies us, because to experience divine love we must feel joy in denying our own appetites for the pleasure of the loved one. We do not lose our own identity in the process. On the contrary, our true identity expands as we render service, and each expression of selflessness intensifies our capacity to experience even more vast dimensions of love. When we are motivated by genuine love to act so selflessly, even more love is available to us."
>
> —Bhaktitīrtha Swami, *Spiritual Warrior II.2*

Genuine love in action counteracts and subdues the faults and weaknesses of human nature.

> "Working sanely and diligently, she pleased her very powerful husband, giving up all lust, pride, envy, greed, sinful activities and vanity."
>
> —*Śrīmad Bhāgavatam* 3.23.3

Misunderstandings in marital relationships usually arise from one or more of the above defects, i.e. lust, pride, envy, greed, sinful activities and vanity. These are the enemies that we need to fight against, rather than each other.

> "Here are some of the qualities of a great husband's great wife. Kardama Muni is great by spiritual qualification. Such a husband is called *tejīyāṁsam*, most powerful. Although a wife may be equal to her husband in advancement in spiritual consciousness, she should not be vainly proud. Sometimes it happens that the wife comes from a very rich family, as did Devahūti, the daughter of Emperor Svāyambhuva Manu. She could have been very proud of her parentage, but that is forbidden. The wife should not be proud of her parental position. She must always be submissive to the husband and must give up all vanity. As soon as the wife becomes proud of her parentage, her pride creates great misunderstanding between the husband and wife, and their nuptial life is ruined. Devahūti was very careful about that, and therefore it is said here that she gave up pride completely."
>
> —*Śrīmad Bhāgavatam* 3.23.3 Bhaktivedanta purport

As conditioned souls in this material world, our tendency is to rebel against God, and we do not like to surrender to Him. However the secret of our real happiness and peace lies in that surrender. Similarly, for those of us who are conditioned souls in female bodies, while we do not like to submit to our husbands, when we take a humble position and give priority to them, we naturally feel happier and more peaceful.

> "So we should remain *tad-adhīna*, always under Kṛṣṇa. That is our perfection. In the Western countries—they rebel. If women are advised to remain under the control of the husband, that is an insult to them. They cannot tolerate it. But actually we see in India that a wife who remains under the guidance of the husband is happy. That's a practical fact. Therefore, in the *Manu-saṁhitā* it is advised, *na striyam svatantram arhati*. Women should be always protected. Protection does not mean negligence, no. Protection means to give her all facilities. That is protection. Just like a father gives protection to the children."
>
> —Bhaktivedanta lecture, *Śrīmad Bhāgavatam* 3.28.18
> Nairobi 27/10/1975

Just as a woman depends on her husband for protection, similarly a man depends on his wife for encouragement. This is explained in reference to the activities of Mahārāja Priyavrata.

> "*Kṣatriyas* and *gṛhasthas*, however, actually need the encouragement of their wives in order to execute their duties. Indeed, a *gṛhastha* or *kṣatriya* cannot properly execute his responsibilities without the association of his wife. Śrī Caitanya Mahāprabhu personally admitted that a *gṛhastha* must live with a wife. *Kṣatriyas* were even allowed to have many wives to encourage them in discharging the duties of government. The association of a good wife is

necessary in a life of *karma* and political affairs. To execute his duties properly, therefore, Mahārāja Priyavrata took advantage of his good wife Barhiṣmatī, who was always very expert in pleasing her great husband by properly dressing herself, smiling, and exhibiting her feminine bodily features. Queen Barhiṣmatī always kept Mahārāja Priyavrata very encouraged, and thus he executed his governmental duty very properly."

—*Śrīmad Bhāgavatam* 5.1.29 Bhaktivedanta purport

A married man becomes empowered by the support and encouragement of his wife to succeed in all his endeavours. A woman is the energy of a man, and the power to inspire him lies in her hands.

"As far as the women class are concerned, they are accepted as a power of inspiration for men. As such, women are more powerful than men. Mighty Julius Caesar was controlled by a Cleopatra."

—*Śrīmad Bhāgavatam* 1.9.27 Bhaktivedanta purport

To Favour the Husband's Relatives and Friends

"...To be equally well disposed toward the husband's relatives and friends..."

—*Śrīmad Bhāgavatam* 7.11.25

According to the extended family system that was prevalent in Vedic society, a married woman would live not only with her husband, but also with his parents and other relatives.

> "In your country, family does not mean father and mother, only wife and children. But in our country, according to Vedic civilisation, family is a large conception. Father, mother, brother, sister, sister's son, brother's son..."
>
> —Bhaktivedanta lecture, *Śrīmad Bhāgavatam* 1.3.17
> Los Angeles 22/9/1972

A bride would become part of her husband's family and render service to his parents, as Draupadī served Kuntī-devī.

> "Personally I wait every day with food, drink, and clothes upon the revered and truthful Kuntī, that mother of heroes. I never show any preference for myself over her in matters of food and attire, and I never verbally reprove that princess who is equal to the Earth herself in forgiveness."
>
> —*Mahābhārata, Vana-parva* 15.231

When a woman marries, she enters a relationship not only with her husband, but also with all those who are dear to him. A chaste wife accepts her husband's relatives and friends as her own and treats them with due respect and affection. As a married woman conquers the heart of her husband by her devoted service, similarly she can conquer the hearts of his relatives by accepting them as her own family members and serving them.

> "Be the ruler of your husband's father. Be the ruler of your husband's mother. Be the ruler of your husband's sisters. Be the ruler of your husband's brothers."
>
> —*Sāma Veda, Brāhmaṇa* 1.2.20

To Follow the Vows of the Husband

"...To follow the vows of the husband..."
—*Śrīmad Bhāgavatam* 7.11.25

Spiritual advancement in human life requires some voluntary acceptance of austerity.

ṛṣabha uvāca
nāyaṁ deho deha-bhājāṁ nṛloke
kaṣṭān kāmān arhate viḍ-bhujāṁ ye
tapo divyaṁ putrakā yena sattvaṁ
śuddhyed yasmād brahma-saukhyaṁ tv anantam

"Lord Ṛṣabhadeva told His sons: My dear boys, of all the living entities who have accepted material bodies in this world, one who has been awarded this human form should not work hard day and night simply for sense gratification, which is available even for dogs and hogs who eat stool. One should engage in penance and austerity to attain the divine position of devotional service. By such activity, one's heart is purified, and when one attains this position, he attains eternal, blissful life, which is transcendental to material happiness and which continues forever."
—*Śrīmad Bhāgavatam* 5.5.1

Those who practise a spiritual discipline take voluntary vows to abstain from irreligious activities that would impede their advancement.

> "The four sinful activities are illicit sex, meat-eating, intoxication and gambling. These are the means by which one gets another material body that is full of miseries."
>
> —*Śrīmad Bhāgavatam* 5.5.4 Bhaktivedanta purport

By following the four regulative principles or, in other words, by abstaining from the four sinful activities, one becomes situated in *sattva-guṇa*, the mode of goodness. Spiritual practitioners may also take vows to engage in daily prayer or meditation, according to the path they are following. For example, initiated members of the International Society for Krishna Consciousness vow to chant at least sixteen rounds per day on prayer beads (i.e. sixteen times one hundred and eight) of the Hare Kṛṣṇa *mahā-mantra.*

> "As far as our ISKCON movement is concerned, we simply ask that one observe the four prohibitive rules, chant sixteen rounds and, instead of indulging in luxurious eating for the tongue, simply accept *prasāda* offered to the Lord."
>
> —*Śrīmad Bhāgavatam* 4.8.72 Bhaktivedanta purport

The process of chanting the Hare Kṛṣṇa *mahā-mantra* not only situates the chanter in the mode of goodness, but also has the power to elevate the serious chanter to the transcendental platform of *śuddha-sattva*, pure goodness, and ultimately to bestow *kṛṣṇa-prema*, pure love of God.

> "By chanting the holy name of the Lord, one dissolves his entanglement in material activities. After this, one becomes very much attracted to Kṛṣṇa, and thus dormant love for Kṛṣṇa is awakened."
>
> —*Śrī Caitanya-caritāmṛta, Madhya-līlā* 15.109

According to traditional Vedic culture, it is not necessary for a woman to accept initiation from a spiritual master. Simply by serving a husband who is initiated, and following his vows, she receives the same spiritual benefit.

> "The nuptial ceremony is stated to be the Vedic sacrament for women and to be equal to the initiation, serving the husband equivalent to the residence in the house of the teacher, and the household duties the same as the daily worship of the sacred fire."
>
> —*Manu-saṁhitā* 2.67

In modern society, where men and women both have access to the same level of education, most spiritual masters give initiation to women as well as men. A husband and wife who are both initiated can support and encourage each other by following their vows together.

> "The wife is expected to be of the same category as the husband. She must be prepared to follow the principles of the husband, and then there will be happy life. If the husband is a devotee and the wife is materialistic, there cannot be any peace in the home. The wife must see the tendencies of the husband and must be prepared to follow him."
>
> —*Śrīmad Bhāgavatam* 3.23.4-5 Bhaktivedanta purport

By following in the footsteps of a devotee husband, a woman can attain liberation along with him.

> "A woman does not need to attain high qualifications, but if she simply follows in the footsteps of her husband, who must be a devotee, then both husband and wife attain liberation and are promoted to the Vaikuṇṭhalokas."
>
> —*Śrīmad Bhāgavatam* 4.23.26 Bhaktivedanta purport

Samanuvrata is the vow of a chaste wife to adapt herself according to the situation and mentality of her husband, and to follow him faithfully.

> "From *Mahābhārata* we learn that when Gāndhārī understood that her would-be husband, Dhṛtarāṣṭra, was blind, she immediately began to practice blindness herself. Thus she covered her eyes and played the part of a blind woman. She decided that since her husband was blind, she must also act like a blind woman, otherwise she would be proud of her eyes, and her husband would be seen as inferior. The word *samanuvrata* indicates that it is the duty of a wife to adopt the special circumstances in which the husband is situated. Of course, if the husband is as great as Kardama Muni, then a very good result accrues from following him. But even if the husband is not a great devotee like Kardama Muni, it is the wife's duty to adapt herself according to his mentality. That makes married life very happy.
>
> —*Śrīmad Bhāgavatam* 3.23.4-5 Bhaktivedanta purport

The concept of adapting oneself according to the mentality of the husband does not imply a devaluation of one's own individual personality. It is a natural part of the process of building a harmonious marital relationship. As a wife gets to know her husband by serving him, she learns how his mind works and thus how to encourage him and make him happy. By adapting herself in this way, according to the mentality of her husband, a chaste wife does not become weak or insipid. Queen Gāndhārī, who vowed to follow her husband by blindfolding herself for the rest of her life, developed great mystic power.

> "Gāndhārī was a powerful ascetic, although she was living the life of a faithful wife and a kind mother."
> —*Śrīmad Bhāgavatam* 1.9.48 Bhaktivedanta purport

The *Rāmāyaṇa* recounts how Lord Rāmacandra, at the request of his stepmother and to protect his father's promise to her, gave up his entitlement to the crown of Ayodhyā and went into exile. His chaste wife Sītā-devī, who had been brought up in luxury as a princess, chose to follow the vow of her husband to live in the forest as an ascetic for fourteen years.

> "Rāmacandra requested His wife, 'Oh, you cannot go with Me. It is very difficult. You are a king's daughter, and you are brought up in such a nice way, and you are so beautiful. You cannot go. You cannot take the trouble of living in the forest.' So she replied, 'Oh, I am your wife, married wife. I must go even if you go to hell.' This is an ideal wife. She could have refused:

'Oh, your father has ordered you to go to the forest. You can go. I shall go to my father's house or I shall remain here.' No. This is an ideal wife. She must be prepared to accept any circumstances of the husband. Not that when the husband is rich the wife is very faithful, and when he has become poor or he's going to the forest the wife gives up his company. No. 'Wife' means the better half. She must abide. Just as a shadow follows the reality, similarly the wife is the shadow of the husband. Wherever the husband goes, she must go. Whatever the husband wants, she must carry it out. Of course in this country this understanding is interpreted differently, that the wife is made into a slave. But actually it is not so. When Sītā was kidnapped in the jungle, Rāmacandra had foreseen that 'she is beautiful, she is young, and we shall be in the open jungle, perhaps some demons may come,' and it actually happened. So for Sītā, Lord Rāmacandra massacred the whole family of Rāvaṇa, only for Sītā. As the husband, so the wife. The wife was so faithful that she could not remain alone. She must accompany the husband even in the forest. And the husband was so faithful that, 'Oh, my wife has been kidnapped,' so He massacred the whole family of Rāvaṇa."

—Bhaktivedanta lecture, *Śrī Rāmanavamī*, Hawaii 27/03/1969

By following the principles of chastity, women develop supernatural powers. When Sītā-devī was kidnapped by Rāvaṇa, she was able to stave off his advances by the power of her chastity, and eventually he died as a result of her curse.

> "O greatly fortunate one, you came under the influence of lusty desires, and therefore you could not understand the influence of mother Sītā. Now, because of her curse, you have been reduced to this state, having been killed by Lord Rāmacandra."
>
> —*Śrīmad Bhāgavatam* 9.10.27

Lord Rāmacandra, of course, was not a mere mortal, but an incarnation of God.

> "Being prayed for by the demigods, the Supreme Personality of Godhead, the Absolute Truth Himself, directly appeared with His expansion and expansions of the expansion. Their holy names were Rāma, Lakṣmaṇa, Bharata and Śatrughna. These celebrated incarnations thus appeared in four forms as the sons of Mahārāja Daśaratha."
>
> —*Śrīmad Bhāgavatam* 9.10.2

Similarly, mother Sītā was not an ordinary woman, but the eternal consort of Lord Rāmacandra.

> "When the Lord appeared as Rāmacandra, she became Sītā-devī, and when He descended in His original form as Lord Kṛṣṇa, she was Princess Rukmiṇī. In Lord Viṣṇu's many other incarnations, she always appeared as the Lord's consort."
>
> —Baladeva Vidyābhūṣaṇa, *Prameya-ratnāvalī*

Nevertheless, it is possible for a mortal woman to develop similar powers of chastity by following the principles exemplified by Sītā-devī.

> "Not only was mother Sītā powerful, but any woman who follows in the footsteps of mother Sītā can also become similarly powerful."
> —*Śrīmad Bhāgavatam* 9.10.27 Bhaktivedanta purport

Whatever is the status of the husband, there is no bar on chastity. Among the most famous examples of chaste women in history are Sītā, the wife of the Supreme Lord; Mandodarī, the wife of a great demon; Draupadī, the wife of five great devotees; and Gāndhārī, the wife of a weak-minded blind king. The husbands could not be more different, but the wives are all equally famed for their chastity.

> "Whenever we find a description of ideal chaste women, mother Sītā is among them. Mandodarī, the wife of Rāvaṇa, was also very chaste. Similarly, Draupadī was one of five exalted chaste women. As a man must follow great personalities like Brahmā and Nārada, a woman must follow the path of such ideal women as Sītā, Mandodarī and Draupadī. By staying chaste and faithful to her husband, a woman enriches herself with supernatural power."
> —*Śrīmad Bhāgavatam* 9.10.27 Bhaktivedanta purport

Rāvaṇa was a demon, inimical to God, but his chaste wife, Mandodarī, is emulated as an ideal wife. While she did not necessarily endorse all the actions of her husband, she always remained faithful to him. If a husband deviates from religious principles, out of human weakness, a chaste wife does not condemn him but continues to serve him while trying to help him to get back on track. A wife can offer good advice to her husband and, provided she offers it with respect and affection, then a reasonable man will be receptive. Rāvaṇa was not receptive to good advice because he was a demon, but still Mandodarī did not desert him. Of course, Rāvaṇa was not an ordinary demon, but a pure devotee who was temporarily playing the part of a demon to assist Lord Rāmacandra in His earthly pastimes. Although Rāvaṇa was so powerful that all the demigods were afraid of him, he became powerless when confronted with the chastity of Sītā-devī to her Lord.

> "Mother Sītā was very submissive, faithful, shy and chaste, always understanding the attitude of her husband. Thus by her character and her love and service she completely attracted the mind of the Lord."
> —*Śrīmad Bhāgavatam* 9.10.55

While Sita was not only an ideal chaste wife, but also the eternal consort of the Supreme Lord, she nevertheless relished hearing the instructions of Anasūyā, the chaste wife of Atri Muni, which were spoken for the benefit of all women.

> "Worlds that are attended with great prosperity await those women to whom their husband is dear, no matter whether he lives in a city or in a forest, whether his circumstances are propitious or adverse. In the eyes of women who are blessed with a noble disposition, the husband is the highest deity, no matter whether he is ill-mannered or licentious or entirely devoid of riches. Though deeply pondering, I do not see for a

woman a friend greater than the husband and more capable of yielding one's desired object at all places like the imperishable fruit of one's austerities, O princess of the Videha kingdom!"

—*Śrīmad Vālmīki-Rāmāyaṇa, Ayodhyā-kāṇḍa* 117.23-5

Rāma and Sītā conducted their earthly pastimes according to *dharma*, to set an ideal example for all married couples.

"As Lord Rāmacandra is the ideal husband (*eka-patnī-vrata*), mother Sītā is the ideal wife. Such a combination makes family life very happy. *Yad yad ācarati śreṣṭhas tat tad evetaro janaḥ*: whatever example a great man sets, common people follow. If the kings, the leaders, and the *brāhmaṇas*, the teachers, would set forth the examples we receive from Vedic literature, the entire world would be heaven; indeed, there would no longer be hellish conditions within this material world."

—*Śrīmad Bhāgavatam* 9.10.55 Bhaktivedanta purport

While there are differences between *dharma* for men and *dharma* for women, it is important to remember that these bodily designations are temporary. Those who are in female bodies in this life may have occupied male bodies in the previous life, and vice versa.

"If someone is too attached to his wife, naturally he thinks of his wife at the time of death, and in his next life he takes the body of a woman. Similarly, if a woman thinks of her husband at the time of death, naturally she gets the body of a man in the next life.

> In the Hindu scriptures, therefore, woman's chastity and devotion to man is greatly emphasized. A woman's attachment to her husband may elevate her to the body of a man in her next life, but a man's attachment to a woman will degrade him, and in his next life he will get the body of a woman."
>
> —*Śrīmad Bhāgavatam* 3.31.41 Bhaktivedanta purport

While every living entity is originally female from a spiritual point of view, in the material world a male body has advantages over a female body in various aspects, such as intelligence, clarity of mind, strength and capacity for performing austerity, which are considered to be favourable for spiritual advancement.

> "We should always remember, as it is stated in *Bhagavad-gītā*, that both the gross and subtle material bodies are dresses; they are the shirt and coat of the living entity. To be either a woman or a man only involves one's bodily dress. The soul in nature is actually the marginal energy of the Supreme Lord. Every living entity, being classified as energy, is supposed to be originally a woman, or one who is enjoyed. In the body of a man there is a greater opportunity to get out of the material clutches; there is less opportunity in the body of a woman."
>
> —*Śrīmad Bhāgavatam* 3.31.41 Bhaktivedanta purport

By following the principles of chastity, a married woman can either graduate to the body of a man in her next life or attain liberation.

> "O Mahārāja Parīkṣit, by observing their husband progressing in spiritual existence, Saubhari Muni's wives were also able to enter the spiritual world by his spiritual power, just as the flames of a fire cease when the fire is extinguished."
>
> —*Śrīmad Bhāgavatam* 9.6.55

A husband and wife are a spiritual team. A faithful wife who helps her husband to make spiritual advancement, by serving, assisting and encouraging him, shares the benefit of his advancement and progresses along with him.

> "As stated in *Bhagavad-gītā* (9.32), *striyo vaiśyās tathā śūdrās te 'pi yānti parāṁ gatim*. Women are not considered very powerful in following spiritual principles, but if a woman is fortunate enough to get a suitable husband who is spiritually advanced and if she always engages in his service, she also gets the same benefit as her husband. Here it is clearly said that the wives of Saubhari Muni also entered the spiritual world by the influence of their husband. They were unfit, but because they were faithful followers of their husband, they also entered the spiritual world with him. Thus a woman should be a faithful servant of her husband, and if the husband is spiritually advanced, the woman will automatically get the opportunity to enter the spiritual world."
>
> —*Śrīmad Bhāgavatam* 9.6.55 Bhaktivedanta purport

Anyone, whether man or woman, who takes shelter of the Supreme Lord and serves His devotees, becomes eligible to go back home, back to Godhead.

māṁ hi pārtha vyapāśritya
ye 'pi syuḥ pāpa-yonayaḥ
striyo vaiśyās tathā śūdrās
te 'pi yānti parāṁ gatim

"O son of Pṛthā, those who take shelter in Me, though they be of lower birth—women, *vaiśyas* [merchants] and *śūdras* [workers]—can attain the supreme destination."

—*Bhagavad-gītā As It Is* 9.32

Chapter Five

Pati-dharma

Duties for Married Men

To Protect the Wife
To be Faithful to the Wife
To Maintain the Wife and Children
To be a Servant of God
To Deliver Dependants from Material Existence

Chapter Five

Pati-dharma

—Duties for Married Men—

"For a woman, her lover, friend, kin, desires, wealth, life—all that she seeks—are compounded in one, namely her husband and lord; in the same way a man sees his properly wedded wife. Thus, shall you both view each other."

—Bhavabhūti, *Mālatī-mādhava* 6

As a wife's duty is to serve her husband, similarly a husband's duty is to serve his wife by protecting, honouring, maintaining and guiding her.

To Protect the Wife

According to religious principles, the duty of a husband is to provide protection for his wife.

"'Husband' means one who takes charge of a girl for life, and 'wife' means one who has resolved to serve her husband throughout her life. That is the meaning

> of 'husband' and 'wife'. When the wife is in danger, the husband's duty is to give her protection, at any cost."
>
> —Bhaktivedanta lecture, *Śrīmad Bhāgavatam* 1.15.50
> Los Angeles 27/12/1973

The protection of women is a fundamental principle of Vedic social culture.

> "The protection of women maintains the chastity of society, by which we can get a good generation for peace, tranquillity and progress of life."
>
> —*Śrīmad Bhāgavatam* 1.8.5 Bhaktivedanta purport

This principle was spectacularly demonstrated in action by Lord Rāmacandra during His transcendental pastimes on earth.

> "Another aspect of the Lord's instructions is that one who accepts a wife must be a faithful husband and give her full protection. Human society is divided into two classes of men—those who strictly follow the religious principles and those who are devotees. By His personal example, Lord Rāmacandra wanted to instruct both of them how to fully adopt the discipline of the religious system and how to be a beloved and dutiful husband. Otherwise He had no reason to undergo apparent tribulations. One who strictly follows religious principles must not neglect to provide all facilities for the complete protection of

> his wife. There may be some suffering because of this, but one must nevertheless endure it. That is the duty of a faithful husband. By His personal example, Lord Rāmacandra demonstrated this duty."
>
> —*Śrīmad Bhāgavatam* 5.19.5 Bhaktivedanta purport

When His wife Sītā-devī was abducted by Rāvaṇa, the king of the demons, Lord Rāma was living in exile in the forest, with no army at His disposal. He formed an army of monkeys and bears, armed with rocks and trees, and together they built a bridge of stones across the sea to Laṅkā and waged war against Rāvaṇa with his army of demons. When Rāvaṇa refused to return Sītā, Lord Rāma defeated and killed him and was reunited with His beloved wife.

> "Lord Rāmacandra could have produced hundreds and thousands of Sītās from His pleasure energy, but just to show the duty of a faithful husband, He not only rescued Sītā from the hands of Rāvaṇa but also killed Rāvaṇa and all the members of his family."
>
> —*Śrīmad Bhāgavatam* 5.19.5 Bhaktivedanta purport

Similarly, the *Mahābhārata* recounts how the five Pāṇḍava brothers waged war against their cousins and defeated them to restore the honour of their chaste wife Draupadī, who had been dishonoured in the court of Hastināpura.

> "Once Draupadī was dragged out, and attempts were made to insult her by stripping her naked in the vicious assembly of the Kurus. The Lord saved

> Draupadī by supplying an immeasurable length of cloth."
>
> —*Śrīmad Bhāgavatam* 1.8.24 Bhaktivedanta purport

A husband's responsibility to protect his wife continues for life.

> "Marriage between the husband and wife means that the husband must forever be responsible for the wife's well-being and protection in all cases. That does not mean that now there is agreement between us, therefore I am responsible, but as soon as there is some disagreement, then I immediately flee the scene and become so-called renounced."
>
> —*Letters from Śrīla Prabhupāda* 15/9/1972

In case a husband decides to enter the *sannyāsa-āśrama* later on, his responsibility is to first make provision for the ongoing care and protection of his wife, which is traditionally managed by grown-up sons. A *gṛhastha* is also responsible for the protection of his daughters until they are married.

> "Actually, a woman should be given protection at every stage of life. She should be given protection by the father in her younger days, by the husband in her youth, and by the grown-up sons in her old age. This is proper social behavior according to the *Manu-saṁhitā*."
>
> —*Bhagavad-gītā As It Is* 16.7 purport

To be Faithful to the Wife

A further religious principle for husbands that was exemplified by Lord Rāmacandra is to be faithful to the wife. Lord Rāma accepted only Sītā-devī as His wife and vowed to have no connection with any other woman.

eka-patnī-vrata-dharo
rājarṣi-caritaḥ śuciḥ
sva-dharmaṁ gṛha-medhīyaṁ
śikṣayan svayam ācarat

> "Lord Rāmacandra took a vow to accept only one wife and have no connection with any other women. He was a saintly king, and everything in His character was good, untinged by qualities like anger. He taught good behavior for everyone, especially for householders, in terms of *varṇāśrama-dharma*. Thus He taught the general public by His personal activities."
>
> —*Śrīmad Bhāgavatam* 9.10.54

Polygamy for men was acceptable in Vedic society, and especially kings were known to keep many wives. Lord Rāmacandra could have accepted any number of wives, but He demonstrated a perfect example of faithfulness and self-control by accepting only one wife, and promising her that He would never accept another.

> "*Eka-patnī-vrata*, accepting only one wife, was the glorious example set by Lord Rāmacandra. One should

not accept more than one wife. In those days, of course, people did marry more than one wife. Even Lord Rāmacandra's father accepted more wives than one. But Lord Rāmacandra, as an ideal king, accepted only one wife, mother Sītā. When mother Sītā was kidnapped by Rāvaṇa and the Rākṣasas, Lord Rāmacandra, as the Supreme Personality of Godhead, could have married hundreds and thousands of Sītās, but to teach us how faithful He was to His wife, He fought with Rāvaṇa and finally killed him. The Lord punished Rāvaṇa and rescued His wife to instruct men to have only one wife. Lord Rāmacandra accepted only one wife and manifested sublime character, thus setting an example for householders. A householder should live according to the ideal of Lord Rāmacandra, who showed how to be a perfect person. Being a householder or living with a wife and children is never condemned, provided one lives according to the regulative principles of *varṇāśrama-dharma*. Those who live in accordance with these principles, whether as householders, *brahmacārīs* or *vānaprasthas*, are all equally important."

—*Śrīmad Bhāgavatam* 9.10.54 Bhaktivedanta purport

While Lord Rāmacandra set an ideal example by accepting only one wife, at the same time polygamy for men is not considered to be sinful. Because the female population is usually greater than the male population, the system of polygamy was accepted in Vedic culture to ensure protection for every woman.

> "Generally in every society the female population is greater in number than the male population. Therefore if it is a principle in the society that all girls should be married, unless polygamy is allowed it will not be possible. If all the girls are not married there is a good chance of adultery, and a society in which adultery is allowed cannot be very peaceful or pure. In our Kṛṣṇa consciousness society we have restricted illicit sex. The practical difficulty is to find a husband for each and every girl. We are therefore in favor of polygamy, provided, of course, that the husband is able to maintain more than one wife."
>
> —*Śrī Caitanya-caritāmṛta, Ādi-līlā* 14.58 Bhaktivedanta purport

Bhaktivedanta Swami Prabhupāda was in favour of polygamy because he wished to see every woman protected and taken care of. However, he was eventually obliged to prohibit polygamy among his disciples to protect their integrity and reputation, since it was (and still is) illegal in the West.

> "But you must consider very carefully the possibility of becoming scandalized in the public for breaking their laws in this way. And in future also the devotees who are neophyte may not understand our policy in this connection, and we could gradually wind up attracting a class of men who are very eager for unlimited sex life only. These things must be avoided at all cost."
>
> —*Letters from Śrīla Prabhupāda* 9/1/1973

While polygamy is not socially acceptable at present in the Western world, illicit sex and prostitution are unfortunately rampant. If polygamy were to be legalised, there would be more opportunity for all women to be protected and less scope for prostitution, adultery and divorce.

> "Every person must get married. Every woman especially must get married. If the women outnumber the men, some men can accept more than one wife. In that way there will be no prostitution in society. If men can marry more than one wife, illicit sex life will be stopped."
>
> —*Śrī Caitanya-caritāmṛta, Madhya-līlā* 7.128
> Bhaktivedanta purport

It is more honourable for a man to marry two wives and take care of both of them, than to marry one wife and commit adultery with another woman, or to abandon one wife and marry another.

> "People have become so degraded in this age that on the one hand they restrict polygamy and on the other hand they hunt for women in so many ways. Many business concerns publicly advertise that topless girls are available in this club or in that shop. Thus women have become instruments of sense enjoyment in modern society. The *Vedas* enjoin, however, that if a man has the propensity to enjoy more than one wife—as is sometimes the propensity for men in the higher

social order, such as the *brāhmaṇas, kṣatriyas* and *vaiśyas*, and even sometimes the *śūdras*—he is allowed to marry more than one wife. Marriage means taking complete charge of a woman and living peacefully without debauchery. At the present moment, however, debauchery is unrestricted. Nonetheless, society makes a law that one should not marry more than one wife. This is typical of a demoniac society."

—*Śrīmad Bhāgavatam* 4.26.6 Bhaktivedanta purport

Within a polygamous marriage, a man is expected to be equally faithful to both or all of his wives. As a chaste wife concerns herself with the pleasure of her husband, similarly a faithful husband is concerned about the happiness of his wife.

"In that family, where the husband is pleased with his wife and the wife with her husband, happiness will assuredly be lasting."

—*Manu-saṁhitā* 3.60

And as a chaste wife respects her husband as a servant of God, in the same way a faithful husband respects his wife as a servant of the Lord.

"Do not consider your wife as one meant for your service. Instead, respect her as a servitor of Kṛṣṇa."

—Gaurakiśora Bābājī (*Bābājī Mahārāja*)

As a man becomes happy when he is loved, respected, valued and appreciated by his wife, similarly a woman becomes happy when she is loved, respected, valued and appreciated by her husband. A faithful husband, who values his wife as a devotee of the Lord, can take inspiration from her devotion. While women may be less intelligent than men, at the same time they tend to more easily accept the authority of God.

> "Women in general are unable to speculate like philosophers, but they are blessed by the Lord because they believe at once in the superiority and almightiness of the Lord, and thus they offer obeisances without reservation. The Lord is so kind that He does not show special favor only to one who is a great philosopher. He knows the sincerity of purpose. For this reason only, women generally assemble in great number in any sort of religious function. In every country and in every sect of religion it appears that the women are more interested than the men. This simplicity of acceptance of the Lord's authority is more effective than showy insincere religious fervor."
>
> —*Teachings of Queen Kuntī* 3

Men are generally endowed with more intelligence than women (for example, in the fields of philosophy, science, technology, engineering, business, politics, etc.), as well as superior strength, determination, decisiveness, detachment, and capacity for austerity. There are also other good qualities that tend to abound in women more than men, such as intuition, empathy, patience, adaptability, submissiveness, and devotion. When male qualities and female qualities are combined together in a co-operative partnership, there is great opportunity for spiritual advancement. The *yajñic brāhmaṇas* of Vṛndāvana, who were too busy with their fire sacrifice to feed Kṛṣṇa and Balarāma, learned a profound lesson from their wives, who left aside everything to serve the Lord.

> "Women in general, being very simple at heart, can very easily take to Kṛṣṇa consciousness, and when they develop love of Kṛṣṇa they can easily get liberation from the clutches of *māyā*, which are very difficult for even so-called intelligent and learned men to surpass. The *brāhmaṇas* continued: 'According to Vedic injunction, women are not allowed to undergo the purificatory process of initiation by the sacred thread, nor are they allowed to live as *brahmacāriṇīs* in the *āśrama* of the spiritual master, nor are they advised to undergo the strict disciplinary procedures, nor are they very expert in discussing the philosophy of self-realization. And by nature they are not very pure, nor are they very much attached to auspicious activities. Therefore, how wonderful it is that these women have developed transcendental love for Kṛṣṇa, the Lord of all mystic *yogīs*! They have surpassed all of us in firm faith and devotion unto Kṛṣṇa.'"
>
> —*Kṛṣṇa the Supreme Personality of Godhead* 23

Material intelligence cannot help one to make advancement in spiritual knowledge, unless it is accompanied by humility and devotion to God. By engagement in devotional service to the Lord, one develops spiritual intelligence, which can be possessed in equal measure by either a man or a woman, since it is not confined by bodily designations.

> "In *Bhagavad-gītā* (9.32) Lord Kṛṣṇa says: 'O son of Pṛthā, those who take shelter in Me—though they be lowborn, women, *vaiśyas*, or *śūdras*—can approach the supreme destination.' Thus although women, *śūdras*, and *vaiśyas* are ordinarily considered to belong to a lower class, when one becomes a devotee he or she goes beyond such designations. Women, *śūdras*, and *vaiśyas* are ordinarily regarded as less intelligent, but if one takes to Kṛṣṇa consciousness one is the most intelligent."
>
> —*Teachings of Queen Kuntī* 3

A chaste wife can become the source of all good intelligence by protecting the husband from external allurements and engaging in spiritual activities together with him.

> "But if one gets a chaste wife, accepted through a religious marriage ritual, she can be of great help when one is threatened by the many dangerous situations of life. Actually such a wife can become the source of all good intelligence. With such a good wife, the family's engagement in the devotional service of the Lord actually makes a home a *gṛhastha-āśrama*, or household dedicated to spiritual cultivation."
>
> —*Śrīmad-Bhāgavatam* 4.26.16 Bhaktivedanta purport

A faithful husband respects and appreciates the woman who is his constant assistant for pursuing the four goals of married life.

> "Kardama Muni wanted to have a wife of like disposition because a wife is necessary to assist in spiritual and material advancement. It is said that a wife yields the fulfillment of all desires in religion, economic development and sense gratification. If one has a nice wife, he is to be considered a most fortunate man. In astrology, a man is considered fortunate who has great wealth, very good sons, or a very good wife. Of these three, one who has a very good wife is considered the most fortunate."
>
> —*Śrīmad Bhāgavatam* 3.21.15 Bhaktivedanta purport

Those who chant the holy names of the Lord develop a mood of humility and offer respect to each other.

tṛṇād api sunīcena
taror api sahiṣṇunā
amāninā mānadena
kīrtanīyaḥ sadā hariḥ

> "One should chant the holy name of the Lord in a humble state of mind, thinking oneself lower than a straw in the street. One should be more tolerant than a tree, devoid of all sense of false prestige, and ready to offer all respects to others. In such a state of mind, one can chant the holy name of the Lord constantly."
>
> —Lord Caitanya, *Śikṣāṣṭaka* 3

According to Vedic culture, the husband and wife do not address each other by name. This tradition helps to maintain mutual respect and to protect a relationship from descending into 'familiarity that breeds contempt'.

> "A wife is addressed as 'devī', not by her name. The husband should address his wife as 'devī'. They must be like devī. 'Devī' means goddess, and the wife must address the husband as 'lord'. This is the system."
>
> —Bhaktivedanta lecture, *Śrīmad Bhāgavatam* 1.15.51
> Los Angeles 28/12/1973

Whichever terms of address a couple may choose to adopt, it is more respectful to avoid calling each other by name. Furthermore, a cultured man treats all other women, except for his wife, as mothers.

mātṛvat para-dāreṣu
para-dravyeṣu loṣṭravat
ātmavat sarva-bhūteṣu
yaḥ paśyati sa paṇḍitaḥ

> "One who considers another's wife as his mother, another's possessions as a lump of dirt and treats all other living beings as he would himself, is considered to be learned."
>
> —*Śrī Cāṇakya Nīti-śāstra* 12.14

To Maintain the Wife and Children

A faithful husband takes care of his wife with honour and provides her with nice clothes and ornaments.

> "Women must be honoured and adorned by their fathers, brothers, husbands, and brothers-in-law, who desire their own welfare."
>
> —*Manu-saṁhitā* 3.55

The husband's responsibility is to maintain his wife and children with the necessities of life.

> "Family life, according to the Vedic system or any system, is a responsible life for maintaining the wife and children."
>
> —Bhaktivedanta lecture, *Śrīmad Bhāgavatam* 6.1.26
> Honolulu 26/5/1976

Where polygamy is accepted, a husband is responsible for maintaining all of his wives and children adequately.

> "You cannot imitate Kṛṣṇa, neither can you marry sixteen thousand women, but you can marry—that is Vedic civilisation—more than one wife. Every female must be married, so where are so many husbands? Therefore, polygamy was allowed, but the man who marries must be able to maintain his wife very nicely. That is Hindu or Vedic civilisation. That is *kuṭumba, kuṭumba-bharaṇa*, maintaining the family."
>
> —Bhaktivedanta lecture, *Śrīmad Bhāgavatam* 2.1.3
> Paris 12/6/1974

The husband's duty is to keep his wife satisfied by providing her with children, a comfortable home, good food, and nice clothes and ornaments. He should also make sure that she has as much help as she needs to carry out her household duties.

> "A man is allowed, if he is able, to marry more than one wife. To have more than one wife does not mean sense enjoyment. The wife must be maintained very respectfully. She must have a good house, good ornaments, good food, good servants and good children. Then one can marry, but not simply for sense gratification."
>
> —Bhaktivedanta lecture, *Śrīmad Bhāgavatam* 5.5.1-2 London 13/9/1969

While women's sexual appetite is greater than men's, their lusty desire is not necessarily consciously focussed on sex, but is typically sublimated and diffused in various directions. A woman can be satisfied by being provided with children and material facilities such as a nice house, good food, nice clothes, etc. When a wife has all her desires satisfied, then both husband and wife can peacefully engage in religious activities.

> "Women in general are very much sexually inclined. Indeed, it is said that a woman's sex desire is nine times stronger than a man's. It is therefore a man's duty to keep a woman under his control by satisfying her, giving her ornaments, nice food and clothes, and

engaging her in religious activities. Of course, a woman should have a few children and in this way not be disturbing to the man."
—*Śrīmad Bhāgavatam* 4.27.1 Bhaktivedanta purport

To be a Servant of God

A husband and wife who co-operate together as a team can both share the benefit of each other's devotional activities.

kṛtam ekatareṇāpi
dam-patyor ubhayor api
patnyāṁ kuryād anarhāyāṁ
patir etat samāhitaḥ

"Between the husband and wife, one person is sufficient to execute this devotional service. Because of their good relationship, both of them will enjoy the result. Therefore if the wife is unable to execute this process, the husband should carefully do so, and the faithful wife will share the result."
—*Śrīmad Bhāgavatam* 6.19.18

Whether devotional service is executed by a husband or a wife, in either case the other will share in the resulting spiritual benefit. However, it is generally the man, with his superior mental and physical stamina, who is more equipped to play the leading role in self-discipline and practice of austerity.

> "The relationship between husband and wife is firmly established when the wife is faithful and the husband sincere. Then even if the wife, being weaker, is unable to execute devotional service with her husband, if she is chaste and sincere she shares half of her husband's activities."
>
> —*Śrīmad Bhāgavatam* 6.19.18 Bhaktivedanta purport

The relationship between husband and wife is so close that they are said to be two halves of the same body.

> "According to the Vedic conception of family life, the husband gives half his body to his wife, and the wife gives half of her body to her husband. In other words, a husband without a wife or a wife without a husband is incomplete."
>
> —*Śrīmad Bhāgavatam* 4.4.3 Bhaktivedanta purport

Where there is any religious ritual to be performed, such as a fire sacrifice for example, a husband and wife traditionally participate together.

> "According to Vedic principle, religious rituals must be executed by the husband and wife together."
>
> —*Kṛṣṇa the Supreme Personality of Godhead* 23

There are also many devotional practices that can be easily carried out by women as well as men, such as Deity worship for example, and for which responsibility can be shared by both husband and wife together. A wife who helps her husband by sharing his religious responsibilities is known as the 'better half'.

> "O respectful one, a wife is so helpful that she is called the better half of a man's body because of her sharing in all auspicious activities. A man can move without anxiety entrusting all responsibilities to his wife."
> —*Śrīmad Bhāgavatam* 3.14.19
>
> Bhaktivedanta purport:
> "By the Vedic injunction, the wife is accepted as the better half of a man's body because she is supposed to be responsible for discharging half of the duties of the husband. A family man has a responsibility to perform five kinds of sacrifices, called *pañca-yajña*, in order to get relief from all kinds of unavoidable sinful reaction incurred in the course of his affairs."

The five kinds of sacrifices called *pañca-yajña*, traditionally performed by householders, are listed as follows.

> *"adhyāpanaṁ brahma-yajñaḥ*
> *pitṛ-yajñas tu tarpaṇam*
> *homo daivo balir bhauto*
> *nṛ-yajño 'tithi-pūjanam*

> "By performing oblations with ghee, the demigods are satisfied. By studying the *Vedas*, *brahma-yajña* is performed, and by this the great sages are satisfied. Offering oblations of water before one's forefathers is called *pitṛ-yajña*. By offering tribute, *bhūta-yajña* is performed. By properly receiving guests, *nṛ-yajña* is performed."
> —*Śrī Caitanya-caritāmṛta, Madhya-līlā* 22.141
> Bhaktivedanta purport

The recommended sacrifice for this age is *saṅkīrtana-yajña*, or the congregational chanting of the holy names of the Lord. By satisfying the Supreme Personality of Godhead, the *saṅkīrtana-yajña* automatically satisfies the demigods, sages, forefathers, et al, just as water poured on the roots of a tree nourishes all the branches and leaves. Householders who regularly perform *saṅkīrtana-yajña* are no longer obliged to perform the traditional *pañca-yajña*.

> "There are five *yajñas* and five kinds of indebtedness—indebtedness to the demigods, great sages, forefathers, living entities and common men. Therefore one has to perform five kinds of *yajñas*, but when one takes to *saṅkīrtana-yajña* (the chanting of the Hare Kṛṣṇa *mantra*) one doesn't have to perform any other *yajña*."
>
> —*Śrī Caitanya-caritāmṛta, Madhya-līlā* 22.141
> Bhaktivedanta purport

Along with *saṅkīrtana-yajña*, couples can also engage together in other auspicious activities such as Deity worship and serving Vaiṣṇavas.

prabhu kahena,—'kṛṣṇa-sevā', 'vaiṣṇava-sevana'
'nirantara kara kṛṣṇa-nāma-saṅkīrtana'

> "Śrī Caitanya Mahāprabhu replied, 'Without cessation continue chanting the holy name of Lord Kṛṣṇa. Whenever possible, serve Him and His devotees, the Vaiṣṇavas.'"
>
> —*Śrī Caitanya-caritāmṛta, Madhya-līlā* 15.104

The most meaningful purpose of marriage between two souls is to co-operate together for their mutual advancement in spiritual life. A man should regard his wife as a spiritual life partner rather than a partner for sense gratification.

> "When a man becomes qualitatively like the cats and dogs, he forgets his duties in cultivating spiritual values, and thus he accepts his wife as a sense gratificatory agency. When the wife is accepted as a sense gratificatory agency, personal beauty is the main consideration, and as soon as there is a break in personal sense gratification, there is disruption or divorce. But when husband and wife aim at spiritual advancement by mutual co-operation, there is no consideration of personal beauty or the disruption of so-called 'love'. In the material world there is no question of love. Marriage is actually a duty performed in mutual co-operation as directed in the authoritative scriptures for spiritual advancement. Therefore marriage is essential in order to avoid the life of cats and dogs, who are not meant for spiritual enlightenment."
>
> —*Śrīmad Bhāgavatam* 3.14.19 Bhaktivedanta purport

As a wife can conquer the heart of her husband, not by battling with him, but by serving him with love and submission, similarly a husband can conquer the heart of his wife, not by overindulgence in sex, but by loving care and kindness. (Where we use the word "love" here, we refer to spiritual or selfless love rather than the "so-called love" that is referred to in the above quotation.) By keeping himself and his wife engaged in devotional service, a man can avoid becoming overly attracted to his wife for sense gratification.

> "A systematic family life as enjoined in the *Vedas* is better than an irresponsible sinful life. If a husband and wife combine together in Kṛṣṇa consciousness and live together peacefully, that is very nice. However, if a husband becomes too much attracted by his wife and forgets his duty in life, the implications of materialistic life will again resume. Śrīla Rūpa Gosvāmī has therefore recommended, *anāsaktasya viṣayān* (*Bhakti-rasāmṛta-sindhu* 1.2.255). Without being attached by sex, the husband and wife may live together for the advancement of spiritual life. The husband should engage in devotional service, and the wife should be faithful and religious according to the Vedic injunctions. Such a combination is very good. However, if the husband becomes too much attracted to the wife due to sex, the position becomes very dangerous... The great politician Cāṇakya Paṇḍita has said: *bhāryā rūpavatī śatruḥ*—a beautiful wife is an enemy. Of course every woman in the eyes of her husband is very beautiful. Others may see her as not very beautiful, but the husband, being very much attracted to her, sees her always as very beautiful. If the husband sees the wife as very beautiful, it is to be assumed that he is too much attracted to her. This attraction is the attraction of sex."
>
> —*Śrīmad Bhāgavatam* 4.27.1 Bhaktivedanta purport

By daily performance of *bhakti-yoga* (such as rising early, chanting 'Hare Kṛṣṇa', Deity worship, etc.), one gradually becomes elevated from the modes of passion and ignorance to the mode of goodness. By becoming situated in the mode of goodness himself, a man can help his wife to also become free from passion and ignorance.

> "The whole world is captivated by the two modes of material nature *rajo-guṇa* and *tamo-guṇa*, passion and ignorance. Generally women are very much passionate and are less intelligent; therefore somehow or other a man should not be under the control of their passion and ignorance. By performing *bhakti-yoga*, or devotional service, a man can be raised to the platform of goodness. If a husband situated in the mode of goodness can control his wife, who is in passion and ignorance, the woman is benefited. Forgetting her natural inclination for passion and ignorance, the woman becomes obedient and faithful to her husband, who is situated in goodness. Such a life becomes very welcome. The intelligence of the man and woman may then work very nicely together, and they can make a progressive march toward spiritual realization. Otherwise, the husband, coming under the control of the wife, sacrifices his quality of goodness and becomes subservient to the qualities of passion and ignorance. In this way the whole situation becomes polluted."
>
> —*Śrīmad Bhāgavatam* 4.27.1 Bhaktivedanta purport

A husband is given the upper hand in the relationship with his wife, not so that he can exploit her, but for this purpose – so that he can elevate her to the mode of goodness for her spiritual advancement. It is not recommended for a husband to spend all day associating with his wife.

> "This is restricted for those who aspire to ascend to the transcendental platform. Even fifty years ago in Hindu society, such association was restricted. A wife could not see her husband during the daytime. Householders even had different residential quarters. The internal quarters of a residential house were for the woman, and the external quarters were for the man."
>
> —*Śrīmad Bhāgavatam* 3.31.40 Bhaktivedanta purport

However, when a husband and wife associate together to perform devotional service to the Lord, then that association becomes purified and spiritualised.

> "In the stage of Kṛṣṇa consciousness, however, such restriction of association may be slackened because if a man's and woman's attachment is not to each other but to Kṛṣṇa, then both of them are equally eligible to get out of the material entanglement and reach the abode of Kṛṣṇa."
>
> —*Śrīmad Bhāgavatam* 3.31.41 Bhaktivedanta purport

To Deliver Dependants from Material Existence

A husband's responsibility to protect his wife extends even beyond this life. He is responsible for protecting her not only from dangers in this life, but also from taking birth again in the material world. This duty was explained by the Lord in His incarnation as Ṛṣabhadeva.

gurur na sa syāt sva-jano na sa syāt
pitā na sa syāj jananī na sā syāt
daivaṁ na tat syān na patiś ca sa syān
na mocayed yaḥ samupeta-mṛtyum

> "One who cannot deliver his dependants from the path of repeated birth and death should never become a spiritual master, a father, a husband, a mother or a worshipable demigod."
>
> —*Śrīmad Bhāgavatam* 5.5.18

The religious responsibility of a husband is to guide his wife spiritually for the rest of his life.

> "Whether your husband likes to take responsibility as your spiritual guide or not, that does not matter. He must do it. It is his duty because he has taken you as his wife. Therefore, he must take full responsibility for you the rest of his life."
>
> —*Letters from Śrīla Prabhupāda* 15/9/1972

One who accepts service from those who are dependent on him is meant to reciprocate with them by delivering them from suffering.

> "Ordinarily, the spiritual master, husband, father, mother or superior relative accepts worship from an inferior relative, but here Ṛṣabhadeva forbids this. First the father, spiritual master or husband must be able to release the dependant from repeated birth and death. If he cannot do this, he plunges himself into the ocean of reproachment for his unlawful activities. Everyone should be very responsible and take charge of his dependants just as a spiritual master takes charge of his disciple or a father takes charge of his son. All these responsibilities cannot be discharged honestly unless one can save the dependant from repeated birth and death."
>
> —*Śrīmad Bhāgavatam* 5.5.18 Bhaktivedanta purport

How does a man become qualified to save his dependants from repeated birth and death? One who is bound cannot free others. First he must see to his own salvation by taking shelter of a bona fide spiritual master.

> "No one can approach the Supreme Personality of Godhead directly. One must approach Him through His pure devotees. Therefore, in the system of Vaiṣṇava activities, the first duty is to accept a devotee as spiritual master and then to render service unto him."
>
> —*The Nectar of Devotion* 12

The credentials of a bona fide spiritual master are that he belongs to an authorised *sampradāya* (ancient succession of spiritual masters) and that his teachings are in accordance with the Vedic scriptures and preceding spiritual masters.

> "The path of spiritual realization is undoubtedly difficult. The Lord therefore advises us to approach a bona fide spiritual master in the line of disciplic succession from the Lord Himself. No one can be a bona fide spiritual master without following this principle of disciplic succession. The Lord is the original spiritual master, and a person in the disciplic succession can convey the message of the Lord as it is to his disciple. No one can be spiritually realized by manufacturing his own process, as is the fashion of foolish pretenders."
>
> —*Bhagavad-gītā As It Is* 4.34 purport

A bona fide spiritual master should also be a pure devotee of the Lord.

> "A *gṛhastha* should accept a spiritual master who is full of devotion and of pure character."
>
> — Bhaktivinoda Ṭhākura, *Śrī Bhaktyāloka* 12

The process for taking shelter of a spiritual master is described as follows.

tad viddhi praṇipātena
paripraśnena sevayā
upadekṣyanti te jñānaṁ
jñāninas tattva-darśinaḥ

> "Just try to learn the truth by approaching a spiritual master. Inquire from him submissively and render

service unto him. The self-realized souls can impart knowledge unto you because they have seen the truth."
—*Bhagavad-gītā As It Is* 4.34

After finding a bona fide spiritual master, serving him, hearing from him and developing faith in him, the next step is to receive spiritual initiation from him.

"When a householder has faith, he should take initiation into the chanting of the Hare Kṛṣṇa *mahā-mantra.*"
— Bhaktivinoda Ṭhākura, *Śrī Bhaktyāloka* 12

The three most important of all the regulative principles of devotional service, as cited by Rūpa Gosvāmī in his *Bhakti-rasāmṛta-sindhu*, are in connection with accepting a spiritual master.

"Out of the twenty, the first three—namely accepting the shelter of a bona fide spiritual master, taking initiation from him and serving him with respect and reverence—are the most important."
—*The Nectar of Devotion* 6

While normally a person accepts only one *dīkṣā-guru* (initiating spiritual master), at the same time he may accept any number of *śikṣā-gurus* (instructing spiritual masters).

"The *dīkṣā-guru* is one but *śikṣā-guru* can be many. In fact all the Vaiṣṇava devotees are *śikṣā-gurus*, but

> both the *dīkṣā-guru* and the many *śikṣā-gurus* are to be equally respected."
>
> —Bhaktivinoda Ṭhākura, *Śrī Harināma-cintāmaṇi* 6

One may receive instructions from any senior Vaiṣṇava, provided they concur with the teachings of the *dīkṣā-guru*, the previous *ācāryas*, and the Vedic scriptures.

> "Kṛṣṇa says that even fire, it is so pure, still there is some defect, there is smoke. So, if you want to find a defect, you'll find one in fire also. But that doesn't matter, fire is fire. Similarly a devotee, an unflinching devotee, without any other desires, who is dedicated to the service of the Lord, he is a *sādhu*. So we have to take shelter of such a *sādhu*. *Ādau gurv-āśrayam*. And a *sādhu* will instruct you. Not by whims, but through *śāstra*. He is a *sādhu*. A *sādhu* will never speak to you anything which is not in the *śāstra*. *Sādhu*, *śāstra*, and *guru*. And a *guru* is a bona fide spiritual master who follows *sādhu* and *śāstra*. Who follows his bona fide spiritual master and who follows the instructions of *śāstra*, he is a *guru*."
>
> —Bhaktivedanta lecture, *Teachings of Lord Caitanya*
> Mumbai 17/3/1971

Similarly, whatever spiritual knowledge a man gives to his wife and family must be in accordance with the teachings of *guru*, *sādhu* and *śāstra*, in order to be effective. On a practical level, a *gṛhastha* can help his wife and family to make spiritual advancement by engaging them in devotional activities. One who has understood the spiritual science of

Kṛṣṇa consciousness, under the guidance of a bona fide spiritual master, becomes qualified to act as a spiritual master himself.

kibā vipra, kibā nyāsī, śūdra kene naya
yei kṛṣṇa-tattva-vettā, sei 'guru' haya

"Whether one is a *brāhmaṇa*, a *sannyāsī* or a *śūdra*, regardless of what he is, he can become a spiritual master if he knows the science of Kṛṣṇa."
—*Śrī Caitanya-caritāmṛta, Madhya-līlā* 8.128

Bhaktivedanta purport:
"Śrīla Bhaktisiddhānta Sarasvatī Ṭhākura also states that although one is situated as a *brāhmaṇa, kṣatriya, vaiśya, śūdra, brahmacārī, vānaprastha, gṛhastha* or *sannyāsī*, if he is conversant in the science of Kṛṣṇa he can become a spiritual master as *vartma-pradarśaka-guru, dīkṣā-guru* or *śikṣā-guru*. The spiritual master who first gives information about spiritual life is called the *vartma-pradarśaka-guru*, the spiritual master who initiates according to the regulations of the *śāstras* is called the *dīkṣā-guru*, and the spiritual master who gives instructions for elevation is called the *śikṣā-guru*."

To become the spiritual master of his wife, and do all that he can to deliver her from the misery of material existence, is the sacred responsibility of a husband. The intelligence that God has given to man is primarily meant to be used for cultivating spiritual knowledge and becoming qualified to liberate his dependants.

> "Kardama Muni was Devahūti's husband, but because he instructed her on how to achieve spiritual perfection, he naturally became her spiritual master also. There are many instances wherein the husband becomes the spiritual master. Lord Śiva also is the spiritual master of his consort, Pārvatī. A husband should be so enlightened that he should become the spiritual master of his wife in order to enlighten her in the advancement of Kṛṣṇa consciousness. Generally *strī*, or woman, is less intelligent than man; therefore, if the husband is intelligent enough, the woman gets a great opportunity for spiritual enlightenment."
>
> —*Śrīmad Bhāgavatam* 3.24.5 Bhaktivedanta purport

A Vaiṣṇava husband accepts service from his wife not only for himself, but on behalf of his spiritual master and the Supreme Personality of Godhead. The greatest gift that he can offer to her in return is to try his best to deliver her from the fearful condition of material existence. When Kardama Muni, having fulfilled his wife's desire for children and provided her with all material comforts, was just about to leave home and take *sannyāsa*, Devahūti placed this request before him.

devahūtir uvāca
sarvaṁ tad bhagavān mahyam
upovāha pratiśrutam
athāpi me prapannāyā
abhayaṁ dātum arhasi

"Śrī Devahūti said: My lord, you have fulfilled all the promises you gave me, yet because I am your surrendered soul, you should give me fearlessness too."

—*Śrīmad Bhāgavatam* 3.23.51

Bhaktivedanta purport:

"Devahūti requested her husband to grant her something without fear. As a wife, she was a fully surrendered soul to her husband, and it is the responsibility of the husband to give his wife fearlessness. How one awards fearlessness to his subordinate is mentioned in the Fifth Canto of *Śrīmad Bhāgavatam*. One who cannot get free from the clutches of death is dependent, and he should not become a spiritual master, nor a husband, nor a kinsman, nor a father, nor a mother, etc. It is the duty of the superior to give fearlessness to the subordinate. To take charge of someone, therefore, either as father, mother, spiritual master, relative or husband, one must accept the responsibility to give his ward freedom from the fearful situation of material existence. Material existence is always fearful and full of anxiety. Devahūti is saying, 'You have given me all sorts of material comforts by your yogic power, and since you are now prepared to go away, you must give me your last award so that I may get free from this material, conditional life.'"

—*Śrīmad Bhāgavatam* 3.23.51

A man who has attained freedom from fear, by taking shelter of Kṛṣṇa, can help his wife to also become fearless in the same way.

> "This is the secret of Kṛṣṇa consciousness—realization that there is no existence besides Kṛṣṇa is the platform of peace and fearlessness."
>
> —*Bhagavad-gītā As It Is* 5.12 purport

One may not feel himself qualified to deliver his dependants, but if he simply takes shelter of Kṛṣṇa, by executing the process of *bhakti-yoga*, and teaches his dependants to do the same, then the Lord will take care of the rest.

> "In the *Bhagavad-gītā* the Lord Himself has claimed Arjuna as His dearmost friend. Every living being is thus related with the Supreme Lord by some sort of affectionate relation, either as servant or as friend or as parent or as an object of conjugal love. Everyone thus can enjoy the company of the Lord in the spiritual realm if he at all desires and sincerely tries for it by the process of *bhakti-yoga*."
>
> —*Śrīmad Bhāgavatam* 1.7.41 Bhaktivedanta purport

Chapter Six

Artha
Economic Development

Varṇa (Natural Occupation)—*Karma-yoga*
Arcana (Deity worship)—*Dana* (Giving in Charity)
Feeding the Hungry—Receiving Guests

Chapter Six

Artha

—Economic Development—

"Charity takes the best form of gifts in sacrifice. All beings depend upon the giver of things. Enemies are avoided by charity. Charity makes friends of people that hate. In charity alone everything else subsists. Therefore it is charity that is extolled as the highest to be obtained."
—*Taittirīya-āraṇyaka* 10.78

AFTER *DHARMA*, THE SECOND GOAL OF household life is known as *artha*, economic development.

"*Dharma-artha-kāma-mokṣa.* Human society, for at least peaceful living, must have religion, *dharma*. *Artha* means economic development, good condition. That is also required. First, human society should be religious, they must have nice economic organisation, and then *kāma*, they must also have a nice arrangement for sense gratification. Sense gratification is not denied. *Dharma, artha, kāma, and mokṣa.* And after that, when one is satisfied, when by religious procedure, one is satisfied in economic development, in satisfaction of the senses, the next need is *mokṣa*. *Mokṣa* means liberation from material bondage. These are the four *arthas*. *Catur-vargaḥ puruṣārthaḥ*. *Puruṣārtha* means the interest of the living entity."

—Bhaktivedanta lecture, *Śrīmad Bhāgavatam* 1.5.1-4
West Virginia 22/5/1969

A responsible householder works to maintain his wife and family, and this is his sacred duty. At the same time however, if he works to accumulate wealth simply for increasing material enjoyment, he becomes entangled in a complex network of *karma*. In other words, he suffers a reaction for every inconvenience or suffering he has caused to any living entity, knowingly or unknowingly, in the course of his activities. And, as long as he continues with his fruitive activities, the karmic reactions also continue, birth after birth.

"The *karma* of those who work with the hope of enjoying the fruits of their labours becomes everlasting and endless and is never destroyed."

—*Śrī Brahma-saṁhitā* 5.54 Bhaktisiddhānta purport

A wise householder can protect himself from becoming bound up to this perpetual cycle of *karma* by regulating his economic development according to religious principles.

"Economic development and sense gratification must be based on religious principles."

—*Śrīmad Bhāgavatam* 4.22.36 Bhaktivedanta purport

One who engages his natural talents in an honest occupation, and engages the fruits of his labour in serving

God, becomes freed from sinful reactions and feels satisfied within himself.

yaḥ sva-dharmeṇa māṁ nityaṁ
nirāśīḥ śraddhayānvitaḥ
bhajate śanakais tasya
mano rājan prasīdati

> "The Supreme Personality of Godhead, Lord Viṣṇu, continued: My dear King Pṛthu, when one situated in his occupational duty engages in My loving service without motive for material gain, he gradually becomes very satisfied within."
>
> —*Śrīmad Bhāgavatam* 4.20.9

This is *artha* according to *dharma*.

> "This is the most auspicious path for a religious householder of the twice-born orders—to selflessly worship the Personality of Godhead with wealth honestly obtained."
>
> —*Śrīmad Bhāgavatam* 10.84.37

Varṇa (Natural Occupation)

According to the Vedic social system known as *varṇāśrama*, each person belongs to one of the four *varṇas* or occupational divisions. The present-day caste system of India is a perversion of this ancient model. The true *varṇa* of an individual is meant to be recognised, not simply by birth in a particular family, but by personal qualities and activities.

> "According to the three modes of material nature and the work associated with them, the four divisions of human society are created by Me."
>
> —Lord Kṛṣṇa, *Bhagavad-gītā As It Is* 4.13

One who is engaged in his rightful occupation, according to his natural skills and propensities, experiences job satisfaction. The four components of society are known as *brāhmaṇas* (priests and teachers), *kṣatriyas* (leaders and warriors), *vaiśyas* (farmers and businessmen), and *śūdras* (artisans and labourers). A person's *varṇa* is identified by his inherent nature and talents, born from the influence of one or two of the three modes of material nature.

> "*Brāhmaṇas, kṣatriyas, vaiśyas* and *śūdras* are distinguished by the qualities born of their own natures in accordance with the material modes, O chastiser of the enemy."
>
> —*Bhagavad-gītā As It Is* 18.41

In ancient Vedic society, the members of the four *varṇas* respected each other and lived peacefully together.

> "The *kṣatriyas* follow the lead of the *brāhmaṇas*, the *vaiśyas* are devoted to the *kṣatriyas*, and the *śūdras* take delight in their own work while serving the other three *varṇas*."
>
> —*Śrīmad Vālmīki-Rāmāyaṇa, Bāla-kāṇḍa* 6.19

Young people who are trained and educated according to their natural *varṇa* can become valuable contributors to society.

> "The social institution known as *varṇāśrama-dharma*—the institution dividing society into four divisions of social life and four occupational divisions or castes—is not meant to divide human society according to birth. Such divisions are in terms of educational qualifications. They are to keep the society in a state of peace and prosperity."
>
> —*Bhagavad-gītā As It Is* 16.1-3 purport

While everyone is influenced by a mixture of the three modes, one of those modes, or sometimes a mixture of two, can be seen to be predominant in the nature of an individual. According to the *varṇāśrama* system, a young person is trained or educated according to his predominant mode(s), and thus equipped for the occupation that naturally suits him. Those who manifest the qualities of the mode of goodness can be educated to become *brāhmaṇas*.

śamo damas tapaḥ śaucaṁ
kṣāntir ārjavam eva ca
jñānaṁ vijñānam āstikyaṁ
brahma-karma svabhāva-jam

> "Peacefulness, self-control, austerity, purity, tolerance, honesty, knowledge, wisdom and religiousness—these are the natural qualities by which the *brāhmaṇas* work."
>
> —*Bhagavad-gītā As It Is* 18.42

Those who manifest the qualities of the mode of passion can be trained to become *kṣatriyas*.

śauryaṁ tejo dhṛtir dākṣyaṁ
yuddhe cāpy apalāyanam
dānam īśvara-bhāvaś ca
kṣātraṁ karma svabhāva-jam

"Heroism, power, determination, resourcefulness, courage in battle, generosity and leadership are the natural qualities of work for the *kṣatriyas.*"
—*Bhagavad-gītā* As It Is 18.43

Those who manifest mixed qualities of passion and ignorance can learn to become *vaiśyas.*

kṛṣi-go-rakṣya-vāṇijyaṁ
vaiśya-karma svabhāva-jam

"Farming, cow protection and business are the natural work for the *vaiśyas.*"
—*Bhagavad-gītā* As It Is 18.44

And those who are predominantly in the mode of ignorance can be engaged as *śūdras.*

paricaryātmakaṁ karma
śūdrasyāpi svabhāva-jam

"And for the *śūdras* there is labor and service to others."
—*Bhagavad-gītā* As It Is 18.44

Each *varṇa* has its own prescribed methods for earning a livelihood. There are six occupational duties prescribed for a *brāhmaṇa*, namely, to study the *Vedas*, to teach Vedic knowledge, to worship the Deity, to teach Deity worship, to give in charity and to accept charity.

> "*Brāhmaṇas* have six occupational duties, of which three are compulsory—namely, studying the *Vedas*, worshiping the Deity and giving charity. By teaching, by inducing others to worship the Deity, and by accepting gifts, the *brāhmaṇas* receive the necessities of life."
>
> —*Śrīmad-Bhāgavatam* 7.11.14 Bhaktivedanta purport

It is also the *brāhmaṇas* who traditionally provide medical and astrological services to the other members of society. *Āyurveda* (medical science) and *jyotiṣa* (astrology) are both propounded in ancient Vedic texts. Those who practise these sciences are known as *vipras*.

> "The specific intelligent class of men who were devoted particularly to the knowledge of the *Vedas* were called the *vipras*, or the graduates of the Vedic knowledge.There are different branches of knowledge in the *Vedas*, of which astrology and pathology are two important branches necessary for the common man. So the intelligent men, generally known as the *brāhmaṇas*, took up all the different branches of Vedic knowledge to guide society. Even the department of military education (*Dhanur-veda*) was also taken up by such intelligent men, and the *vipras* were also teachers of this section of knowledge, as were Droṇācārya, Kṛpācārya, etc."
>
> —*Śrīmad Bhāgavatam* 1.12.29 Bhaktivedanta purport

Vipras belong to the brahminical order but are known as *vipras* to distinguish them from the *brāhmaṇas* who specialise in studying and teaching spiritual knowledge.

> "There is a little difference between the *vipras* and the *brāhmaṇas*. The *vipras* are those who are expert in *karma-kāṇḍa*, or fruitive activities, guiding the society towards fulfilling the material necessities of life, whereas the *brāhmaṇas* are expert in spiritual knowledge of transcendence. This department of knowledge is called *jñāna-kāṇḍa*, and above this there is the *upāsanā-kāṇḍa*. The culmination of *upāsanā-kāṇḍa* is the devotional service of the Lord Viṣṇu, and when the *brāhmaṇas* achieve perfection, they are called Vaiṣṇavas."
>
> —*Śrīmad Bhāgavatam* 1.12.29 Bhaktivedanta purport

Like all *brāhmaṇas*, *vipras* traditionally maintain themselves by accepting charity.

> "Amongst the *karma-kāṇḍa* experts, the *jātaka* expert *vipras* were good astrologers who could tell all the future history of a born child simply by the astral calculations of the time (*lagna*). Such expert *jātaka-vipras* were present during the birth of Mahārāja Parīkṣit, and his grandfather, Mahārāja Yudhiṣṭhira, awarded the *vipras* sufficiently with gold, land, villages, grains and other valuable necessaries of life, which also include cows."
>
> —*Śrīmad Bhāgavatam* 1.12.29 Bhaktivedanta purport

It is the duty of the *kṣatriyas*, or government, to maintain the *vipras*, thus allowing them to provide free services for the benefit of society in general.

> "There is a need of such *vipras* in the social structure, and it is the duty of the state to maintain them comfortably, as designed in the Vedic procedure. Such expert *vipras*, being sufficiently paid by the state, could give free service to the people in general, and thus this department of Vedic knowledge could be available for all."
>
> —*Śrīmad Bhāgavatam* 1.12.29 Bhaktivedanta purport

Anyone who is situated in the mode of goodness can become trained as a *brāhmaṇa* and take up brahminical work. A genuine *brāhmaṇa* is peaceful, free from vices, and conversant with Vedic knowledge. A *brāhmaṇa* should not become anyone's paid servant, but he can be maintained by the state, as mentioned above, to provide a public service. A *brāhmaṇa* who is a teacher should provide knowledge that is free from deception and cheating.

A *kṣatriya* is a leader, law enforcer or warrior. The main duties of the *kṣatriya* are to protect the innocent, to govern society according to the teachings of the *brāhmaṇas*, and to punish aggressors and criminals. *Kṣatriyas* may also perform any of the six activities of a *brāhmaṇa*, except for accepting charity.

> "For a *brāhmaṇa* there are six occupational duties. A *kṣatriya* should not accept charity, but he may perform

> the other five of these duties. A king or *kṣatriya* is not allowed to levy taxes on *brāhmaṇas*, but he may make his livelihood by levying minimal taxes, customs duties, and penalty fines upon his other subjects."
>
> —*Śrīmad Bhāgavatam* 7.11.14

The prescribed occupational duties for *vaiśyas* and *śūdras* are described as follows.

> "The mercantile community should always follow the directions of the *brāhmaṇas* and engage in such occupational duties as agriculture, trade, and protection of cows. For the *śūdras* the only duty is to accept a master from a higher social order and engage in his service."
>
> —*Śrīmad Bhāgavatam* 7.11.15

> "*Śūdras* must work; sometimes they should engage in occupational duties as cloth manufacturers, weavers, blacksmiths, goldsmiths, brass-smiths, and so on, or else they should engage in hard labor to produce food grains."
>
> —*Śrīmad Bhāgavatam* 7.14.10 Bhaktivedanta purport

Out of the four *varṇas*, the *śūdras* are the only ones who can be employed by others, according to Vedic culture. These are in essence the main duties of the four *varṇas*. Unfortunately today there is a great deal of work that is executed, not for the overall benefit of society, but to satisfy the greed and ambition of materialistic opportunists.

> "Development of factories and mills is called *ugra-karma*, or pungent activities, and such activities deteriorate the finer sentiments of the human being and society to form a dungeon of demons."
>
> —*Śrīmad Bhāgavatam* 1.11.12 Bhaktivedanta purport

A householder can avoid *ugra-karma* by keeping his work as simple and natural as possible and beneficial to others. In case of an emergency situation, for practical purposes, anyone, except for a *kṣatriya*, may carry out the duties of others and accept their means of livelihood.

> "Except in a time of emergency, lower persons should not accept the occupational duties of those who are higher. When there is such an emergency, of course, everyone but the *kṣatriya* may accept the means of livelihood of others."
>
> —*Śrīmad Bhāgavatam* 7.11.17

(The terms "lower" and "higher" are used here with reference to the different types of work that people do and bear no reflection on their personal worth as human beings.) The present chaotic condition of society can be considered an emergency situation, since there is a shortage of qualified *brāhmaṇas* to provide spiritual guidance. For this reason, people who have not been trained from childhood as *brāhmaṇas* and have not been consecrated from birth with traditional Vedic rites are being trained as adults to become *brāhmaṇas*.

> "At the present moment, society is in a chaotic condition, and everyone has given up the cultivation

> of spiritual life, which is especially meant for the *brāhmaṇas*. Because spiritual culture has been stopped all over the world, there is now an emergency, and therefore it is now time to train those who are considered lower and condemned, so that they may become *brāhmaṇas* and take up the work of spiritual progress."
>
> —*Śrīmad Bhāgavatam* 7.11.17 Bhaktivedanta purport

People who are born in the West or in meat-eating families are viewed by some Hindu caste-*brāhmaṇas* as lower and condemned or, in other words, they are considered to be unqualified to become *brāhmaṇas* in the same lifetime. However, according to the original ethos of the *varṇāśrama* system, anyone who is inclined to study spiritual knowledge and to follow religious principles, while avoiding sinful activities, can be trained to become a *brāhmaṇa*. To follow *varna-dharma* means simply to acknowledge and appreciate whatever natural talents and propensities God has given to us and to engage them in His service.

> "The occupational duty of a *brāhmaṇa* is certainly in the mode of goodness, but if a person is not by nature in the mode of goodness, he should not imitate the occupational duty of a *brāhmaṇa*. For a *kṣatriya*, or administrator, there are so many abominable things; a *kṣatriya* has to be violent to kill his enemies, and sometimes a *kṣatriya* has to tell lies for the sake of diplomacy. Such violence and duplicity accompany political affairs, but a *kṣatriya* is not supposed to give

up his occupational duty and try to perform the duties of a *brāhmaṇa*. In the business field also, sometimes a merchant has to tell so many lies to make a profit. If he does not do so, there can be no profit. Sometimes a merchant says, 'Oh, my dear customer, for you I am making no profit,' but one should know that without profit the merchant cannot exist. Therefore it should be taken as a simple lie if a merchant says that he is not making a profit. But the merchant should not think that because he is engaged in an occupation in which the telling of lies is compulsory, he should give up his profession and pursue the profession of a *brāhmaṇa*. That is not recommended. Whether one is a *kṣatriya*, a *vaiśya*, or a *śūdra* doesn't matter, if he serves, by his work, the Supreme Personality of Godhead."

—*Bhagavad-gītā As It Is* 18.47 purport

Any work performed in this world is bound to be imperfect.

"Every endeavor is covered by some fault, just as fire is covered by smoke. Therefore one should not give up the work born of his nature, O son of Kuntī, even if such work is full of fault."

—*Bhagavad-gītā As It Is* 18.48

Even while working in a society that does not recognise the *varṇāśrama* system, one can nevertheless follow the basic principles of *varṇāśrama* simply by using his/her natural qualifications and whatever training one has received to contribute to the welfare of society, whether spiritually, morally, or materially, without promoting sinful activities such as meat-eating, intoxication, gambling, and illicit sex, which lead to degradation and suffering. Other unavoidable faults that one may incur can be counteracted by the remedy of working for the pleasure of the Supreme Lord and engaging the results in His service.

> "When a particular type of occupation is performed for the satisfaction of the Supreme Lord, all the defects in that particular occupation are purified. When the results of work are purified, when connected with devotional service, one becomes perfect in seeing the self within, and that is self-realization."
>
> —*Bhagavad-gītā As It Is* 18.48 purport

While the unavoidable impurities connected with prescribed occupational duties can be cleansed by the process of working for God, bribery and corruption are prohibited.

> "Everyone is prohibited from corrupt earning or spending, and workers are prohibited from accepting bribes."
>
> —Bhaktivinoda Ṭhākura, *Śrī Bhaktyāloka* 12

Money should not be misappropriated or spent for sinful activities. This was explained by Śrī Caitanya Mahāprabhu to Gopīnātha Paṭṭanāyaka, the tax-collector.

> "One who serves the government but misappropriates the government's revenue is liable to be punished by the king. That is the verdict of all revealed scriptures."
>
> —*Śrī Caitanya-caritāmṛta, Antya-līlā* 9.90

> "Do not spend any of the king's revenue. First you should pay the revenue due to the king, and then you may spend the balance for religious and fruitive activities. Don't spend a farthing for sinful activities for which you will be the loser both in this life and the next."
>
> —*Śrī Caitanya-caritāmṛta, Antya-līlā* 9.142-4

Accumulating wealth by sinful means is also prohibited.

> "By following his prescribed duties a *gṛhastha* Vaiṣṇava should accumulate wealth for his maintenance. He should not accumulate wealth by sinful means."
>
> —Bhaktivinoda Ṭhākura, *Śrī Bhaktyāloka* 12

> "These are the different occupational duties by which men should earn their livelihood, and in this way human society should be simple. At the present moment, however, everyone is engaged in technological advancement, which is described in *Bhagavad-gītā* as *ugra-karma*—extremely severe endeavor. This *ugra-karma* is the cause of agitation within the human mind. Men are engaging in many sinful activities and becoming degraded by opening slaughterhouses, breweries and cigarette factories, as well as nightclubs and other establishments for sense enjoyment. In this way they are spoiling their lives."
>
> —*Śrīmad Bhāgavatam* 7.14.10 Bhaktivedanta purport

The fruits of criminal activities that cause suffering to others are not desirable to God. Lord Nityānanda gave the following instructions to Mādhāi, who was previously a *brāhmaṇa* but had been leading the life of a criminal.

> "Now listen carefully, O *brāhmaṇa*. I will take responsibility for all your previous misdeeds if you do not repeat them. No more aggression, violence, looting, or murder; give them up forever. Lead a religious life and chant the holy names of the Supreme Lord. Then later you can also save others. Go and meet other dacoits and murderers and bring them to the path of pure religious life."
>
> —*Śrī Caitanya-bhāgavata, Antya-khaṇḍa* 5.685-8

Karma-yoga

Simply by working according to one's *varṇa*, and engaging the fruits of that work in the service of the Supreme Lord, one can attain perfection.

yataḥ pravṛttir bhūtānāṁ
yena sarvam idaṁ tatam
sva-karmaṇā tam abhyarcya
siddhiṁ vindati mānavaḥ

> "By worship of the Lord, who is the source of all beings and who is all-pervading, a man can attain perfection through performing his own work."
>
> —*Bhagavad-gītā As It Is* 18.46

Work that is performed simply for oneself and one's family is known as *karma*, or fruitive activity, which implicates the worker in a web of karmic reactions. Work that is carried out for the pleasure of the Lord, on the other hand, is called *karma-yoga*. By this shift in consciousness, normal work is transformed from an ordinary material activity into a form of *yoga*, which means 'linking with the Supreme'.

yajñārthāt karmaṇo 'nyatra
loko 'yaṁ karma-bandhanaḥ
tad-arthaṁ karma kaunteya
mukta-saṅgaḥ samācara

> "Work done as a sacrifice for Viṣṇu has to be performed; otherwise work causes bondage in this material world. Therefore, O son of Kuntī, perform your prescribed duties for His satisfaction, and in that way you will always remain free from bondage."
> —*Bhagavad-gītā As It Is* 3.9

Karma-yoga that is performed directly for Kṛṣṇa can also be called *kṛṣṇa-karma*. Whether one is rich or poor, there are unlimited ways of working for Kṛṣṇa.

> "No work should be done by any man except in relationship to Kṛṣṇa. This is called *kṛṣṇa-karma*. One may be engaged in various activities, but one should not be attached to the result of his work; the result should be done only for Him. For example, one may be engaged in business, but to transform that activity into Kṛṣṇa consciousness, one has to do business for Kṛṣṇa. If Kṛṣṇa is the proprietor of the business, then Kṛṣṇa should enjoy the profit of the

business. If a businessman is in possession of thousands and thousands of dollars, and if he has to offer all this to Kṛṣṇa, he can do it. This is work for Kṛṣṇa. Instead of constructing a big building for his sense gratification, he can construct a nice temple for Kṛṣṇa, and he can install the Deity of Kṛṣṇa and arrange for the Deity's service, as is outlined in the authorized books of devotional service. This is all *kṛṣṇa-karma*. One should not be attached to the result of his work, but the result should be offered to Kṛṣṇa, and one should accept as *prasādam* the remnants of offerings to Kṛṣṇa. If one constructs a very big building for Kṛṣṇa and installs the Deity of Kṛṣṇa, one is not prohibited from living there, but it is understood that the proprietor of the building is Kṛṣṇa. That is called Kṛṣṇa consciousness. If, however, one is not able to construct a temple for Kṛṣṇa, one can engage himself in cleansing the temple of Kṛṣṇa; that is also *kṛṣṇa-karma*. One can cultivate a garden. Anyone who has land—in India, at least, any poor man has a certain amount of land—can utilize that for Kṛṣṇa by growing flowers to offer Him. One can sow *tulasī* plants, because *tulasī* leaves are very important and Kṛṣṇa has recommended this in *Bhagavad-gītā*. *Patraṁ puṣpaṁ phalaṁ toyam*. Kṛṣṇa desires that one offer Him either a leaf, or a flower, or fruit, or a little water—and by such an offering He is satisfied. This leaf especially refers to the *tulasī*. So one can sow *tulasī* and pour water on the plant. Thus, even the poorest man can engage in the service of

> Kṛṣṇa. These are some of the examples of how one can engage in working for Kṛṣṇa."
>
> —*Bhagavad-gītā* As It Is 11.55 purport

Whatever activities one is obliged to perform in the normal course of duty can ultimately become *bhakti-yoga*, the highest form of *yoga*, if carried out in a devotional consciousness.

> "This world subsists by constant performance of certain activities. Fill all these activities with meditation of Me. This will destroy the quality that makes those activities appear as acts done by you. They will then be of the nature of My service (*bhakti*)."
>
> —*Śrī Brahma-saṁhitā* 5.61 Bhaktisiddhānta purport

The various stages of advancement in consciousness that can be attained during the performance of regular activities are described as follows by Bhaktisiddhānta Sarasvatī Ṭhākura.

> "Mankind lives by the threefold activities of body, mind and society. Eating, sitting, walking, resting, sleeping, cleansing the body, covering the body, etc., are the various bodily activities; thinking, recollecting, retaining an impression, becoming aware of an entity, feeling pleasure and pain, etc., are the mental feats; marrying, practising reciprocal relationship between the king and subject, practising brotherhood, attending sacrificial meetings, offering oblations, digging wells, tanks, etc., for the benefit of

the people, maintaining one's relations, practising hospitality, observing proper civic conduct, showing due respect to others are the various social activities. When these acts are performed for one's selfish enjoyment, they are called *karma-kāṇḍa*; when the desire for attainment of freedom from activity by knowledge underlies these actions, they are termed *jñāna-yoga* or *karma-yoga*. And when these activities are managed to be performed in a way that is conducive to our endeavour for attainment of *bhakti*, they are called *jñāna-bhakta-yoga*, i.e., the subsidiary devotional practices. But only those activities that are characterised by the principle of pure worship are called *bhakti* proper. My meditation is practised in every act when *bhakti* proper is practised in due time while performing the subsidiary devotional activities in one's intercourse with the ungodly people of this world. In such position, a *jīva* does not become apathetic to Godhead even by performing those worldly activities."

—*Śrī Brahma-saṁhitā* 5.61 Bhaktisiddhānta purport

A *bhakti-yogī* sees everything as the property of the Supreme Lord and accepts for himself only what he needs to maintain his service to the Lord.

īśāvāsyam idam sarvaṁ
yat kiñca jagatyāṁ jagat
tena tyaktena bhuñjīthā
mā gṛdhaḥ kasya svid dhanam

> "Everything animate or inanimate that is within the universe is controlled and owned by the Lord. One should therefore accept only those things necessary for himself, which are set aside as his quota, and one must not accept other things, knowing well to Whom they belong."
>
> —*Śrī Īśopaniṣad* 1

A devotional consciousness is characterised by the mood of accepting one's quota as *prasādam* or mercy of the Supreme Personality of Godhead.

> "The real significance being that, if whatever is accepted is received as a favour vouchsafed by the Supreme Lord, the worldly activity will then cease to be such and will turn into service of Godhead (*bhakti*)."
>
> —*Śrī Brahma-saṁhitā* 5.61 Bhaktisiddhānta purport

Work performed as devotional service is not subject to ordinary laws of *karma* and is free from sinful reactions.

kurvann eveha karmāṇi
jijīviṣec chataṁ samāḥ
evaṁ tvayi nānyatheto 'sti
na karma lipyate nare

> "One may aspire to live for hundreds of years if he continuously goes on doing work in that way, because that sort of work will not bind him to the law of *karma*. And there is no alternative to this way for man."
>
> —*Śrī Īśopaniṣad* 2

Bhaktisiddhānta Sarasvatī Ṭhākura explains the first and second *mantras* of *Śrī Īśopaniṣad* in the following way.

> "The meaning of these two mantras from the *jñāna* point of view is renouncement of the fruits of one's worldly actions; but from the *bhakti* point of view they mean the attainment of Kṛṣṇa's favour (*prasādam*) by their transfer to His account. In this method, which is the path of *arcana*, you should do your duties of the world with the meditation of worshipping Godhead thereby."
>
> —*Śrī Brahma-saṁhitā* 5.61 Bhaktisiddhānta purport

While those who are engaged in fruitive activities are forced to continually suffer and enjoy the results of their *karma*, those who are engaged in devotional service are personally taken care of by the Lord. Whatever suffering they may undergo is understood by them to be a personal benediction from the Lord for their purification, preparing them to ultimately become free from all suffering.

> "God impartially induces the fallen souls to act in the way that is consequent on the deeds of their previous births and to enjoy the fruition of their labours but, out of His great mercy to His devotees, He purges out, by the fire of ordeal, the root of all *karma*, viz., nescience and evil desires."
>
> —*Śrī Brahma-saṁhitā* 5.54 Bhaktisiddhānta purport

He who works with the meditation that it is the Supreme Lord Who is engaging him in that work and Who is to be worshipped by its results, can attain the highest perfection of life.

> "Everyone should think that he is engaged in a particular type of occupation by Hṛṣīkeśa, the master of the senses. And by the result of the work in which one is engaged, the Supreme Personality of Godhead, Śrī Kṛṣṇa, should be worshiped. If one thinks always in this way, in full Kṛṣṇa consciousness, then, by the grace of the Lord, he becomes fully aware of everything. That is the perfection of life. The Lord says in *Bhagavad-gītā* (12.7), *teṣām ahaṁ samuddhartā*. The Supreme Lord Himself takes charge of delivering such a devotee. That is the highest perfection of life. In whatever occupation one may be engaged, if he serves the Supreme Lord he will achieve the highest perfection."
>
> —*Bhagavad-gītā As It Is* 18.46 purport

The perfection of economic development is to work according to one's prescribed occupation for the pleasure of the Lord.

> "If one works according to the *varṇāśrama-dharma* system and does not desire fruitive results, he gets satisfaction gradually. Discharging one's occupational duty as a means of rendering devotional service unto the Supreme Personality of Godhead is the ultimate goal of life. *Bhagavad-gītā* confirms this as the process of *karma-yoga*. In other words, we should act only for the satisfaction and service of the Lord. Otherwise we will be entangled by the resultant actions. Everyone is situated in his occupational duty, but the purpose of material occupations should not be

material gain. Rather, everyone should offer the results of his occupational activities. A *brāhmaṇa* especially should execute his occupational duties not for material gain but to please the Supreme Personality of Godhead. The *kṣatriya, vaiśya* and *śūdra* should work in a similar way. In this material world everyone is engaged in various professional and occupational duties, but the purpose of such activities should be to please the Supreme Personality of Godhead."

—*Śrīmad Bhāgavatam* 4.20.9 Bhaktivedanta purport

Arcana (Deity worship)

Since God is not visible to our material eyes, how do we offer the results of our work to Him? For this reason the Lord appears in the form of the Deity, made of matter, so that we can render personal service to Him. The ancient practice of Deity worship is a beautiful and practical system by which householders of all *varṇas* can offer the fruits of their labour to the Supreme Lord on a regular daily basis within their own homes.

"Devotional service is very simple, and anyone can adopt it. Let one remain what he is; he need only install the Deity of the Supreme Lord in his house. The Deity may be Rādhā-Kṛṣṇa or Lakṣmī-Nārāyaṇa (there are many other forms of the Lord). In this way a *brāhmaṇa, kṣatriya, vaiśya* or *śūdra* can worship the Deity with the results of his honest labor. Regardless of one's occupational duty, one should adopt the devotional means of hearing, chanting, remembering, worshiping, offering everything to the Lord and engaging in His service. In this way one can very easily engage himself in the service of the Lord. When the Lord is pleased with one's service, one's mission in life is fulfilled."

—*Śrīmad Bhāgavatam* 4.20.9 Bhaktivedanta purport

Genuine Deities are constructed according to authoritative Vedic descriptions of the Supreme Personality of Godhead, whether in His original form as Lord Kṛṣṇa (Govinda) or in the forms of His scheduled incarnations.

veṇuṁ kvaṇantam aravinda-dalāyatākṣam
barhāvataṁsam asitāmbuda-sundarāṅgam
kandarpa-koṭi-kamanīya-viśeṣa-śobhaṁ
govindam ādi-puruṣaṁ tam ahaṁ bhajāmi

"I worship Govinda, the primeval Lord, who is adept in playing on His flute, with blooming eyes like lotus petals, with head decked with peacock's feather, with the figure of beauty tinged with the hue of blue clouds, and His unique loveliness charming millions of Cupids."

—*Śrī Brahma-saṁhitā* 5.30

Anyone can set up a simple altar at home and install a small Deity of the Supreme Lord. Even a poor man can satisfy the Lord by offering simple items with love and devotion.

patraṁ puṣpaṁ phalaṁ toyaṁ
yo me bhaktyā prayacchati

tad ahaṁ bhakty-upahṛtam
aśnāmi prayatātmanaḥ

> "If one offers Me with love and devotion a leaf, a flower, fruit or water, I will accept it."
> —Lord Kṛṣṇa, *Bhagavad-gītā As It Is* 9.26

By preparing pure vegetarian food, offering it first to the Lord in His Deity form, and then accepting it as *prasāda* (mercy), families can enjoy eating delicious food and at the same time make spiritual advancement. Food that has been cooked with devotion and offered to God becomes free from *karma.*

yat karoṣi yad aśnāsi
yaj juhoṣi dadāsi yat
yat tapasyasi kaunteya
tat kuruṣva mad-arpaṇam

> "Whatever you do, whatever you eat, whatever you offer or give away, and whatever austerities you perform—do that, O son of Kuntī, as an offering to Me."
> —*Bhagavad-gītā As It Is* 9.27

Householders who are wealthy are recommended to worship the Lord with their opulence.

> "Especially for householder devotees who are opulent in material possessions, the path of Deity worship is strongly recommended. An opulent householder devotee who does not engage his hard-earned money in the service of the Lord is called a miser."
> —*Śrīmad Bhāgavatam* 7.5.23-4 Bhaktivedanta purport

Deity worship should be conducted in accordance with Vedic injunctions and the teachings of *ācāryas* from a bona fide Vaiṣṇava *sampradāya* (disciplic succession), under the direction of a spiritual master who is descended from the same *sampradāya*.

> "In the *Vāyu Purāṇa* an *ācārya* is defined as one who knows the import of all Vedic literature, explains the purpose of the *Vedas*, abides by their rules and regulations, and teaches his disciples to act in the same way."
>
> —*Śrī Caitanya-caritāmṛta, Ādi-līlā* 1.46 Bhaktivedanta purport

For Gauḍīya Vaiṣṇavas, the authorised instructions on Deity worship are derived from the *Hari-bhakti-vilāsa* of Sanātana Gosvāmī. The path of Deity worship is strongly recommended for householders.

> "Especially for the householder devotees, the path of Deity worship is strongly recommended. As far as possible, every householder, by the direction of the spiritual master, must install the Deity of Viṣṇu, forms like Rādhā-Kṛṣṇa, Lakṣmī-Nārāyaṇa or Sītā-Rāma especially, or any other form of the Lord, like Nṛsiṁha, Varāha, Gaura-Nitāi, Matsya, Kūrma, *śālagrāma-śilā* and many other forms of Viṣṇu, like Trivikrama, Keśava, Acyuta, Vāsudeva, Nārāyaṇa and Dāmodara, as recommended in the *Vaiṣṇava-tantras* or *Purāṇas*, and one's family should worship strictly following the directions and regulations of *arcana-vidhi*."
>
> —*Śrīmad Bhāgavatam* 2.3.22 Bhaktivedanta purport

Deity worship can be carried out by all family members who are initiated by a Vaiṣṇava spiritual master. Others can render supporting services.

> "Any member of the family who is above twelve years of age should be initiated by a bona fide spiritual master, and all the members of the household should be engaged in the daily service of the Lord, beginning from morning (4 a.m.) till night (10 p.m.) by performing *maṅgala-ārātrika, nirañjana, arcana, pūjā, kīrtana, śṛṅgāra, bhoga-vaikāli, sandhyā-ārātrika, pāṭha, bhoga* (at night), *śayana-ārātrika*, etc."
>
> —*Śrīmad Bhāgavatam* 2.3.22 Bhaktivedanta purport

Direct services to the Deity include waking the Lord; bathing, dressing and decorating the Deity; offering food, water, cloth, incense, flaming lamps, flowers, fans, and perfume oils; and putting the Lord to rest. Those who are engaged in such personal services to the Lord, with care and attention, become purified and elevated in consciousness.

> "Engagement in such worship of the Deity, under the direction of a bona fide spiritual master, will greatly help the householders to purify their very existence and make rapid progress in spiritual knowledge."
>
> —*Śrīmad Bhāgavatam* 2.3.22 Bhaktivedanta purport

The full daily programme of Deity worship as described above, from 4 a.m. to 10 p.m., is the traditional Vaiṣṇava system, established to serve the Lord in accordance with His various pastimes at different times of the day. This is the way that the Deities are served in large ISKCON temples. To worship in such a way at home requires a committed family of initiates. Where this is not possible or practical, then the programme can be simplified in consultation with the spiritual master. A devotional consciousness is the most important ingredient of Deity worship. While devotion is naturally expressed through service, at the same time, since Deity worship is a regular daily commitment, families should establish a schedule that they can regularly maintain, gradually increasing as and when possible.

> "The best process for making the home pleasant is Kṛṣṇa consciousness. If one is in full Kṛṣṇa consciousness, he can make his home very happy, because this process of Kṛṣṇa consciousness is very easy. One need only chant Hare Kṛṣṇa, Hare Kṛṣṇa, Kṛṣṇa Kṛṣṇa, Hare Hare/ Hare Rāma, Hare Rāma, Rāma Rāma, Hare Hare, accept the remnants of foodstuffs offered to Kṛṣṇa, have some discussion on books like *Bhagavad-gītā* and *Śrīmad-Bhāgavatam*, and engage oneself in Deity worship. These four things will make one happy. One should train the members of his family in this way. The family members can sit down morning and evening and chant together Hare Kṛṣṇa, Hare Kṛṣṇa, Kṛṣṇa Kṛṣṇa, Hare Hare/ Hare Rāma, Hare Rāma, Rāma Rāma, Hare Hare. If one can mold his family life in this way to develop Kṛṣṇa consciousness, following these four principles, then there is no need to change from family life to renounced life."
>
> —*Bhagavad-gītā As It Is* 13.8-12 purport

Engagement in Deity worship is a purifying substitute for unwanted activities that cause degradation.

> "Thus it is the duty of every householder to install Deities of the Lord at home and to begin the process of worshiping along with all of his family members. This will save everyone from such unwanted activities as going to clubs, cinemas and dancing parties, and smoking, drinking, etc. All such nonsense will be forgotten if one stresses the worship of the Deities at home."
>
> —*The Nectar of Devotion* 13

By chanting the holy names of the Lord and engaging in Deity worship, devotees become freed from all bad *karma*.

> "The holy name is so spiritually potent that simply by chanting the holy name one can be freed from the reactions to all sinful activities. What, then, is to be said of those who chant the holy name regularly or worship the Deity regularly? For such purified devotees, freedom from sinful reaction is certainly assured."
>
> —*Śrīmad Bhāgavatam* 6.13.8-9 Bhaktivedanta purport

Those householders who are unable to maintain a temple at home are advised to visit another's temple where regular Deity worship is maintained.

> "If one is unable to maintain a temple at home, he should go to another's temple where all the above performances are regularly executed. Visiting the

> temple of a devotee and looking at the profusely decorated forms of the Lord well dressed in a well-decorated, sanctified temple naturally infuse the mundane mind with spiritual inspiration."
>
> —*Śrīmad Bhāgavatam* 2.3.22 Bhaktivedanta purport

The temple may be small, in a family home, or it may be a large public temple.

> "In many places throughout the world we are constructing communities to give shelter to devotees and worship the Deity in the temple. The Deity cannot be worshiped except by devotees... Therefore, in the temple there must be the Deity of the Lord, and the Lord should be worshiped by the devotees. This combination of the devotees and the Deity creates a first-class transcendental place. Aside from this, if a *gṛhastha* devotee worships the *śālagrāma-śilā*, or the form of the Deity at home, his home also becomes a very great place. It was therefore customary for members of the three higher classes—namely the *brāhmaṇas*, *kṣatriyas* and *vaiśyas*—to worship the *śālagrāma-śilā*, or a small Deity of Rādhā-Kṛṣṇa or Sītā-Rāma in each and every home. This made everything auspicious."
>
> —*Śrīmad Bhāgavatam* 7.14.29 Bhaktivedanta purport

Deity worship, when combined with the chanting of the holy names of the Lord and the reading of scriptures, provides a complete practical and theoretical process for attaining spiritual perfection.

> "Simple theoretical book knowledge is not sufficient for a neophyte devotee. Book knowledge is theoretical, whereas the *arcana* process is practical. Spiritual knowledge must be developed by a combination of theoretical and practical knowledge, and that is the guaranteed way for the attainment of spiritual perfection."
>
> —*Śrīmad Bhāgavatam* 2.3.22 Bhaktivedanta purport

If we simply worship the Deity, without hearing and chanting about the Lord, then the activities of Deity worship may become mechanical. Therefore both processes are essential to complement one another. Deity worship belongs to the *pañcarātriki-mārga*, and hearing and chanting belong to the *bhāgavata-mārga*. The two paths are meant to be followed together, as parallel lines.

> "For the neophyte devotees, it is essential to worship the Deity. But if we simply worship the Deity without hearing about the Lord, (*śravaṇaṁ kīrtanam*—these things are essential), then the Deity worship will be a burden. At a certain point, it will become a burden, and gradually it will be neglected, and the whole thing will be spoiled. So both things should continue: *bhāgavata-mārga* and *pañcarātriki-mārga*. Deity worship is *pāñcarātriki-vidhi*, and *bhāgavata-mārga* is hearing, chanting, like that. Both of them should be accepted, in parallel lines."
>
> —Bhaktivedanta lecture, *Śrīmad Bhāgavatam* 7.6.6
> West Virginia 22/6/1976

Theoretically, we can attain perfection simply by chanting the holy names of the Lord. However, since we are susceptible to the unavoidable contamination that results from living in a material body, Deity worship is also necessary for our purification.

> "By chanting the holy name of the Lord, one can reach the platform of love of Godhead. One might ask, then what is the necessity of being initiated? The answer is that even though the chanting of the holy name is sufficient to enable one to progress in spiritual life to the standard of love of Godhead, one is nonetheless susceptible to contamination because of possessing a material body. Consequently, special stress is given to the *arcana-vidhi*. One should therefore regularly take advantage of both the *bhāgavata* process and *pāñcarātrikī* process."
>
> —*Śrīmad Bhāgavatam* 7.5.23-4 Bhaktivedanta purport

Deity worship helps householders to live a regulated lifestyle and to practise cleanliness.

> "The special purpose of Deity worship is to keep oneself always pure and clean. *Gṛhastha* devotees should be actual examples of cleanliness."
>
> —*Śrīmad Bhāgavatam* 7.5.23-4 Bhaktivedanta purport

As a result of the regular practice of devotional activities, the atmosphere of a home can become transcendental.

> "Thus Svāyambhuva Manu was a saintly king. Although absorbed in material happiness, he was not

> dragged to the lowest grade of life, for he always enjoyed his material happiness in a Kṛṣṇa conscious atmosphere."
>
> —*Śrīmad Bhāgavatam* 3.22.34
>
> Bhaktivedanta purport:
> "The kingly happiness of material enjoyment generally drags one to the lowest grade of life, namely degradation to animal life, because of unrestricted sense enjoyment. But Svāyambhuva Manu was considered as good as a saintly sage because the atmosphere created in his kingdom and home was completely Kṛṣṇa conscious. The case is similar with the conditioned souls in general; they have come into this material life for sense gratification, but if they are able to create a Kṛṣṇa conscious atmosphere, as depicted here or as prescribed in revealed scriptures, by temple worship and household Deity worship, then in spite of their material enjoyment they can make advancement in pure Kṛṣṇa consciousness without a doubt."

A God conscious householder learns to see his home and his family as the property of the Lord, temporarily entrusted into his care.

> "Marriage is for the establishment of Kṛṣṇa's family; producing children is for increasing Kṛṣṇa's servants; offering oblations to the forefathers is for the satisfaction of Kṛṣṇa's servants; feasting is for the gratification of Kṛṣṇa's living entities. All of these activities should be dovetailed in the favorable service

> of Kṛṣṇa; then one will not fall into the grip of unfavorable fruitive activities. 'The body, house, and everything else belong to Kṛṣṇa.' Thinking in this way, one should protect the body, the house, and the community. This is called 'Kṛṣṇa's family'."
>
> —Bhaktivinoda Ṭhākura, *Śrī Bhaktyāloka* 10

Seeing everything as God's property and engaging it all in His service, a *gṛhastha* earns money to facilitate his devotional service to the Lord.

> "As indicated herein, a householder should endeavor to earn money for the execution of *bhakti-yoga—śravaṇaṁ kīrtanaṁ viṣṇoḥ smaraṇaṁ pāda-sevanam/ arcanaṁ vandanaṁ dāsyaṁ sakhyam ātma-nivedanam.* A householder should lead such a life that he gets full opportunity to hear and chant. He should worship the Deity at home, observe festivals, invite friends in and give them *prasāda.* A householder should earn money for this purpose, not for sense gratification."
>
> —*Śrīmad Bhāgavatam* 5.5.3 Bhaktivedanta purport

Dana (Giving in Charity)

Besides serving the Lord directly with the results of his work, a charitable *gṛhastha* also serves the Lord's devotees. The *gṛhastha-āśrama* forms the economic foundation of the *varṇāśrama* system. This means that *gṛhasthas* are traditionally responsible for maintaining not only their own families but also the other three *āśramas.*

> "There are four social orders for cooperation in the endeavor for liberation from material existence. The orders of *brahmacarya*, or pious student life, household life with a wife, retired life and renounced life all depend for successful advancement on the householder who lives with a wife. This cooperation is essential for the proper functioning of the institution of the four social orders and the four spiritual orders of life. The man who lives with a wife has a great responsibility in maintaining the members of the other social orders—the *brahmacārīs*, *vānaprasthas* and *sannyāsīs*."
>
> —*Śrīmad Bhāgavatam* 3.14.18 Bhaktivedanta purport

The four *āśramas* are meant to co-operate together like a family. From an economic point of view, householders are the parents of society, taking care of the members of the other three *āśramas* like their children.

> "Except for the *gṛhasthas*, or the householders, everyone is supposed to engage in the spiritual advancement of life, and therefore the *brahmacārī*, the *vānaprastha* and the *sannyāsī* have very little time to earn a livelihood. They therefore collect alms from the *gṛhasthas*, and thus they secure the bare necessities of life and cultivate spiritual understanding. By helping the other three sections of society cultivate spiritual values, the householder also makes advancement in spiritual life. Ultimately every member of society automatically becomes spiritually advanced and easily crosses the ocean of nescience."
>
> —*Śrīmad Bhāgavatam* 3.14.18 Bhaktivedanta purport

According to the three modes of material nature – goodness, passion and ignorance – there are three ways of giving in charity. Charity in the mode of goodness is described as follows.

> "Charity given out of duty, without expectation of return, at the proper time and place, and to a worthy person is considered to be in the mode of goodness."
>
> —*Bhagavad-gītā* As It Is 17. 20

> Purport:
>
> "In the Vedic literature, charity given to a person engaged in spiritual activities is recommended. There is no recommendation for giving charity indiscriminately. Spiritual perfection is always a consideration. Therefore charity is recommended to be given at a place of pilgrimage and at lunar or solar eclipses or at the end of the month or to a qualified *brāhmaṇa* or a Vaiṣṇava (devotee) or in temples. Such charities should be given without any consideration of return. Charity to the poor is sometimes given out of compassion, but if a poor man is not worth giving charity to, then there is no spiritual advancement. In other words, indiscriminate charity is not recommended in the Vedic literature."

Charity in the mode of passion is described in this way.

> "But charity performed with the expectation of some return, or with a desire for fruitive results, or in a grudging mood, is said to be charity in the mode of passion."
>
> —*Bhagavad-gītā* As It Is 17. 21

Purport:

"Charity is sometimes performed for elevation to the heavenly planets and sometimes with great trouble and with repentance afterwards: 'Why have I spent so much in this way?' Charity is also sometimes given under some obligation, at the request of a superior. These kinds of charity are said to be given in the mode of passion. There are many charitable foundations which offer their gifts to institutions where sense gratification goes on. Such charities are not recommended in the Vedic scripture."

And finally there is charity in the mode of ignorance.

"And charity performed at an impure place, at an improper time, to unworthy persons, or without proper attention and respect is said to be in the mode of ignorance."

—*Bhagavad-gītā As It Is* 17. 22

Purport:

"Contributions for indulgence in intoxication and gambling are not encouraged here. That sort of contribution is in the mode of ignorance. Such charity is not beneficial; rather, sinful persons are encouraged. Similarly, if a person gives charity to a suitable person but without respect and without attention, that sort of charity is also said to be in the mode of darkness."

The scriptures recommend that charity should be given in the mode of goodness.

> "Charity in the mode of goodness is recommended by the scriptures, but charity in the modes of passion and ignorance is not recommended, because it is simply a waste of money."
>
> —*Bhagavad-gītā As It Is* 16.3 purport

Charity in the mode of goodness is given to *brāhmaṇas* and *sannyāsīs*.

> "Only the *brāhmaṇas* and *sannyāsīs* are authorized to accept charity from the householders. Charity is never unproductive or blind. In the *śāstras* charity was offered to persons who deserve to accept charity by dint of spiritual enlightenment."
>
> —*Śrīmad Bhāgavatam* 1.12.14 Bhaktivedanta purport

It is also given at the right time and place. The most liberal charity is traditionally given at *saṁskāra* ceremonies, performed at the time of the passage of the soul into each new chapter of a life, such as birth or marriage, to invoke the blessings of *brāhmaṇas*, demigods, and forefathers.

> "In all the different occasions of *saṁskāras*, especially during the time of birth, marriage and death, wealth is distributed to the *brāhmaṇas* because the *brāhmaṇas* give the highest quality of service in regard to the prime necessity of humankind. It is enjoined in the *śāstras* that as long as a child is joined with the mother by the navel pipe, the child is considered to be of one body with the mother, but as soon as the pipe is cut and the child is separated from the mother, the

> purificatory process of *jātakarman* is performed. The administrative demigods and past forefathers of the family come to see a newly born child, and such an occasion is specifically accepted as the proper time for distributing wealth to the right persons productively for the spiritual advancement of society."
>
> —*Śrīmad Bhāgavatam* 1.12.14 Bhaktivedanta purport

For a father to give away the precious gift of a daughter in marriage is also considered to be a great act of charity – *kanyā-dāna*. Of course there is no comparison in value between a beloved daughter and a material object or money, but there is a similar principle involved in the act of giving. When a father gives his daughter away to a suitable husband, he is supposed to give up all jurisdiction over her. Thus it is a complete act of giving, from the heart. According to Vedic culture, the father of the bride is also expected to host the wedding and to give gifts to the bridegroom in dowry.

> "As stated in the Vedic scriptures, the first-class process is to call the bridegroom to the home of the bride and hand her to him in charity with a dowry of necessary ornaments, gold, furniture and other household paraphernalia. This form of marriage is prevalent among higher-class Hindus even today and is declared in the *śāstras* to confer great religious merit on the bride's father. To give a daughter in charity to a suitable son-in-law is considered to be one of the pious activities of a householder."
>
> —*Śrīmad Bhāgavatam* 3.22.16 Bhaktivedanta purport

A dowry may be large or small, according to one's means.

> "In this way Kardama Muni was married with full opulence to a qualified wife and was endowed with the necessary paraphernalia for household life. In the Vedic way of marriage such a dowry is still given to the bridegroom by the father of the bride; even in poverty-stricken India there are marriages where hundreds and thousands of rupees are spent for a dowry. The dowry system is not illegal, as some have tried to prove. The dowry is a gift given to the daughter by the father to show good will, and it is compulsory. In rare cases where the father is completely unable to give a dowry, it is enjoined that he must at least give a fruit and a flower. As stated in *Bhagavad-gītā*, God can also be pleased even by a fruit and a flower. When there is financial inability and no question of accumulating a dowry by another means, one can give a fruit and flower for the satisfaction of the bridegroom."
>
> —*Śrīmad Bhāgavatam* 3.22.23 Bhaktivedanta purport

The most qualified recipients of monetary charity are those who are engaged in missionary activities for distributing spiritual knowledge to society in general.

> "Charity should be given only to propagate Kṛṣṇa consciousness all over the world. That is charity in the mode of goodness."
>
> —*Bhagavad-gītā As It Is* 16.3 purport

While endeavours to feed the hungry and care for the sick are great altruistic activities, the propagation of spiritual knowledge is considered to be the greatest social welfare work, since it bestows eternal freedom from suffering rather than just temporary relief.

> "By God's favor we sometimes get large quantities of food grains or suddenly receive some contribution or unexpected profit in business. In this way we may get more money than needed. So, how should that be spent? There is no need to accumulate money in the bank merely to increase one's bank balance. Such a mentality is described in *Bhagavad-gītā* (16.13) as *asuric*, demoniac... Actually, if one has more than one requires for his necessities, the extra money should be spent for Kṛṣṇa... The *gṛhasthas* should give contributions for constructing temples of the Supreme Lord and for preaching of *Śrīmad Bhagavad-gītā*, or Kṛṣṇa consciousness, all over the world."
>
> —*Śrīmad Bhāgavatam* 7.14.8 Bhaktivedanta purport

Householders are enjoined to engage fifty percent of their income, if possible, for spreading Kṛṣṇa consciousness.

> "The householders should earn a livelihood by an honorable means and spend fifty percent of their income to propagate Kṛṣṇa consciousness all over the world. Thus a householder should give in charity to institutional societies that are engaged in that way."
>
> —*Bhagavad-gītā As It Is* 16.3 purport

This formula was taught by Rūpa Gosvāmī by his own example.

"The householder should earn money by business or by profession and spend at least fifty percent of his income to spread Kṛṣṇa consciousness; twenty-five percent he can spend for his family, and twenty-five percent he should save to meet emergencies. This example was shown by Rūpa Gosvāmī, so devotees should follow it."
—*Śrīmad Bhāgavatam* 3.21.31 Bhaktivedanta purport

Rūpa Gosvāmī was empowered by Caitanya Mahāprabhu to establish principles of devotional service based on *śāstra* (scripture). Those who follow his teachings are known as *rūpānugas*, or followers of Rūpa Gosvāmī. Although it was when he retired from household life that Rūpa Gosvāmī allocated his wealth according to the above formula, *rūpānugas* aspire to follow his example, as far as possible, even as householders. Kṛṣṇa says in the *Gītā* that, according to how much we surrender to Him, He will reciprocate with us and reward us.

ye yathā māṁ prapadyante
tāṁs tathaiva bhajāmy aham

"As all surrender unto Me, I reward them accordingly."
—*Bhagavad-gītā As It Is* 4.11

By remembering that everything in this world is the property of the Supreme Personality of Godhead, we can avoid becoming attached to the fruits of our labour.

"To give charity is one of the householder's main functions, and he should be prepared to give in charity at least fifty percent of his hard-earned money. In the *brahmacārī* life the training is sufficiently imparted so that one may understand that the world as property belongs to the Supreme Lord, the Personality of Godhead. No one, therefore, can claim to be the proprietor of anything in the world. Therefore, in the life of a householder, which is a sort of license for sex enjoyment, one must give in charity for the service of the Lord."

—*Śrīmad Bhāgavatam* 1.9.27 Bhaktivedanta purport

Householders who cannot afford to give fifty percent should simply give as much as possible for the spiritual welfare of society. Those who misuse their excess wealth for whimsical sense enjoyment accrue bad *karma.*

"One may claim proprietorship to as much wealth as required to maintain body and soul together, but one who desires proprietorship over more than that must be considered a thief, and he deserves to be punished by the laws of nature."

—*Śrīmad Bhāgavatam* 7.14.8

Whatever we have at our disposal, including time and energy, is on loan from the Supreme Proprietor. We can show our gratitude by offering it back to Him.

"Everyone's energy is generated or borrowed from the reservoir of energy of the Lord; therefore, the resultant actions of such energy must be given to the Lord in the shape of transcendental loving service for Him.

> As the rivers draw water from the sea through the clouds and again go down to the sea, similarly our energy is borrowed from the supreme source, the Lord's energy, and it must return to the Lord. That is the perfection of our energy. The Lord, therefore, in the *Bhagavad-gītā* (9.27) says that whatever we do, whatever we undergo as penance, whatever we sacrifice, whatever we eat or whatever we give in charity must be offered to Him (the Lord). That is the way of utilizing our borrowed energy. When our energy is utilized in that way, our energy is purified from the contamination of material inebrieties, and thus we become fit for our original natural life of service to the Lord."
>
> —*Śrīmad Bhāgavatam* 1.9.27 Bhaktivedanta purport

Instead of engaging most of their time and energy in working for money, householders can balance their lives more spiritually by dedicating some of that time and energy for primary devotional activities, such as hearing and chanting about Kṛṣṇa.

> "One should work eight hours at the most to earn his livelihood, and either in the afternoon or in the evening a householder should associate with devotees to hear about the incarnations of Kṛṣṇa and His activities and thus be gradually liberated from the clutches of *māyā*."
>
> —*Śrīmad Bhāgavatam* 7.14.3-4 Bhaktivedanta purport

The first two limbs of devotional service are *śravanaṁ kīrtanam*, hearing and chanting. After hearing, *gṛhasthas* can also share what they have heard with others. Devotees with big hearts like to share the mercy of the Lord with others and thus relieve their suffering.

> "There are two kinds of *mahātmās*. One is the renounced order who are preaching all over the world for the benefit of the society. The *gṛhastha* may not be preaching... but he can preach. Amongst his relatives, family members, and children, he can also preach; he can preach to his friends. Preaching cannot be stopped. You may do it on a small scale or a big scale – the benefit will be *śravanaṁ kīrtanam*. We are preaching. You are hearing , and you are chanting also. This chanting and hearing process should be increased. One should try to become sinless and try to make friendship with God. Then our lives will be successful."
>
> —Bhaktivedanta lecture, *Śrīmad Bhāgavatam* 5.5.2
> Johannesburg 22/10/1975

The responsibility for teaching spiritual knowledge is not confined by considerations of *varṇa* and *āśrama*. A merciful soul, who has received knowledge that can free people from suffering, naturally desires to share this with others.

> "One has to adjust things. Not that 'Because I am a *gṛhastha*, householder, I cannot become a preacher. It is the business of the *sannyāsī* or *brahmacārī*.' No. It is the business of everyone. The whole world is suffering for want of knowledge. The present civilisation is an animal civilisation. They do not know anything beyond eating, sleeping, mating and

defending... Human life is meant for something else: 'What I am? What is God? What is my relationship with God? What is this material world? Why I am here? Where do I have to go next?' So many things one has to learn. *Athāto brahma jijñāsā*. This is human life. Not that we eat and sleep and have sex life and die someday like cats and dogs. Therefore, there is a need of *ācāryas*, teachers, for propagating spiritual knowledge, Kṛṣṇa consciousness."

—Bhaktivedanta lecture
Appearance Anniversary of Bhaktivinoda Ṭhākura
London 3/9/1971

Śrī Caitanya Mahāprabhu, during His tour of South India, took a meal one day at the home of a *gṛhastha brāhmaṇa* named Kūrma. Kūrma became so inspired by the association of the Lord that he desired to immediately give up his family life and travel with Mahāprabhu. The Lord instructed him to simply remain at home, chant the Hare Kṛṣṇa *mahā-mantra*, and teach the instructions of Lord Kṛṣṇa to others.

prabhu kahe,—"aiche bāt kabhu nā kahibā
gṛhe rahi' kṛṣṇa-nāma nirantara laibā

yāre dekha, tāre kaha 'kṛṣṇa'-upadeśa
āmāra ājñāya guru hañā tāra' ei deśa"

"Śrī Caitanya Mahāprabhu replied, 'Don't speak like that again. Better to remain at home and chant the holy name of Kṛṣṇa always. Instruct everyone to follow the orders of Lord Śrī Kṛṣṇa as they are given in the *Bhagavad-gītā* and *Śrīmad-Bhāgavatam*. In this

> way become a spiritual master and try to liberate everyone in this land.'"
>
> —*Śrī Caitanya-caritāmṛta, Madhya-līlā* 7.127-8

The Lord did not encourage the *brāhmaṇa* Kūrma to give up his family responsibilities, but rather to stay in his position and perfect his life by chanting and sharing spiritual knowledge with others. Mahāprabhu gave this same instruction to all the householders who invited Him to their homes during His tour of South India.

> "At whosever house Śrī Caitanya accepted His alms by taking *prasādam*, He would convert the dwellers to His *saṅkīrtana* movement and advise them just as He advised the *brāhmaṇa* named Kūrma."
>
> —*Śrī Caitanya-caritāmṛta, Madhya-līlā* 7.130

Householders can share their spiritual knowledge with family, friends and whomever they meet. This is the topmost charity and the greatest welfare work for human society. The great Vaiṣṇava *ācārya* Bhaktivinoda Ṭhākura spearheaded the nineteenth century revival of the *saṅkīrtana* movement and wrote over a hundred books, all while remaining at home as a *gṛhastha*.

> "Although he was a *gṛhastha*, householder, a government officer, and a magistrate, still he was an *ācārya*. So, from his dealings, from his life, we should learn how one can become a preacher in any stage of life. It doesn't matter what he is."
>
> —Bhaktivedanta lecture
> Appearance Anniversary of Bhaktivinoda Ṭhākura
> London 3/9/1971

Feeding the Hungry

The most basic form of charity and the duty of every householder is to feed the hungry. Before eating, a *gṛhastha* first feeds the children, older members of the family, *brāhmaṇas*, and invalids. In addition, according to Vedic culture, he is enjoined to step outside of his house onto the road and call out three times "Is anyone hungry?" before he sits down to eat.

> "It is the duty of a householder to feed first of all the children, the old members of the family, the *brāhmaṇas*, and the invalids. Besides that, an ideal householder is required to call for any unknown hungry man to come and dine before he himself goes to take his meals. He is required to call for such a hungry man thrice on the road. The neglect of this prescribed duty of a householder, especially in the matter of the old men and children, is unpardonable."
> —*Śrīmad Bhāgavatam* 1.14.43 Bhaktivedanta purport

A *gṛhastha* is prepared to sacrifice his own meal, if necessary, to feed others.

> "According to Vedic principles, a householder, before taking lunch, should go outside and shout very loudly to see if there is anyone without food. In this way he invites people to take *prasādam*. If someone comes, the householder offers him *prasādam*, and if there is not much left, he should offer his own portion to the guest. If no one responds to his call, the householder

> can accept his own lunch. Thus the householder's life is also a kind of austerity. Because of this, the householder's life is called the *gṛhastha-āśrama*."
>
> —*Śrī Caitanya-caritāmṛta, Madhya-līlā* 3.41
> Bhaktivedanta purport

In Vedic society *brahmacārīs* and *sannyāsīs* would be out collecting alms and they depended on the *gṛhasthas* to feed them. Even today, in India, there are still wandering mendicants who depend on householders to feed them. In the West, however, it is not very common to find hungry people wandering around in residential neighbourhoods. Otherwise, wherever a householder encounters the poor and the hungry, he should treat them with compassion. The best kind of food to give is *kṛṣṇa-prasāda*, since it not only nourishes the body but also benefits the soul.

> "Even earned wealth is obtained by the mercy of God. It is not the incorrect use of wealth if some portion of mercy is given to requesting poor people – it is its proper use! To distribute mercy (*prasāda*) is the compulsory duty of householder Vaisnavas. Even though their (poor people's) miserableness has been obtained through the fault of their own *karma*, they are still God's people. Therefore, to give them help is the compulsory duty of well-to-do people."
>
> —Bhaktisiddhānta Sarasvatī (*A Ray of Viṣṇu)*

A charitable householder treats even the animals as if they were his own children by feeding them with *prasāda*.

mṛgoṣṭra-khara-markākhu-
sarīsṛp khaga-makṣikāḥ
ātmanaḥ putravat paśyet
tair eṣām antaraṁ kiyat

"One should treat animals such as deer, camels, asses, monkeys, mice, snakes, birds and flies exactly like one's own son. How little difference there is between children and these innocent animals."
—*Śrīmad Bhāgavatam* 7.14.9

According to Vedic culture, food should be grown organically, without the use of pesticides, since the deliberate killing of any innocent creature, however small, is forbidden. A learned person with spiritual vision does not discriminate between one species of life and another, but sees the soul and the Supersoul in the heart of every living entity.

vidyā-vinaya-sampanne
brāhmaṇe gavi hastini
śuni caiva śva-pāke ca
paṇḍitāḥ sama-darśinaḥ

"The humble sages, by virtue of true knowledge, see with equal vision a learned and gentle *brāhmaṇa*, a cow, an elephant, a dog and a dog-eater (outcaste)."
—*Bhagavad-gītā As It Is* 5.18

Because animals are innocent and vulnerable like children, a merciful householder protects them as he protects his own children.

"Like children, the unintelligent animals are also sons of the Supreme Personality of Godhead, and therefore a Kṛṣṇa conscious person, even though a householder, should not discriminate between children and poor animals. Unfortunately, modern society has devised many means for killing animals in different forms of life. For example, in the agricultural fields there may be many mice, flies and other creatures that disturb production, and sometimes they are killed by pesticides. In this verse, however, such killing is forbidden. Every living entity should be nourished by the food given by the Supreme Personality of Godhead. Human society should not consider itself the only enjoyer of all the properties of God; rather, men should understand that all the other animals also have a claim to God's property. In this verse even the snake is mentioned, indicating that a householder should not be envious even of a snake. If everyone is fully satisfied by eating food that is a gift from the Lord, why should there be envy between one living being and another?"

—*Śrīmad Bhāgavatam* 7.14.9 Bhaktivedanta purport

Receiving Guests

Anyone who enters the home of a *gṛhastha* as a guest should be served without reservation. This principle was personally demonstrated by Śrī Caitanya Mahāprabhu when He was living as a householder.

> "In this way the Lord satisfied all His guests and taught the world how to behave as a perfect householder. The foremost duty of a householder is to serve his guests. If a householder happily serves his guests without duplicity and according to his ability he is considered hospitable."
>
> —*Śrī Caitanya-bhāgavata, Ādi- khaṇḍa* 14.21, 26

When Kṛṣṇa's uncle Akrūra travelled from Mathurā to Vṛndāvana, he was received with great honour by Kṛṣṇa and Balarāma. Thus the Supreme Lord personally taught the world in which mood a guest should be received at home.

> "Taking him by the hand, Kṛṣṇa and Balarāma brought him to Their sitting room, where They offered him a very nice sitting place and water for washing his feet. They also worshiped him with a suitable presentation of honey mixed with other ingredients. When Akrūra was thus comfortably seated, Kṛṣṇa and Balarāma offered him a cow in charity and then brought very palatable dishes, and Akrūra accepted them. When Akrūra finished eating, Balarāma gave him betel nut and spices, as well as pulp of sandalwood, just to make him more pleased and comfortable. The Vedic system of receiving a guest was completely observed by Lord Kṛṣṇa Himself to teach all others how to receive a guest at home. Kṛṣṇa and Balarāma welcomed Akrūra in a way just befitting his exalted position."
>
> —*Kṛṣṇa the Supreme Personality of Godhead* 38

Those who are unable to provide elaborate gifts can offer a more simple reception, according to their means. The mood of service is more important than the external details.

> "If the host is a poor man, he should at least offer a straw mat as a sitting place and a glass of water to drink."
>
> —*Kṛṣṇa the Supreme Personality of Godhead* 38

The act of offering *prasāda* to Vaisnava guests is one of the six loving exchanges, as described in *The Nectar of Instruction,* that nourish relationships between devotees.

> "We should also invite pure devotees to our home, offer them *prasāda* and be prepared to please them in all respects. This is called *bhuṅkte bhojayate caiva.*"
>
> —*The Nectar of Instruction* 4 purport

To fail to properly receive a Vaiṣṇava guest is considered to be a great sin for a householder.

> "If a person fails to properly welcome a Vaiṣṇava who has come to his house, it becomes like a crematorium, which the forefathers will avoid. There is no greater sinner than one who fails to receive, according to his means, a Vaiṣṇava who has come from a distant place."
>
> —*Skanda Purāṇa*

Even an enemy, if he comes to the home as a guest, should be respected as a guest and not treated as an enemy. This is one of the principles of real hospitality.

"The law of reception in the codes of the Vedic principles states that even if an enemy is received at home, he must be received with all respects. He should not be given a chance to understand that he has come into the house of an enemy."

—*Śrīmad Bhāgavatam* 1.18.28 Bhaktivedanta purport

Chapter Seven

Kāma

Sense Gratification

Eating, Sleeping, Mating & Defending
The Shackles of Sex—Religious Sex Life
Educating Children—*Garbhādāna-saṁskāra*
Family Planning—*Dama* (Self-control)
From *Kāma* to *Prema*

Chapter Seven

Kāma

—Sense Gratification—

"By self-control alone, becoming serene of mind, people perform good deeds. Sages attain to heaven by self-control. Control of the mind stands four-square to all attempts against it. In self-control alone everything else exists. Therefore, it is control that is regarded as the highest to be achieved."

—*Taittirīya-āraṇyaka* 10.78

THE THIRD GOAL OF MARRIED LIFE IS KNOWN as *kāma* (sense gratification) or, in other words, the supply chain to the four basic bodily demands, for eating, sleeping, mating and defending.

"Therefore, in the Vedic civilisation, there are four principles: *dharma, artha, kāma, mokṣa. Dharma* means to understand religious principles; and economic development, because we require money, after all, to keep the body fit, that is also required. *Kāma* means sense gratification. *Āhāra-nidrā-bhaya-*

> *maithunaṁ ca*. To eat, to make arrangement for eating, to make arrangement for sleeping, to make arrangement for sense gratification, and to make arrangement for defence – these are necessities of the body. These activities are called *kāma*. And, at last, to become liberated, *mokṣa*. *Mokṣa* means to get out of the entanglement of the material, miserable condition of life."
>
> —Bhaktivedanta lecture, *Śrīmad Bhāgavatam* 1.2.9
> Detroit 3/8/1975

While the natural proclivity of the soul is to love God, when a soul falls down to the mundane world and enters a material body, that loving propensity is transformed into lust, or the desire for material sense gratification.

> "When a living entity comes in contact with the material creation, his eternal love for Kṛṣṇa is transformed into lust, in association with the mode of passion."
>
> —*Bhagavad-gītā As It Is* 3.37 purport

The Vedic scriptures explain that while all living entities are part and parcel of the Absolute Truth, the Supreme Personality of Godhead, they are also endowed with partial independence as individuals. For those of us who misuse our independence to turn away from the Lord, our love for Him becomes transformed into lust, and we enter the material world to try to satisfy our separate desires.

> "The Supreme Personality of Godhead expanded Himself into many for His ever-increasing spiritual

> bliss, and the living entities are parts and parcels of this spiritual bliss. They also have partial independence, and by misuse of their independence, when the service attitude is transformed into the propensity for sense enjoyment, they come under the sway of lust. This material creation is created by the Lord to give facility to the conditioned souls to fulfill these lustful propensities, and when completely baffled by prolonged lustful activities, the living entities begin to enquire about their real position."
>
> *Bhagavad-gītā* As *It Is* 3.37 purport

The progressive social system of four successive *āśramas* is meant to help people to become gradually freed, step by step, from the influence of lusty desires.

> "Generally, unless one enjoys material happiness, one cannot attain renunciation. *Varṇāśrama* therefore gives the opportunity for gradual elevation. Yadu, the son of Mahārāja Yayāti, explained that he was unable to give up his youth, for he wanted to use it to attain the renounced order in the future."
>
> —*Śrīmad Bhāgavatam* 9.18.40 Bhaktivedanta purport

When Maharaja Yayāti asked his sons if any of them would be willing to give their youth in exchange for his old age, his oldest son Yadu refused, for the following reason.

> "Yadu replied: My dear father, you have already achieved old age, although you also were a young man. But I do not welcome your old age and invalidity, for

> unless one enjoys material happiness, one cannot attain renunciation."
>
> —*Śrīmad Bhāgavatam* 9.18.40

Yadu was a pure devotee of the Lord and desired to engage in devotional service, but at the same time he was fully aware of the potential obstructions that could be presented by youthful lusty desires. He wanted to make provision for the fulfilment of any material desires that may appear so that his future spiritual path would be clear of impediments. In this way he was teaching the principles of *varṇāśrama* culture for the benefit of people in general.

> "The ultimate principle of religion is to engage oneself in devotional service to the Lord. Mahārāja Yadu was very eager to engage himself in the Lord's service, but there was an impediment: during youth the material desire to enjoy the material senses is certainly present, and unless one fully satisfies these lusty desires in youth, there is a chance of one's being disturbed in rendering service to the Lord. We have actually seen that many *sannyāsīs* who accept *sannyāsa* prematurely, not having satisfied their material desires, fall down because they are disturbed. Therefore the general process is to go through *gṛhastha* life and *vānaprastha* life and finally come to *sannyāsa* and devote oneself completely to the service of the Lord."
>
> —*Śrīmad Bhāgavatam* 9.18.40 Bhaktivedanta purport

In fact, Mahārāja Yadu was not an ordinary person, and his choice to enter *gṛhastha-āśrama* was of special significance, for it was in his dynasty that the Supreme Personality of Godhead later appeared on earth in His original form as Lord Kṛṣṇa.

Eating, Sleeping, Mating and Defending

As *artha* can be regulated according to *dharma*, similarly *kāma* can be regulated according to *dharma* in such a way that activities of the senses can pave the way to *mokṣa*, liberation, instead of degradation. The activity of eating, for example, becomes purified by accepting only *kṛṣṇa-prasādam*, vegetarian food that has been offered to God.

> "The devotees of the Lord are released from all kinds of sins because they eat food that is offered first for sacrifice. Others, who prepare food for personal sense enjoyment, verily eat only sin."
>
> —*Bhagavad-gītā As It Is* 3.13

Foods in the mode of goodness, which are recommended in the scriptures, are suitable for offering to God and are healthy for the body and mind.

> "In the past, great authorities selected those foods that best aid health and increase life's duration, such as milk products, sugar, rice, wheat, fruits and vegetables. These foods are very dear to those in the mode of goodness."
>
> —*Bhagavad-gītā As It Is* 17.10 purport

Regulated patterns of eating and sleeping are conducive for the practice of *yoga*.

> "There is no possibility of one's becoming a *yogī*, O Arjuna, if one eats too much or eats too little, sleeps too much or does not sleep enough."
>
> —*Bhagavad-gītā As It Is* 6.16

A *yogī* eats and sleeps only as much as necessary to maintain the body in a healthy condition. Fasting on designated days is also conducive for spiritual advancement.

> "The Kṛṣṇa conscious person observes fasting as it is recommended in the scriptures. He does not fast or eat more than is required, and he is thus competent to perform *yoga* practice. One who eats more than required will dream very much while sleeping, and he must consequently sleep more than is required. One should not sleep more than six hours daily. One who sleeps more than six hours out of twenty-four is certainly influenced by the mode of ignorance. A person in the mode of ignorance is lazy and prone to sleep a great deal. Such a person cannot perform *yoga*."
>
> —*Bhagavad-gītā As It Is* 6.16 purport

Even the state of sleep can also become spiritualised by the practice of hearing about Kṛṣṇa before going to bed.

> "...Family members sit down, hold Hare Kṛṣṇa *kīrtana*, hear narrations from *Śrīmad-Bhāgavatam* and

> *Bhagavad-gītā* and enjoy music before going to bed. The atmosphere created by this *saṅkīrtana* movement lives in their hearts, and while sleeping they also dream of the singing and glorification of the Lord. In such a way, perfection of Kṛṣṇa consciousness can be attained."
>
> —*Śrīmad Bhāgavatam* 3.22.33 Bhaktivedanta purport

The act of mating can be regulated according to *dharma* by being confined to religious marriage.

> "According to scriptural injunctions, one is forbidden to engage in sex relationships with any women other than one's wife. All other women are to be considered as one's mother."
>
> —*Bhagavad-gītā As It Is* 3.34 purport

Within marriage, sex can be further regulated according to religious principles by being engaged exclusively for its divine purpose, which is to beget children.

> "Similarly, sex life, according to religious principles (*dharma*), should be for the propagation of children, not otherwise. The responsibility of parents is then to make their offspring Kṛṣṇa conscious."
>
> —*Bhagavad-gītā As It Is* 7.11 purport

Defence is acceptable according to religious principles for the lawful protection of dependants. The religious duty of a *kṣatriya* is to protect the citizens who are under his care and the religious duty of a husband is to protect his wife and children. There are six kinds of aggressors who are allowed to be punished by death, according to the *Manu-saṁhitā*.

> "According to Vedic injunctions there are six kinds of aggressors: (1) a poison giver, (2) one who sets fire to the house, (3) one who attacks with deadly weapons, (4) one who plunders riches, (5) one who occupies another's land, and (6) one who kidnaps a wife. Such aggressors are at once to be killed, and no sin is incurred by killing such aggressors."
>
> —*Bhagavad-gītā As It Is* 1.36 purport

While modern laws in most countries of the world do not allow citizens to kill aggressors, responsible husbands still do whatever is necessary, within the law, to protect their families. Defence can become devotional service if it is engaged in the service of the Lord or His devotees.

> "Hanumān, the great servitor of Lord Rāma, exhibited his wrath by burning the golden city of Rāvaṇa, but by doing so he became the greatest devotee of the Lord. Here also, in *Bhagavad-gītā*, the Lord induces Arjuna to engage his wrath upon his enemies for the satisfaction of the Lord. Therefore, lust and wrath, when they are employed in Kṛṣṇa consciousness, become our friends instead of our enemies."
>
> —*Bhagavad-gītā As It Is* 3.37 purport

The Shackles of Sex

Of all the varieties of sensual allurement that bind the conditioned soul to material existence, the root catalyst is sex desire.

> "In the material world, the centre of all activities is sex, and thus this material world is called *maithunya-agara*, or the shackles of sex life. In the ordinary prison house, criminals are kept within bars; similarly, the criminals who are disobedient to the laws of the Lord are shackled by sex life."
>
> —*Bhagavad-gītā* As *It Is* 3.39 purport

Since it is shackles of sex life that bind us to the prison of the material world, the pursuit of celibacy is a key component of spiritual life.

> "If you stop sex life, then you become spiritually advanced, and if you indulge in sex life, then you will be materially enthusiastic. That is the difference between Western and Eastern culture. The whole Eastern culture is based on how to stop sex life, and here in the Western countries, how to increase sex life."
>
> —*Conversations with Śrīla Prabhupāda*
> Morning walk, Johannesburg 18/10/1975

The unrestricted pursuit of sense enjoyment is diametrically opposed to the endeavour for spiritual advancement in human life. Sex life is therefore prohibited within three of the four *āśramas*. Only within *gṛhastha-āśrama* is there some allowance for sex life.

> "Sex life is the cause of material bondage, and therefore it is prohibited in three *āśramas* and is allowed only in the *gṛhastha-āśrama*."
> —*Śrīmad Bhāgavatam* 3.14.20 Bhaktivedanta purport

A faithful husband and chaste wife co-operate together in all the four departments of *gṛhastha-āśrama*, namely *dharma*, *artha*, *kāma* and *mokṣa*, and in this way they help each other to make gradual spiritual advancement.

> "A faithful wife is supposed to cooperate with her husband in fulfilling all material desires so that he can then become comfortable and execute spiritual activities for the perfection of life."
> —*Śrīmad Bhāgavatam* 3.14.17 Bhaktivedanta purport

Married couples uphold moral standards in society by protecting each other from becoming involved in illicit affairs.

> "The bodily senses are considered plunderers of the fort of the body. The wife is supposed to be the commander of the fort, and therefore whenever there is an attack on the body by the senses, it is the wife who protects the body from being smashed. The sex demand is inevitable for everyone, but one who has a fixed wife is saved from the onslaught of the sense

> enemies. A man who has a good wife does not create a disturbance in society by corrupting virgin girls."
> —*Śrīmad Bhāgavatam* 3.14.20 Bhaktivedanta purport

While it is the duty of a faithful wife to protect her husband by fulfilling his desires, and vice versa, a *gṛhastha* should also endeavour to refrain from engaging in irreligious sex life with his wife. According to religious principles, the rightful purpose of sexual intercourse is to beget children.

> "Her sex desire was like a mad elephant, and therefore it was the prime duty of her husband to give her all protection by fulfilling her desire... In *Bhagavad-gītā* sexual intercourse for begetting children is accepted as righteous... In Diti's appeal to her husband for sex, it was not exactly that she was afflicted by sex desires, but she desired sons... Therefore Kaśyapa was supposed to satisfy his bona fide wife."
> —*Śrīmad Bhāgavatam* 3.14.10-11 Bhaktivedanta purports

According to Vedic civilisation, even within marriage, sex life is restrained and regulated in the interests of spiritual advancement.

> "Similarly, the householders, who have some license for sense gratification, perform such acts with great restraint. Sex life, intoxication and meat-eating are general tendencies of human society, but a regulated householder does not indulge in unrestricted sex life and other sense gratification. Marriage on the principles of religious life is therefore current in all

civilized human society because that is the way for restricted sex life. This restricted, unattached sex life is also a kind of *yajña* because the restricted householder sacrifices his general tendency toward sense gratification for higher, transcendental life."

—*Bhagavad-gītā* As *It Is* 4.26 purport

Religious Sex Life

When sex life is regulated according to scriptural injunctions, it can be transformed from an impediment into a stepping-stone for spiritual progress.

"Vedic civilization offers us all knowledge in the *śāstras*, and if we live a regulated life under the direction of *śāstras* and *guru*, all our material desires will be fulfilled; at the same time we will be able to go forward to liberation."

—*Śrīmad Bhāgavatam* 4.22.34 Bhaktivedanta purport

The act of sex can be either sinful or religious, depending on how it is applied. Casual sex is degrading for the soul, but the same act becomes sacred when it is used for lawful procreation.

dharmāviruddho bhūteṣu
kāmo 'smi bharatarṣabha

"I am sex life which is not contrary to religious principles, O lord of the Bhāratas."

—Lord Kṛṣṇa, *Bhagavad-gītā* 7.11

The divine purpose of sex life within marriage is to provide new human bodies for pious souls to facilitate their spiritual advancement. Thus it is a service that assists the Lord in fulfilling His ultimate purpose for creating the material world, which is to give everyone the opportunity to return back home to His spiritual kingdom. Although it is the propensity for sex life that binds the conditioned souls to the prison house of the material world, they can engage the same sexual propensity to serve the higher purpose of God's creation by marrying, procreating children and setting them on course for spiritual liberation. Only when sex is dovetailed in this way does it become free from karmic reaction. This is *kāma* according to *dharma*.

> "This material world is created to give the conditioned souls a chance for rejuvenation for going back home, back to Godhead, and therefore generation of the living being is necessary for upkeep of the purpose of creation. Sexual pleasure is an impetus for such action, and as such one can serve the Lord even in the act of such sexual pleasure. The service is counted when the children born of such sexual pleasure are properly trained in God consciousness. The whole idea of material creation is to revive the dormant God consciousness of the living entity. In forms of life other than the human form, sexual pleasure is prominent without any motive of service for the mission of the Lord. But in the human form of life the conditioned soul can render service to the Lord by creating progeny suitable for the attainment of

> salvation. One can beget hundreds of children and enjoy the celestial pleasure of sexual intercourse, provided he is able to train the children in God consciousness. Otherwise begetting children is on the level of the swine. Rather, the swine is more expert than the human being because the swine can beget a dozen piglets at a time, whereas the human being can give birth to only one at a time. So one should always remember that the genitals, sexual pleasure, the woman and the offspring are all related in the service of the Lord, and one who forgets this relationship in the service of the Supreme Lord becomes subjected to the threefold miseries of material existence by the laws of nature."
>
> —*Śrīmad Bhāgavatam* 2.10.26 Bhaktivedanta purport

Marriage is meant for producing good children who will become assets to society.

> "The aim of married life is to produce nice children, Kṛṣṇa conscious children. That is the best service to the human society, produce nice children."
>
> —Bhaktivedanta lecture, wedding, Montreal 22/7/1968

Educating Children

The sacred responsibility of parents is to teach their children to become devotees of the Supreme Lord.

> "If one is determined to make spiritual advancement, he will not beget a child unless able to make that child

> a devotee. As stated in *Śrīmad-Bhāgavatam* (5.5.18), *pitā na sa syāt*: one should not become a father unless one is able to protect his child from *mṛtyu*, the path of birth and death."
>
> —*Śrīmad Bhāgavatam* 10.3.33 Bhaktivedanta purport

Conscientious parents raise their children to become God conscious from an early age.

> "Like Śrī Sunīti, every mother should train her child to become a devotee like Dhruva Mahārāja. Sunīti instructed her son, even at the age of five years, to be unattached to worldly affairs and to go to the forest to search out the Supreme Lord. She never desired that her son remain at home comfortably without ever undertaking austerities and penances to achieve the favor of the Supreme Personality of Godhead. Every mother, like Sunīti, must take care of her son and train him to become a *brahmacārī* from the age of five years and to undergo austerities and penances for spiritual realization. The benefit will be that if her son becomes a strong devotee like Dhruva, certainly not only will he be transferred back home, back to Godhead, but she will also be transferred with him to the spiritual world, even though she may be unable to undergo austerities and penances in executing devotional service."
>
> —*Śrīmad Bhāgavatam* 4.12.34 Bhaktivedanta purport

The traditional Vedic system of education for boys is to be trained as *brahmacārī* in the guru's *āśrama*, otherwise known as *gurukula*.

> "In the system of *varṇāśrama-dharma*, which is the beginning of actual human life, small boys after five years of age are sent to become *brahmacārī* at the guru's *āśrama*, where these things are systematically taught to boys, be they king's sons or sons of ordinary citizens. The training was compulsory not only to create good citizens of the state, but also to prepare the boy's future life for spiritual realization. The irresponsible life of sense enjoyment was unknown to the children of the followers of the *varṇāśrama* system. The boy was even injected with spiritual acumen before being placed by the father in the womb of the mother. Both the father and the mother were responsible for the boy's success in being liberated from the material bondage. That is the process of successful family planning. It is to beget children for complete perfection. Without being self-controlled, without being disciplined and without being fully obedient, no one can become successful in following the instructions of the spiritual master, and without doing so, no one is able to go back to Godhead."
>
> —*Śrīmad Bhāgavatam* 1.5.24 Bhaktivedanta purport

Where there is no *gurukula*, the onus is on parents to train children at home by teaching them the spiritual knowledge of *Bhagavad-gītā* and by engaging them in devotional service.

> "In all the schools, colleges and universities, and at home, all children and youths should be taught to hear about the Supreme Personality of Godhead. In other

words, they should be taught to hear the instructions of *Bhagavad-gītā*, to put them into practice in their lives, and thus to become strong in devotional service, free from fear of being degraded to animal life. Following *bhāgavata-dharma* has been made extremely easy in this age of Kali. The *śāstra* says:

harer nāma harer nāma
harer nāmaiva kevalam
kalau nāsty eva nāsty eva
nāsty eva gatir anyathā
(Bṛhan-nāradīya Purāṇa)

One need only chant the Hare Kṛṣṇa *mahā-mantra*. Everyone engaged in the practice of chanting the Hare Kṛṣṇa *mahā-mantra* will be completely cleansed, from the core of his heart, and be saved from the cycle of birth and death."

—*Śrīmad Bhāgavatam* 7.6.1 Bhaktivedanta purport

Along with studying, chanting Hare Kṛṣṇa, and playing, children can also be engaged in active service to channel their restless minds and senses in a positive direction. By carrying out simple chores, they can learn to become servants of God. Children require a healthy balance of both love and discipline to be happy and secure and make spiritual progress.

"Encourage them to chant as much *japa* as possible, but there is no question of force or punishment. Try as far as possible to discipline them with love and affection, so that they develop a taste for austerity of life and think it great fun to serve Kṛṣṇa in many ways."

—*Letters from Śrīla Prabhupāda* 10/1/1972

To teach by example is the most effective form of training. When children see that their teachers or parents are 'walking the talk', the children become more inclined to take seriously the instructions that they are given. According to the teachings of Cāṇakya Pandit, children can be chastised from the age of five to sixteen years, but after that they should be treated with friendship by parents.

"Indulge your son up to his fifth year, and strictly discipline him for the next ten years. But when he reaches the age of sixteen, treat him as a friend."

—*Śrī Cāṇakya Nīti-śāstra* 3.18

"If you try to force them after sixteen, they may rebel and leave altogether, as is happening in the Western countries."

— *Conversations with Śrīla Prabhupāda*, Dallas, July 1975

Children who are raised in Kṛṣṇa consciousness can even become responsible later for delivering their parents, should the need arise.

"The purpose of accepting a wife in religious marriage, as sanctioned in the *Vedas*, is to have a *putra*, a son qualified to deliver his father from the darkest region of hellish life. Marriage is not intended for sense gratification but for getting a son fully qualified to deliver his father. But if a son is raised to become an unqualified demon, how can he deliver his father from hellish life? It is therefore the duty of a father to become a Vaiṣṇava and raise his children to become Vaiṣṇavas; then even if by chance the father falls into a hellish life in his next birth, such a son can deliver him, as Mahārāja Pṛthu delivered his father."

—*Śrīmad Bhāgavatam* 4.21.46 Bhaktivedanta purport

Garbhādāna-saṁskāra

A *saṁskāra* is a sanctifying ceremony, or rite of passage, traditionally performed at the time of major life events such as conception, birth, initiation, marriage, and death. The word *saṁskāra* also indicates an impression built up in the mind from experiences of previous lives and the present life. The purpose of the *saṁskāra* ceremony is to purify the mental *saṁskāra* from the influence of mundane impressions and to create a favourable atmosphere for spiritual evolution.

"There are many purificatory processes for advancing a human being to spiritual life. The marriage ceremony, for example, is considered to be one of these sacrifices. It is called *vivāha-yajña*. *Vivāha-yajña*, the marriage ceremony, is meant to regulate the human mind so that it may become peaceful for spiritual advancement. For most men, this *vivāha-yajña* should be encouraged even by persons in the renounced order of life. All prescribed sacrifices are meant for achieving the Supreme Lord."

—*Bhagavad-gītā As It Is* 18.5 purport

The *saṁskāra* that is performed at the time of conception is called *garbhādhāna-saṁskāra*, traditionally carried out at an auspicious time for inviting a pious soul to take birth.

"The *saṁskāras* of the school of *sanātana-dharma* (man's eternal engagement) are highly suitable for creating an atmosphere for taking advantage of good stellar influences, and therefore *garbhādhāna-saṁskāra*, or the first seedling purificatory process prescribed for the higher castes, is the beginning of all pious acts to receive a good pious and intelligent class of men in human society. There will be peace and prosperity in the world due to good and sane population only; there is hell and disturbance only because of the unwanted, insane populace addicted to sex indulgence."

—*Śrīmad Bhāgavatam* 1.12.12 Bhaktivedanta purport

Part of the observance of *garbhādhāna-saṁskāra*, as of other *saṁskāras*, was formerly a ceremony to which *brāhmaṇas* and relatives would be invited.

"Then the first principle is, even if it is taken for begetting child, it is not secret. *Garbhādāna-saṁskāra*. There should be a function, all the *brāhmaṇas* and relatives should come, and there will be a ceremony, and everyone will know that this man is going to now have sex for begetting children."

—*Conversatons with Śrīla Prabhupāda*
Morning walk, Johannesburg 18/10/1975

While the social functions connected with *garbhādāna* are no longer widely observed, the other conditions for inviting pious progeny, as described in *Śrīmad-Bhāgavatam* 3.14, can still be fulfilled. There it is recounted how Diti, the wife of Kaśyapa Muni, approached her husband for sexual union at the time of his evening meditation. Her husband, although he would have preferred to wait for a more suitable time, agreed to fulfil her desire. Afterwards, he reprimanded her as follows.

"The learned Kaśyapa said: Because of your mind's being polluted, because of defilement of the particular time, because of your negligence of my directions, and because of your being apathetic to the demigods, everything was inauspicious."

—*Śrīmad Bhāgavatam* 3.14.38

Bhaktivedanta purport:

"The conditions for having good progeny in society are that the husband should be disciplined in religious and regulative principles and the wife should be faithful to the husband. In *Bhagavad-gītā* (7.11) it is said that sexual intercourse according to religious principles is a representation of Kṛṣṇa consciousness. Before engaging in sexual intercourse, both the

> husband and the wife must consider their mental condition, the particular time, the husband's direction, and obedience to the demigods. According to Vedic society, there is a suitable auspicious time for sex life, which is called the time for *garbhādhāna*."

Since Diti's mental condition was disturbed and she did not respect her husband's direction to wait for an auspicious time, according to the timetable of the administrative demigods, she gave birth to two demons. The junctions between day and night are known as *sandhyās*, traditionally observed as times for prayer and meditation. These times are inauspicious for procreation.

> "This particular time is most inauspicious because at this time the horrible-looking ghosts and constant companions of the lord of the ghosts are visible."

etasyāṁ sādhvi sandhyāyāṁ
bhagavān bhūta-bhāvanaḥ
parīto bhūta-parṣadbhir
vṛṣeṇāṭati bhūtarāṭ

> "Lord Śiva, the king of the ghosts, sitting on the back of his bull carrier, travels at this time, accompanied by ghosts who follow him for their welfare."
>
> —*Śrīmad Bhāgavatam* 3.14.23-4

Lord Śiva is the most revered of all the demigods and the greatest devotee of the Supreme Lord.

vaiṣṇavānāṁ yathā śambhuḥ

"Lord Śambhu (Śiva) is the greatest of Vaiṣṇavas."
—*Śrīmad Bhāgavatam* 12.13.16

Lord Śiva is so merciful that he gives shelter to ghosts, souls who are lost in the material world and bereft of a physical body.

> "Ghosts are bereft of a physical body because of their grievously sinful acts, such as suicide. Lord Śiva, being very kind to the ghosts, sees that although they are condemned, they get physical bodies. He places them into the wombs of women who indulge in sexual intercourse regardless of the restrictions on time and circumstance."
> —*Śrīmad Bhāgavatam* 3.14.24 Bhaktivedanta purport

The Vaiṣṇava procedures and *mantras* for *garbhādhāna-saṁskāra* can be found in *Sat-kriyā-sāra-dīpikā* by Gopāla Bhaṭṭa Gosvāmī. Alternatively, couples can simply chant the names of God.

> "There may be discrepancies in pronouncing the *mantras* and observing the regulative principles, and, moreover, there may be discrepancies in regard to time, place, person and paraphernalia. But when Your Lordship's holy name is chanted, everything becomes faultless."
> —*Śrīmad Bhāgavatam* 8.23.16

Śrīla Prabhupāda instructed his disciples to chant fifty rounds on beads (i.e. fifty times one hundred and eight) of the Hare Kṛṣṇa *mahā-mantra* before engaging in sexual intercourse for procreation.

> "You have asked me some questions about the functions of sex life in Kṛṣṇa consciousness, and the basic principle is that it should be avoided as far as possible. However, if it is unavoidable, then it should be utilized only for begetting Kṛṣṇa conscious children. In that case, the husband and wife should chant at least fifty rounds before going to sex. The recommended period is six days after the menstruation period."
>
> —*Letters from Śrīla Prabhupāda* 18/1/1969

The chanting of fifty rounds is an excellent practice for inviting a spiritually advanced soul to take birth. Anyone who is unable to reach fifty rounds should nevertheless chant as many as possible. The profuse chanting of the Hare Kṛṣṇa *mahā-mantra* serves to purify the consciousness, to create an auspicious atmosphere, and to invite a pious soul to enter the womb. To obtain blessings for the performance of *garbhādhāna-saṁskāra*, an ideal *gṛhastha* first requests permission from his spiritual master.

> "All the rules and regulations apply equally to the householder and the *sannyāsī*, the member of the renounced order of life. The *gṛhastha*, however, is given permission by the spiritual master to indulge in sex during the period favorable for procreation."
>
> —*Śrīmad Bhāgavatam* 7.12.11

During the time of pregnancy, sex life should be avoided.

> "Similarly, according to religious injunctions a man is restricted to enjoy sex only once in a month, after the menstrual period of the wife, and if the wife is pregnant, he is not allowed sex life at all. That is the law for human beings."
>
> —*Śrīmad Bhāgavatam* 4.27.5 Bhaktivedanta purport

This is another reason why polygamy was practised in Vedic society.

> "A man is allowed to keep more than one wife because he cannot enjoy sex when the wife is pregnant. If he wants to enjoy sex at such a time, he may go to another wife who is not pregnant. These are laws mentioned in the *Manu-saṁhitā* and other scriptures."
>
> —*Śrīmad Bhāgavatam* 4.27.5 Bhaktivedanta purport

Family Planning

The purpose of *garbhādhāna-saṁskāra* is to produce a good quality population.

> "To check the increase of demoniac population, the Vedic civilization enacted so many rules and regulations of social life, the most important of which is the *garbhādhāna* process for begetting good children."
>
> —*Śrīmad Bhāgavatam* 3.17.15 Bhaktivedanta purport

The inherent qualities of a person to be born are determined at the time of conception, according to the surrounding atmosphere and the consciousness of the parents.

> "According to Vedic literature, the superior and inferior varieties found in the human social system, *varṇāśrama*, are due to pious and sinful modes of family planning. Thus piety and sin are constant points of reference in the Vedic analysis of the components of a given situation—namely the material ingredients, place, age and time. Indeed, the *Vedas* reveal the existence of material heaven and hell, which are certainly based on piety and sin."
>
> —*Śrīmad Bhāgavatam* 11.20.2

Vedic literatures also give information on how a husband and wife can influence the gender of the child to be produced from their union.

> "The circumstances for creating good children are mentioned in *kāma-śāstra*, the scripture in which suitable arrangements are prescribed for factually glorious sex life. Everything needed is mentioned in the scriptures—what sort of house and decorations there should be, what sort of dress the wife should have, how she should be decorated with ointments, scents and other attractive features, etc. With these requisites fulfilled, the husband will be attracted by her beauty, and a favorable mental situation will be created. The mental situation at the time of sex life

may then be transferred into the womb of the wife, and good children can come out of that pregnancy. Sexual intercourse in which the husband is attracted to the wife is sure to produce a male child, but sexual intercourse based on attraction of the wife for the husband may produce a girl. That is mentioned in the *Āyur-veda*. When the passion of the woman is greater, there is a chance of a girl's being born. When the passion of the man is greater, then there is the possibility of a son."

—*Śrīmad Bhāgavatam* 3.23.11 Bhaktivedanta purport

Now that the *garbhādhāna-saṁskāra* is no longer performed by the majority of the population, the world has become afflicted by *varṇa-saṅkara*, accidental progeny who may become liabilities rather than assets to society.

"In *Bhagavad-gītā* Arjuna informed Kṛṣṇa that if there is unwanted population (*varṇa-saṅkara*), the entire world will appear to be hell. People are very anxious for peace in the world, but there are so many unwanted children born without the benefit of the *garbhādhāna* ceremony, just like the demons born from Diti. Diti was so lusty that she forced her husband to copulate at a time which was inauspicious, and therefore the demons were born to create disturbances."

—*Śrīmad Bhāgavatam* 3.17.15 Bhaktivedanta purport

Modern governments, instead of teaching people how to produce pious children, encourage them to adopt artificial means of birth control.

> "Instead of being encouraged to adopt artificial means of birth control, people should be educated in Kṛṣṇa consciousness because only then will they understand their responsibility to their children. If one can beget children who will be devotees and be taught to turn aside from the path of birth and death (*mṛtyu-saṁsāra-vartmani*), there is no need of birth control. Rather, one should be encouraged to beget children. Artificial means of birth control have no value. Whether one begets children or not, a population of men who are like cats and dogs will never make human society happy. It is therefore necessary for people to be educated spiritually so that instead of begetting children like cats and dogs, they will undergo austerities to produce devotees. This will make their lives successful."
>
> —*Śrīmad Bhāgavatam* 10.3.33 Bhaktivedanta purport

Contraception is considered to be sinful because it defies the authority of God and interferes with His arrangements for other living entities.

> "Contraception deteriorates the womb so that it no longer is a good place for the soul. That is against the order of God. By the order of God, a soul is sent to a particular womb, but by this contraceptive he is denied that womb and has to be placed in another. That is disobedience to the Supreme. For example, take a man who is supposed to live in a particular apartment. If the situation there is so disturbed that he cannot enter the apartment, then he is put at a great disadvantage.

> That is illegal interference and is punishable."
> —Letter from Śrīla Prabhupāda to Dr Wilfred G. Bigelow

Even more sinful than this is abortion, when a child takes shelter in the womb of a mother and, instead of being protected and nurtured by her, is killed by her.

> "Illicit sex creates pregnancies, and these unwanted pregnancies lead to abortion. Those involved become implicated in these sins, so much so that they are punished in the same way the next life. Thus in the next life they also enter the womb of a mother and are killed in the same way."
> —*Śrīmad Bhāgavatam* 5.14.9 Bhaktivedanta purport

The Vedic concept of birth control is simply to educate people how to control the senses, refrain from illicit sex, and engage their sexual propensities for religious procreation.

> "According to Vedic civilization, procreation should not be contrary to religious principles, and then the birthrate will be controlled. As stated in *Bhagavad-gītā* (7.11), *dharmāviruddho bhūteṣu kāmo'smi*: sex not contrary to religious principles is a representation of the Supreme Lord. People should be educated how to give birth to good children through *saṁskāras*, beginning with the *garbhādhāna-saṁskāra*; birth should not be controlled by artificial means, for this will lead to a civilization of animals. If one follows

religious principles, he automatically practices birth control, because if one is spiritually educated he knows that the after-effects of sex are various types of misery (*bahu-duḥkha-bhāja*). One who is spiritually advanced does not indulge in uncontrolled sex. Therefore, instead of being forced to refrain from sex or refrain from giving birth to many children, people should be spiritually educated, and then birth control will automatically follow."

—*Śrīmad Bhāgavatam* 10.3.33 Bhaktivedanta purport

If every child were to be conceived in God consciousness, there would be peace all over the world.

"In having sex life to beget children, one should observe the process for begetting nice children. If each and every householder in every family observes the Vedic system, then there are nice children, not demons, and automatically there is peace in the world. If we do not follow regulations in life for social tranquillity, we cannot expect peace. Rather, we will have to undergo the stringent reactions of natural laws."

—*Śrīmad Bhāgavatam* 3.17.15 Bhaktivedanta purport

Dama (Self-control)

Sense control is an essential part of spiritual development and is therefore important for all four *āśramas*. Even *gṛhasthas* are meant to abstain from sex life when it is not favourable for procreation.

> "Then as far as *dama* (self-control) is concerned, it is not only meant for other orders of religious society, but is especially meant for the householder. Although he has a wife, a householder should not use his senses for sex life unnecessarily. There are restrictions for the householders even in sex life, which should only be engaged in for the propagation of children. If he does not require children, he should not enjoy sex life with his wife. Modern society enjoys sex life with contraceptive methods or more abominable methods to avoid the responsibility of children. This is not in the transcendental quality, but is demoniac. If anyone, even if he is a householder, wants to make progress in spiritual life, he must control his sex life and should not beget a child without the purpose of serving Kṛṣṇa. If he is able to beget children who will be in Kṛṣṇa consciousness, one can produce hundreds of children, but without this capacity one should not indulge only for sense pleasure."
>
> —*Bhagavad-gītā* As *It Is* 16.1-3 purport

Unrestricted sex life is not only contrary to religious principles, but it also diminishes memory and energy by wasting semen.

> "If semen is not discharged unnecessarily, one becomes extremely strong in memory, determination, activity and the vitality of one's bodily energy."
>
> —*Śrīmad Bhāgavatam* 7.11.8-12 Bhaktivedanta purport

Whether it is time to abstain or time to procreate, the principle of self-control remains paramount. At the time of procreation, the senses are controlled by the performance of *garbhādhāna-saṁskāra* for producing qualified progeny.

> "According to Vedic principles, before creating progeny one must fully control the senses. This control takes place through the *garbhādhāna-saṁskāra*."
>
> —*Śrīmad Bhāgavatam* 10.3.33

When it is time to abstain, one can learn to control the senses by becoming sober enough to tolerate the itch.

> "Sex life is compared to the rubbing of two hands to relieve an itch. *Gṛhamedhis*, so-called *gṛhasthas* who have no spiritual knowledge, think that this itching is the greatest platform of happiness, although actually it is a source of distress. The *kṛpaṇas*, the fools who are just the opposite of *brāhmaṇas*, are not satisfied by repeated sensuous enjoyment. Those who are *dhīra*, however, who are sober and who tolerate this itching, are not subjected to the sufferings of fools and rascals."
>
> —*Śrīmad Bhāgavatam* 7.9.45

The ability to tolerate the itch is developed by the regular practice of devotional activities in Kṛṣṇa consciousness. Sense control cannot be achieved in a vacuum. It requires the observance of a lifestyle that is conducive for mental equilibrium, and participation in spiritual and cultural activities that satisfy the mind and senses.

> "But much better is to follow the injunction of the *śāstras*: simply try to tolerate the itching sensation

> and avoid so much pain. This is real psychology. That itching sensation can be tolerated if one practices Kṛṣṇa consciousness. Then one will not be very attracted by sex life."
>
> —*Beyond Illusion and Doubt* 13

Indulgence in sense gratification gives quick relief from the itch, but then compounds the problem.

> "It is said in the *Manu-smṛti* that lust cannot be satisfied by any amount of sense enjoyment, just as fire is never extinguished by a constant supply of fuel."
>
> —*Bhagavad-gītā* As *It Is* 3.39 purport

One who can tolerate the itch, while at the same time developing a higher taste for spiritual enjoyment, attains long-term relief in due course of time. Unregulated sex life, which produces negative *karma* and misery, is known as happiness in the mode of passion.

> "That happiness which is derived from contact of the senses with their objects and which appears like nectar at first but poison at the end is said to be of the nature of passion."
>
> —*Bhagavad-gītā* As *It Is* 18.38

Those who can renounce this flashing happiness and thereby avoid its concomitant suffering, by controlling the senses, can enjoy long-term happiness in the mode of goodness.

"That which in the beginning may be just like poison but at the end is just like nectar and which awakens one to self-realization is said to be happiness in the mode of goodness."

—*Bhagavad-gītā* As *It Is* 18.37

The power of lust affects not only the external senses, but also the mind and the intelligence.

indriyāṇi mano buddhir
asyādhiṣṭhānam ucyate
etair vimohayaty eṣa
jñānam āvṛtya dehinam

"The senses, the mind and the intelligence are the sitting places of this lust. Through them lust covers the real knowledge of the living entity and bewilders him."

—*Bhagavad-gītā* As *It Is* 3.40

The mind is the most subtle of all the senses and the most difficult to conquer.

mamaivāṁśo jīva-loke
jīva-bhūtaḥ sanātanaḥ
manaḥ-ṣaṣṭhānīndriyāṇi
prakṛti-sthāni karṣati

"The living entities in this material world are My eternal fragmental parts. Due to conditioned life, they are struggling very hard with the six senses, which include the mind."

—*Bhagavad-gītā* As *It Is* 15.7

However, to try to control the senses without controlling the mind is more or less a futile endeavour.

> "One who restrains the senses of action but whose mind dwells on sense objects certainly deludes himself and is called a pretender."
>
> —*Bhagavad-gītā* As *It Is* 3.6

Since the intelligence is higher than the mind, one who uses his intelligence to understand the constitutional position of the soul as a servant of God can influence the mind to surrender to Him, and then the other senses will automatically follow.

> "If by intelligence one engages one's mind in Kṛṣṇa consciousness, by complete surrender unto the Supreme Personality of Godhead, then automatically the mind becomes stronger, and even though the senses are very strong, like serpents, they will be no more effective than serpents with broken fangs."
>
> —*Bhagavad-gītā* As *It Is* 3.42 purport

A mind that is directed by spiritual intelligence, instead of being influenced by lust, can command all the senses to engage in devotional activities.

tasmāt tvam indriyāṇy ādau
niyamya bharatarṣabha
pāpmānaṁ prajahi hy enaṁ
jñāna-vijñāna-nāśanam

"Therefore, O Arjuna, best of the Bhāratas, in the very beginning curb this great symbol of sin (lust) by

> regulating the senses, and slay this destroyer of knowledge and self-realization."
>
> —*Bhagavad-gītā* As *It Is* 3.41

While a mind that is controlled by higher intelligence is the greatest friend of the soul, an uncontrolled mind is the worst enemy.

> "For him who has conquered the mind, the mind is the best of friends; but for one who has failed to do so, his mind will remain the greatest enemy."
>
> —*Bhagavad-gītā* As *It Is* 6.6

Lust is born from the mode of passion, one of the three energies of *māyā* that imprison us in the material world. Only by surrendering the intelligence, mind and senses in the service of the Lord and Master of the material energy can we become protected from her powerful influence. Otherwise we are insignificant in the face of such a formidable opponent.

daivī hy eṣā guṇa-mayī
mama māyā duratyayā
mām eva ye prapadyante
māyām etāṁ taranti te

> "This divine energy of Mine, consisting of the three modes of material nature, is difficult to overcome. But those who have surrendered unto Me can easily cross beyond it."
>
> —*Bhagavad-gītā* As *It Is* 7.14

Sense control begins with the tongue. The tongue can be controlled by being engaged in chanting the holy names of the Lord and eating *kṛṣṇa-prasāda*.

> "Similarly, the demands of the body can be divided into three categories—the demands of the tongue, the belly and the genitals. One may observe that these three senses are physically situated in a straight line, as far as the body is concerned, and that the bodily demands begin with the tongue. If one can restrain the demands of the tongue by limiting its activities to the eating of *prasāda*, the urges of the belly and the genitals can automatically be controlled."
>
> —*The Nectar of Instruction* 1 purport

Control of the tongue also requires vigilance to avoid the pitfall of overeating.

> "After taking his dinner and having his thirst and hunger satisfied, King Purañjana felt some joy within his heart. Instead of being elevated to a higher consciousness, he became captivated by Cupid, and was moved by a desire to find his wife, who kept him satisfied in his household life."
>
> —*Śrīmad Bhāgavatam* 4.26.13

> Bhaktivedanta purport:
>
> "This verse is very significant for those desiring to elevate themselves to a higher level of Kṛṣṇa consciousness. When a person is initiated by a

> spiritual master, he changes his habits and does not eat undesirable eatables or engage in the eating of meat, the drinking of liquor, illicit sex or gambling. *Sāttvika-āhāra*, foodstuffs in the mode of goodness, are described in the *śāstras* as wheat, rice, vegetables, fruits, milk, sugar, and milk products. Simple food like rice, *dhal*, *capātīs*, vegetables, milk and sugar constitute a balanced diet, but sometimes it is found that an initiated person, in the name of *prasāda*, eats very luxurious foodstuffs. Due to his past sinful life he becomes attracted by Cupid and eats good food voraciously. It is clearly visible that when a neophyte in Kṛṣṇa consciousness eats too much, he falls down. Instead of being elevated to pure Kṛṣṇa consciousness, he becomes attracted by Cupid."

In case of accidental fall-down, the repentant *gṛhastha* continues to worship the Lord with faith and conviction.

> "Having awakened faith in the narrations of my glories, being disgusted with all material activities, knowing that all sense gratification leads to misery, but still being unable to renounce all sense enjoyment, My devotee should remain happy and worship Me with great faith and conviction. Even though he is sometimes engaged in sense enjoyment, My devotee knows that all sense gratification leads to a miserable result, and he sincerely repents such activities."
>
> —Lord Kṛṣṇa, *Śrīmad Bhāgavatam* 11.20.27-8

The religious principle of limiting sex life solely to planned procreation presents a serious challenge for married couples of today. Within Vedic society polygamy was socially acceptable and families were typically much larger than they are today. The artificial economic pressures of modern materialistic society have made child-raising into a costly business for parents. Today there is less scope for procreation than before, and less support for celibacy. The battle to control the senses is difficult to win alone.

> "The senses are so strong and impetuous, O Arjuna, that they forcibly carry away the mind even of a man of discrimination who is endeavoring to control them."
>
> —*Bhagavad-gītā* As *It Is* 2.60

With the association and support of like-minded people, and by participating in spiritual programmes and devotional activities, couples can repel the onslaughts of *māyā* by filling up their lives with Kṛṣṇa consciousness. Any circumstantial discrepancies that may nonetheless arise, due to past material conditioning, can be counteracted by the continuing practice of devotional service.

> "The devotee, in the beginning, may sometimes fall from the standard, but still he should be considered superior to all other philosophers and yogīs. One who always engages in Kṛṣṇa consciousness should be understood to be a perfectly saintly person. His accidental nondevotional activities will diminish, and he will soon be situated without any doubt in

complete perfection. The pure devotee has no actual chance to fall down, because the Supreme Godhead personally takes care of His pure devotees. Therefore, the intelligent person should take directly to the process of Kṛṣṇa consciousness and happily live in this material world. He will eventually receive the supreme award of Kṛṣṇa."

—*Bhagavad-gītā As It Is* 9.34 purport

For most aspiring *yogīs*, learning to conquer the senses is a gradual process. In case of human error, the recommended system of atonement for *bhakti-yogīs* is simply to continue to engage in devotional service.

"My dear Uddhava, just as a blazing fire turns firewood into ashes, similarly, devotion unto Me completely burns to ashes sins committed by My devotees."

—Lord Kṛṣṇa, *Śrīmad-Bhāgavatam* 11.14.19

Those who continually engage in devotional service with enthusiasm, confidence, and patience will gradually become purified and freed from all *anarthas* (undesirable habits).

utsāhān niścayād dhairyāt
tat-tat-karma-pravartanāt
saṅga-tyāgāt sato vṛtteḥ
ṣaḍbhir bhaktiḥ prasidhyati

"There are six principles favorable to the execution of pure devotional service: (1) being enthusiastic, (2) endeavoring with confidence, (3) being patient, (4)

> acting according to regulative principles (such as *śravaṇaṁ kīrtanaṁ viṣṇoḥ smaraṇam*—hearing, chanting and remembering Kṛṣṇa), (5) abandoning the association of nondevotees, and (6) following in the footsteps of the previous *ācāryas*. These six principles undoubtedly assure the complete success of pure devotional service."
>
> —*The Nectar of Instruction* 3

The holy name of the Lord, when chanted without offence, has the power to nullify the reactions to all sinful activities.

> "Simply by chanting one holy name of Hari, a sinful man can counteract the reactions to more sins than he is able to commit."
>
> —*Bṛhad-viṣṇu Purāṇa*

To commit sinful activities intentionally, however, with the idea of becoming purified afterwards by chanting the holy name of the Lord, is considered to be the most serious of the ten offences against the holy name.

> "The seventh offence is to commit sins intentionally on the strength of the holy name. In the scriptures it is said that one can be liberated from the effects of all sinful actions simply by chanting the holy name of the Lord. One who takes advantage of this transcendental method and continues to commit sins on the expectation of neutralizing the effects of sins by chanting the holy name of the Lord is the greatest offender at the feet of the holy name. Such an offender

> cannot purify himself by any recommended method of purification."
>
> —*Śrīmad Bhāgavatam* 2.1.11 Bhaktivedanta purport

In case of unintentional fall-down, a Vaiṣṇava husband and wife can continue to respect each other as devotees of the Lord by remembering that those who are steadily engaged in devotional service are considered to be saintly.

api cet su-durācāro
bhajate mām ananya-bhāk
sādhur eva sa mantavyaḥ
samyag vyavasito hi saḥ

> "Even if one commits the most abominable action, if he is engaged in devotional service he is to be considered saintly because he is properly situated in his determination."
>
> —*Bhagavad-gītā As It Is* 9.30

Faults and weaknesses are products of temporary material conditioning, while the soul and devotional service are eternal. To denigrate a Vaiṣṇava, or a servant of God, is the first of the ten offences against the holy name.

> "One can deliver himself from the effects of all sins by surrendering himself unto the Lord. One can deliver himself from all offences at the feet of the Lord by taking shelter of His holy name. But one cannot protect himself if one commits an offence at the feet of the holy name of the Lord. Such offences are

mentioned in the *Padma Purāṇa* as being ten in number. The first offence is to vilify the great devotees who have preached about the glories of the Lord."

—*Śrīmad Bhāgavatam* 2.1.11 Bhaktivedanta purport

This is known as the 'mad elephant' offence.

"To commit an offence against a devotee is very dangerous in devotional service. Lord Caitanya therefore said that an offence to a devotee is just like a mad elephant run loose; when a mad elephant enters a garden, it tramples all the plants. Similarly, an offence unto the feet of a pure devotee murders one's position in devotional service."

—*Śrīmad Bhāgavatam* 3.15.39 Bhaktivedanta purport

A husband and wife can avoid condemning each other for indiscrepancies by remembering that their real common enemy is *kāma*, lust.

"Arjuna said: O descendant of Vṛṣṇi, by what is one impelled to sinful acts, even unwillingly, as if engaged by force?"

śrī-bhagavān uvāca
kāma eṣa krodha eṣa
rajo-guṇa-samudbhavaḥ
mahāśano mahā-pāpmā
viddhy enam iha vairiṇam

"The Supreme Personality of Godhead said: It is lust only, Arjuna, which is born of contact with the

> material mode of passion and later transformed into wrath, and which is the all-devouring sinful enemy of this world."
>
> —*Bhagavad-gītā As It Is* 3.36-7

The "all-devouring sinful enemy of this world" is not an enemy to be trifled with. A person who is facing challenges in this area needs to be supported by his partner with kindness and patience in the mode of goodness. If lusty desire is repressed, unsatisfied lust transforms into wrath, in the mode of passion, and then degenerates into illusion, in the mode of ignorance, which binds the soul to the material world.

> "When lust is unsatisfied, it turns into wrath; wrath is transformed into illusion, and illusion continues the material existence."
>
> —*Bhagavad-gītā As It Is* 3.37 purport

Lust can be tamed only by being rechannelled into higher occupations.

A Higher Taste

Self-control is a brahminical quality in the mode of goodness. Without Kṛṣṇa consciousness, however, even great *yogīs* who perform severe austerities and penances can become victimised by attacks of the senses.

> "There are many learned sages, philosophers and transcendentalists who try to conquer the senses, but

> in spite of their endeavors, even the greatest of them sometimes fall victim to material sense enjoyment due to the agitated mind. Even Viśvāmitra, a great sage and perfect *yogī*, was misled by Menakā into sex enjoyment, although the *yogī* was endeavoring for sense control with severe types of penance and *yoga* practice. And, of course, there are so many similar instances in the history of the world. Therefore, it is very difficult to control the mind and senses without being fully Kṛṣṇa conscious."
>
> —*Bhagavad-gītā* As *It Is* 2.60 purport

Control over the senses cannot be achieved artificially or in a vacuum. A poisonous snake may be restrained by force, but as soon as it is released it will bite. An expert snake charmer, however, can control the snake by *mantras*. Similarly, to try to control the senses by force alone is a fruitless endeavour, but by the process of hearing and chanting the Hare Kṛṣṇa *mahā-mantra*, one can tame the senses.

> "The senses are compared to poisonous snakes, but the senses of a *bhakta* engaged in the service of the Lord are like snakes with their poisonous fangs removed."
>
> —*Śrīmad Bhāgavatam* 5.17.3 Bhaktivedanta purport

By directing the senses towards spiritual activities, one experiences a superior substitute for mundane habits. Only by cultivating a higher taste can one become detached from inferior pursuits.

viṣayā vinivartante
nirāhārasya dehinaḥ
rasa-varjaṁ raso 'py asya
paraṁ dṛṣṭvā nivartate

> "The embodied soul may be restricted from sense enjoyment, though the taste for sense objects remains. But, ceasing such engagements by experiencing a higher taste, he is fixed in consciousness."
> —*Bhagavad-gītā* As It Is 2.59

This truth was vividly expressed by the great saint and devotee, Yāmunācārya.

> "Since my mind has been engaged in the transcendental loving service of Kṛṣṇa, realizing ever-new pleasure in Him, whenever I think of sex pleasure, I spit at the thought and my lips curl with distaste."

The cultivation of a higher taste, by practice of devotional service to Kṛṣṇa, is the ultimate secret of success in the battle to conquer the senses.

> "As illustrated in the above-mentioned verse of Śrī Yāmunācārya, a sincere devotee of the Lord shuns all material sense enjoyment due to his higher taste for spiritual enjoyment in the association of the Lord. That is the secret of success. One who is not, therefore, in Kṛṣṇa consciousness, however powerful he may be in controlling the senses by artificial repression, is

sure ultimately to fail, for the slightest thought of sense pleasure will agitate him to gratify his desires."

—*Bhagavad-gītā* As *It Is* 2.62 purport

Haridāsa Ṭhākura, the *ācārya* of the holy name, was not attracted by the idea of sex life, even when tempted by Māyā-devī in person, because he was constantly absorbed in chanting the Hare Kṛṣṇa *mahā-mantra*.

"One who is not Kṛṣṇa conscious is subjected to material desires while contemplating the objects of the senses. The senses require real engagements, and if they are not engaged in the transcendental loving service of the Lord, they will certainly seek engagement in the service of materialism. In the material world everyone, including Lord Śiva and Lord Brahmā—to say nothing of other demigods in the heavenly planets—is subjected to the influence of sense objects, and the only method to get out of this puzzle of material existence is to become Kṛṣṇa conscious."

—*Bhagavad-gītā* As *It Is* 2.62 purport

By engaging the mind and senses in the service of the Lord, one can transform his attachment for material sense gratification into attachment for the Lord.

"When the cause of the mind's restlessness is sense gratification and this restlessness is the main obstacle in the practice of devotional service, then all sensual activities should be dovetailed in the service of the

> Lord and the attachment to sense gratification should be transformed into attachment for the Lord. Then the mind becomes fixed in devotional service by taking shelter of that attachment."
>
> —Bhaktivinode Thakur, *Śrī Bhaktyāloka* 6

The transcendental form, qualities and pastimes of the Supreme Personality of Godhead are so attractive that, by becoming attached to Him, one can conquer over mundane lust.

> "If you increase your Kṛṣṇa consciousness, love for Kṛṣṇa, then you will forget this lust. That is the only way. There is no other second way. To conquer over lust, one has to take shelter of Madana-mohana. *Madana* means lust, Cupid, and Kṛṣṇa is Madana-mohana. He can enchant Cupid also."
>
> —*Conversations with Śrīla Prabhupāda*
> Morning walk, Los Angeles 26/6/1975

By hearing about Kṛṣṇa's *rasa-līlā* with the *gopīs,* as recounted in the *Tenth Canto* of *Śrīmad-Bhāgavatam,* from a realised soul, and by understanding the transcendental nature of these pastimes, one can become free from lusty desire for material sense gratification.

> "Everyone has got lusty desires, but if one is actually advanced and he hears from a realised person about the meaning of Kṛṣṇa's *rasa* dance, then the result will be *hṛd-roga-kāmam.* We have got a heart disease, which means lusty desire. *Hṛd-roga-kāmam apahinoti:*

> 'It becomes vanquished.' If one actually hears Kṛṣṇa's *rasa-līlā*, then no more material lusty desires, this is the result."
>
> —Bhaktivedanta lecture, *Śrīmad Bhāgavatam* 3.28.18
> Nairobi 27/10/1975

Devotees become attached to Kṛṣṇa by hearing about His transcendental pastimes and by rendering personal service to Him. Deity worship is a practical process for keeping Kṛṣṇa at the centre of household life, and is especially recommended for householders.

> "*Gṛhastha* devotees, however, are generally engaged in material activities, and therefore if they do not take to Deity worship, their falling down is positively assured."
>
> —*Śrīmad Bhāgavatam* 7.5.23-4 Bhaktivedanta purport

The practical process of *bhakti-yoga*, which protects the practitioner from material contamination, is to engage all the senses in devotional service. This principle was exemplified by Mahārāja Ambarīṣa.

> "Mahārāja Ambarīṣa always engaged his mind in meditating upon the lotus feet of Kṛṣṇa, his words in describing the glories of the Lord, his hands in cleansing the Lord's temple, and his ears in hearing the words spoken by Kṛṣṇa or about Kṛṣṇa. He engaged his eyes in seeing the Deity of Kṛṣṇa, Kṛṣṇa's temples and Kṛṣṇa's places like Mathurā and Vṛndāvana. He engaged his sense of touch in touching the bodies of

the Lord's devotees. He engaged his sense of smell in smelling the fragrance of *tulasī* offered to the Lord, and he engaged his tongue in tasting the Lord's *prasāda*. He engaged his legs in walking to the holy places and temples of the Lord, his head in bowing down before the Lord, and all his desires in serving the Lord, twenty-four hours a day. Indeed, Mahārāja Ambarīṣa never desired anything for his own sense gratification. He engaged all his senses in devotional service, in various engagements related to the Lord. This is the way to increase attachment for the Lord and be completely free from all material desires."

—*Śrīmad-Bhāgavatam* 9.4.18-20

The most effective way to protect oneself from falling down is to keep all the senses engaged in the service of the Lord. Couples who keep themselves fully engaged in activities of devotional service are left with neither the time, the energy, nor the inclination to engage in whimsical sense gratification. One who has lost his taste for mundane sense gratification can withdraw his/her senses from material sense objects without any artificial endeavour.

"One who is able to withdraw his senses from sense objects, as the tortoise draws its limbs within the shell, is firmly fixed in perfect consciousness."

—*Bhagavad-gītā* As It Is 2.58

From *Kāma* to *Prema*

That which is generally known as 'love' between a man and a woman in this world, when carefully analysed, can be more accurately understood to be lust. It is not surprising that the two feelings are commonly confused, considering that lust is actually the material transformation of our original love for God.

> "Lust is actually an egocentric misdirection of the love that is our birthright – a love inherent in all creation. Because we are part and parcel of a loving God, in our natural state we share in that love. Here in the material world, though, we are not in our natural state, and the self-centered energy of lust has caused us to forget our birthright."
>
> —Bhaktitīrtha Swami, *Spiritual Warrior II*. 3

The main difference between lust and love is that lust is selfish whereas love is selfless. When we are under the influence of lust, we desire to satisfy our own senses. Pure love, on the other hand, is characterised by the sole desire to satisfy the beloved.

> "Lust and love have different characteristics, just as iron and gold have different natures."
>
> —*Śrī Caitanya-caritāmṛta, Ādi-līlā* 4.164

Pure love is known as *prema*, the spiritual love that is experienced by the pure devotee in relationship with Kṛṣṇa.

> "The desire to gratify one's own senses is *kāma* (lust), but the desire to please the senses of Lord Kṛṣṇa is *prema* (love)."
>
> —*Śrī Caitanya-caritāmṛta, Ādi-līlā* 4.165

Since *kāma* is a material transformation of *prema*, the secret of how to become free from *kāma* is to gradually transform it back into its original state of *prema*, pure love of God, by engagement in devotional service.

> "The object of lust is only the enjoyment of one's own senses. But love caters to the enjoyment of Lord Kṛṣṇa, and thus it is very powerful."
>
> —*Śrī Caitanya-caritāmṛta, Ādi-līlā* 4.166

Every one of us has an eternal blissful loving relationship with the Supreme Personality of Godhead, which is free from all material contamination.

> "Bhaktisiddhānta Sarasvatī Ṭhākura says that material lust should never be attributed to Kṛṣṇa, who is full of transcendental knowledge. Material lust cannot be engaged in the service of the Lord, for it is applicable to materialists, not to Kṛṣṇa. Only *prema*, or love of Godhead, is applicable for the satisfaction of Kṛṣṇa. *Prema* is full service rendered unto the Lord. The lusty affairs of the *gopīs* actually constitute the topmost love of Godhead because the *gopīs* never act for their own personal satisfaction. They are simply pleased by engaging other *gopīs* in the service of the Lord. The *gopīs* derive more transcendental pleasure from

> indirectly engaging other *gopīs* in the service of Kṛṣṇa than from engaging in His service themselves. That is the difference between material lust and love of Godhead. Lust applies to the material world, and love of Godhead applies only to Kṛṣṇa."
>
> —*Śrī Caitanya-caritāmṛta, Madhya-lila* 8.215
> Bhaktivedanta purport

When we begin to reawaken our dormant love for Kṛṣṇa, our relationships with each other also become more loving and less lustful. By advancing in Kṛṣṇa consciousness and willingly abstaining from sex life, married couples develop more pure and spiritual relationships between themselves and experience feelings of genuine love for one another. The loving dealings between the *gopīs* and Kṛṣṇa are completely pure and transcendental, with no tinge of mundane lust.

> "The predominated *gopīs* were bound to Kṛṣṇa in such pure love. For them there was no question of sexual love based on sense gratification. Their only engagement in life was to see Kṛṣṇa happy in all respects, regardless of their own personal interests. They dedicated their souls only for the satisfaction of the Personality of Godhead, Śrī Kṛṣṇa. There was not the slightest tinge of sexual love between the *gopīs* and Kṛṣṇa."
>
> —*Śrī Caitanya-caritāmṛta, Ādi-līlā* 4.165
> Bhaktivedanta purport

The taste of *prema*, pure love for Kṛṣṇa, is so sublime and transcendental that it overpowers and replaces mundane lusty desires, which have no connection with the eternal soul. Kāmadeva means Cupid, and Kṛṣṇa is also known as Kāmadevāya, the transcendental Cupid in the spiritual world. Kṛṣṇa is actually the original Cupid, the God of love, who attracts all living entities by His transcendental amorous pastimes.

> "It is also stated in the *Gopāla-tāpanī Upaniṣad* that when Kṛṣṇa is spoken of as Cupid, one should not think of Him as the Cupid of this material world. As already explained, Vṛndāvana is the spiritual abode of Kṛṣṇa, and the word Cupid is also spiritual and transcendental. One should not take the material Cupid and Kṛṣṇa to be on the same level. The material Cupid represents the attraction of the external flesh and body, but the spiritual Cupid is the attraction by which the Supersoul attracts the individual soul. Actually lust and sex are there in spiritual life, but when the spirit soul is embodied in material elements, that spiritual urge is expressed through the material body and is therefore pervertedly reflected. When one actually becomes conversant in the science of Kṛṣṇa consciousness, he can understand that his material desire for sex is abominable, whereas spiritual sex is desirable."
>
> —*Teachings of Lord Caitanya* 31

When the word "sex" is combined with the word "spiritual", as above, it has nothing to do with sex as it is understood in material terms. It is an entirely different activity, pure and transcendental. The conjugal pastimes of Śrī Kṛṣṇa with Śrīmatī Rādhārāṇī and the other *gopīs* can never be gross or mundane. Their mutual dealings are supremely cultured and refined, never tinged by selfishness or material lust, but constantly driven by their unending emotions of sublime love for one another.

"Kṛṣṇa's *rāsa* dance should never be compared to any kind of material dance, such as a ball dance or a society dance. The *rāsa* dance is a completely spiritual performance. In order to establish this fact, Kṛṣṇa, the supreme mystic, expanded Himself into many forms and stood beside each *gopī*. Placing His hands on the shoulders of the *gopīs* on both sides of Him, He began to dance in their midst. The mystic expansions of Kṛṣṇa were not perceived by the *gopīs* because Kṛṣṇa appeared alone to each of them. Each *gopī* thought that Kṛṣṇa was dancing with her alone. Above that wonderful dance flew many airplanes carrying the denizens of the heavenly planets, who were very eager to see the wonderful dance of Kṛṣṇa with the *gopīs*. The Gandharvas and Kinnaras began to sing, and, accompanied by their respective wives, all the Gandharvas began to shower flowers on the dancers."

—*Kṛṣṇa the Supreme Personality of Godhead* 33

Chapter Eight

Mokṣa
Liberation

Developing Detachment—Spiritualising Relationships
Simple Living—*Vānaprastha-āśrama*
Five Kinds of Liberation
Bhakti (Pure Devotional Service)
Pañcama-puruṣārtha (The Fifth Goal)

Chapter Eight

Mokṣa

—Liberation—

je-dina gṛhe, bhajana dekhi,
gṛhete goloka bhāya

"Goloka Vṛndāvana appears in my home whenever I see the worship and service of Lord Hari going on there."
—Bhaktivinoda Ṭhākura, *Gītāvalī*

OF THE FOUR GOALS OF HUMAN LIFE, *mokṣa* is the ultimate. While *varṇāśrama-dharma*, *artha* and *kāma* are temporary goals pertaining to the material body, *mokṣa* is eternal. The fourth goal of human life is to attain eternal liberation from the material world and its four major sources of suffering, namely birth, death, old age and disease.

"Kṛṣṇa says in *Bhagavad-gītā* (3.19) that the real sufferings of the material world are four—*janma-mṛtyu-jarā-vyādhi* (birth, death, old age and disease).

> In the history of the world, no one has been successful in conquering these miseries imposed by material nature."
>
> —*Śrīmad Bhāgavatam* 7.9.19 Bhaktivedanta purport

Vedic literatures explain that even those who reach the highest planets in the material universe eventually face death, because the material body is perishable and can never become immortal. Freedom from the four miseries of material life is attainable only by entrance into the eternal spiritual world, the transcendental abode of the Supreme Personality of Godhead, which lies beyond all the mundane material universes.

ā-brahma-bhuvanāl lokāḥ
punar āvartino 'rjuna
mām upetya tu kaunteya
punar janma na vidyate

> "From the highest planet in the material world down to the lowest, all are places of misery wherein repeated birth and death take place. But one who attains to My abode, O son of Kuntī, never takes birth again."
>
> —*Bhagavad-gītā As It Is* 8.16

The purpose of the *varṇāśrama* system is to situate each person in the position that is most favourable for his/her progress towards liberation from birth and death. By remaining in that position and executing prescribed duties for the service of God, everyone can gradually become elevated.

> "...Not everyone is competent to be liberated from material bondage. It is everyone's duty, therefore, to enjoy according to his present position, but under the direction of the Lord or the *Vedas*. The *Vedas* are considered to be the direct words of the Lord. The Lord gives us the opportunity to enjoy material life as we want, and at the same time He gives directions for the modes and processes of abiding by the *Vedas* so that gradually one may be elevated to liberation from material bondage. The conditioned souls who have come to the material world to fulfill their desires to lord it over material nature are bound by the laws of nature. The best course is to abide by the Vedic rules; that will help one to be gradually elevated to liberation."
>
> —*Śrīmad Bhāgavatam* 3.21.16 Bhaktivedanta purport

Gṛhasthas become eligible for *mokṣa* by following their *dharma*, according to *varna* and *āśrama*, while dovetailing activities of *artha* and *kāma* in the service of the Supreme Lord, thus developing spiritual knowledge, detachment, and devotion.

> "When religion, economic development and sense gratification are adjusted, liberation from this material birth, death, old age and disease is assured."
>
> —*Śrīmad-Bhāgavatam* 4.22.36 Bhaktivedanta purport

Whatever spiritual progress one has achieved in life is revealed at the time of death. The next destination of the soul is determined by one's consciousness at that time.

yaṁ yaṁ vāpi smaran bhāvaṁ
tyajaty ante kalevaram
taṁ tam evaiti kaunteya
sadā tad-bhāva-bhāvitaḥ

"Whatever state of being one remembers when he quits his body, O son of Kuntī, that state he will attain without fail."

—*Bhagavad-gītā As It Is* 8.6

Those who take shelter of the Supreme Personality of Godhead at the time of death can attain liberation from birth, death, old age, and disease, and go back home, back to Godhead.

anta-kāle ca mām eva
smaran muktvā kalevaram
yaḥ prayāti sa mad-bhāvaṁ
yāti nāsty atra saṁśayaḥ

"And whoever, at the end of his life, quits his body, remembering Me alone, at once attains My nature. Of this there is no doubt."

—*Bhagavad-gītā As It Is* 8.5

A person's state of consciousness at the time of death is a reflection of the consciousness and activities he or she has developed in life. To remember the Lord at the time of death requires practice.

"One cannot suddenly remember the Supreme Lord at death; one must have practiced some *yoga* system, especially the system of *bhakti-yoga*. Since one's mind at death is very disturbed, one should practice transcendence through *yoga* during one's life."

—*Bhagavad-gītā As It Is* 8.10 purport

One who has become used to remembering the Lord in daily life will be able to take shelter of Him at the time of death.

tasmāt sarveṣu kāleṣu
mām anusmara yudhya ca
mayy arpita-mano-buddhir
mām evaiṣyasy asaṁśayaḥ

"Therefore, Arjuna, you should always think of Me in the form of Kṛṣṇa and at the same time carry out your prescribed duty of fighting. With your activities dedicated to Me and your mind and intelligence fixed on Me, you will attain Me without doubt."

—*Bhagavad-gītā As It Is* 8.7

Developing Detachment

The common purpose of all the different processes of *yoga* is to empower the practitioner to develop detachment from matter.

"The greatest common understanding for all *yogīs* is complete detachment from matter, which can be achieved by different kinds of *yoga*."

—*Śrīmad Bhāgavatam* 3.32.27

The system of four *āśramas* also is meant to facilitate gradual detachment from matter by performance of austerity.

> "The entire *varṇāśrama-dharma* society is meant for *tapasya*. Without *tapasya*, or austerity, no human being can get liberation."
>
> —*Bhagavad-gītā As It Is* 16.1-3 purport

While members of the other three *āśramas* openly manifest detachment by renunciation of material possessions, the *gṛhastha* develops detachment internally, by regulating *artha* and *kāma* according to *dharma*, while externally appearing to be attached.

> "While working to earn his livelihood as much as necessary to maintain body and soul together, one who is actually learned should live in human society unattached to family affairs, although externally appearing very much attached."
>
> —*Śrīmad Bhāgavatam* 7.14.5

Not only husbands but also wives are advised to cultivate internal detachment from family affairs.

> "A woman, therefore, should consider her husband, her house and her children to be the arrangement of the external energy of the Lord for her death, just as the sweet singing of the hunter is death for the deer."
>
> —*Śrīmad Bhāgavatam* 3.31.42

Married couples who are interested in spiritual progress try to avoid becoming overly attached to each other for material enjoyment.

> "In these instructions of Lord Kapiladeva it is explained that not only is woman the gateway to hell for man, but man is also the gateway to hell for woman. It is a question of attachment. A man becomes attached to a woman because of her service, her beauty and many other assets, and similarly a woman becomes attached to a man for his giving her a nice place to live, ornaments, dress and children. It is a question of attachment for one another. As long as either is attached to the other for such material enjoyment, the woman is dangerous for the man, and the man is also dangerous for the woman."
>
> —*Śrīmad Bhāgavatam* 3.31.42 Bhaktivedanta purport

While these attachments are considered to be dangerous for those who are aspiring for spiritual advancement, the solution recommended by the Vaiṣṇava *ācāryas* is not to file for a divorce. Rather, they advise husbands and wives to remain together and, at the same time, focus on increasing their attachment to Kṛṣṇa.

> "But if the attachment is transferred to Kṛṣṇa, both of them become Kṛṣṇa conscious, and then marriage is very nice. Śrīla Rūpa Gosvāmī therefore recommends:
>
> *anāsaktasya viṣayān*
> *yathārham upayuñjataḥ*

nirbandhaḥ kṛṣṇa-sambandhe
yuktaṁ vairāgyam ucyate
(*Bhakti-rasāmṛta-sindhu* 1.2.255)"
—*Śrīmad Bhāgavatam* 3.31.42 Bhaktivedanta purport

> This verse translates as follows: "When one is not attached to anything, but at the same time accepts everything in relation to Kṛṣṇa, one is rightly situated above possessiveness."

This concept of *yukta-vairāgya*, as described by Rūpa Gosvāmī, is a core principle of Vaiṣṇava philosophy in practice. Instead of renouncing the world by rejecting matter, a *yukta-vairāgī* renounces by engaging everyone and everything in devotional service to the Lord. This is a beautifully practical process of spiritual life and is the secret of transcendence for *gṛhasthas*.

> "Man and woman should live together as householders in relationship with Kṛṣṇa, only for the purpose of discharging duties in the service of Kṛṣṇa. Engage the children, engage the wife and engage the husband, all in Kṛṣṇa conscious duties, and then all these bodily or material attachments will disappear. Since the via medium is Kṛṣṇa, the consciousness is pure, and there is no possibility of degradation at any time."
> —*Śrīmad Bhāgavatam* 3.31.42 Bhaktivedanta purport

As long as family members are engaged in devotional service to Kṛṣṇa, there is no danger of material attachment or degradation.

vāsudeve bhagavati
bhakti-yogaḥ prayojitaḥ
janayaty āśu vairāgyaṁ
jñānaṁ ca yad ahaitukam

"By rendering devotional service unto the Personality of Godhead, Śrī Kṛṣṇa, one immediately acquires causeless knowledge and detachment from the world."
—*Śrīmad Bhāgavatam* 1.2.7

Those who try to detach themselves from the material world by renouncing all material possessions and meditating on the impersonal Brahman are obliged to undergo severe penances and austerities.

kleśo 'dhikataras teṣām
avyaktāsakta-cetasām
avyaktā hi gatir duḥkhaṁ
dehavadbhir avāpyate

"For those whose minds are attached to the unmanifested, impersonal feature of the Supreme, advancement is very troublesome. To make progress in that discipline is always difficult for those who are embodied."
—*Bhagavad-gītā As It Is* 12.5

Devotees of the Lord, on the other hand, naturally develop detachment from matter by transferring their attachment to Kṛṣṇa. This is achieved by the simple and joyful process of engaging the senses in devotional service to the Lord.

ataḥ śrī-kṛṣṇa-nāmādi
na bhaved grāhyam indriyaiḥ
sevonmukhe hi jihvādau
svayam eva sphuraty adaḥ

> "The material senses cannot appreciate Kṛṣṇa's holy name, form, qualities and pastimes. When a conditioned soul renders service by using his tongue to chant the Lord's holy name and taste the remnants of the Lord's food, his tongue is purified, and he gradually comes to understand who Kṛṣṇa really is."
> —*Bhakti-rasāmṛta-sindhu* 1.2.234

Spiritualising Relationships

As a *gṛhastha* develops detachment from material possessions by engaging them in the service of God, the same principle can also be applied to bodily relationships.

> "As for detachment from children, wife and home, it is not meant that one should have no feeling for these. They are natural objects of affection. But when they are not favorable to spiritual progress, then one should not be attached to them."
> —*Bhagavad-gītā As It Is* 13.8-12 purport

Family affection cannot be cut off artificially, but can be spiritualised by the process of *bhakti-yoga*. This is explained in connection with the prayers of Kuntīdevī, who prayed to Lord Kṛṣṇa to cut off her ties of affection to her relatives so that her heart could repose on Him alone.

atha viśveśa viśvātman
viśva-mūrte svakeṣu me
sneha-pāśam imaṁ chindhi
dṛḍhaṁ pāṇḍuṣu vṛṣṇiṣu

tvayi me 'nanya-viṣayā
matir madhu-pate 'sakṛt
ratim udvahatād addhā
gaṅgevaugham udanvati

"O Lord of the universe, soul of the universe, O personality of the form of the universe, please, therefore, sever my tie of affection for my kinsmen, the Pāṇḍavas and the Vṛṣṇis. O Lord of Madhu, as the Ganges forever flows to the sea without hindrance, let my attraction be constantly drawn unto You without being diverted to anyone else."
—*Śrīmad Bhāgavatam* 1.8.41-2

By asking the Lord to sever her tie of affection for her kinsmen, Kuntīdevī was referring to family affection in connection with bodily relationships. However, since she and her relatives were all eternal associates of Lord Kṛṣṇa, she was actually related with them spiritually.

> "Her affection for the Pāṇḍavas and the Vṛṣṇis is not out of the range of devotional service because the service of the Lord and the service of the devotees are identical. Sometimes service to the devotee is more valuable than service to the Lord. But here the affection of Kuntīdevī for the Pāṇḍavas and the Vṛṣṇis was due to family relation. This tie of affection in

terms of material relation is the relation of *māyā* because the relations of the body or the mind are due to the influence of the external energy. Relations of the soul, established in relation with the Supreme Soul, are factual relations. When Kuntīdevī wanted to cut off the family relation, she meant to cut off the relation of the skin. The skin relation is the cause of material bondage, but the relation of the soul is the cause of freedom. This relation of the soul to the soul can be established by the via medium of the relation with the Supersoul. Seeing in the darkness is not seeing. But seeing by the light of the sun means to see the sun and everything else which was unseen in the darkness. That is the way of devotional service."

—*Śrīmad Bhāgavatam* 1.8.42 Bhaktivedanta purport

Relationships of the body bind the soul to material existence. The same relationships however, when raised to the spiritual platform by devotional service to the Lord, can become liberating. As eternal souls, our relationships with each other are originally pure and spiritual in connection with our eternal Master. When we come in contact with the material energy, under the influence of false ego, we identify ourselves with our minds and bodies, and our close relationships become infected by separatist desires for control and enjoyment. Relationships can become purified again by reconnection with the Supreme Personality of Godhead in devotional service. When family members serve God together, they learn to appreciate each other as servants of God, and thus their relationships with each other become gradually spiritualised. When dormant love of God is reawakened in the heart, it is accompanied by spiritual love and empathy for all living entities, since they are all part and parcel of Him.

> "God is the center of love, and since everything is God's expansion, the lover of God is a lover of everyone."
>
> —*Beyond Illusion and Doubt* 7

Real detachment is attained by seeing every person as the Lord's servant and every object as His property.

vidyā-vinaya-sampanne
brāhmaṇe gavi hastini
śuni caiva śva-pāke ca
paṇḍitāḥ sama-darśinaḥ

> "The humble sages, by virtue of true knowledge, see with equal vision a learned and gentle *brāhmaṇa*, a cow, an elephant, a dog and a dog-eater (outcaste)."
>
> —*Bhagavad-gītā As It Is* 5.18

One who engages himself, his family members and his possessions in the service of the Lord can attain perfect detachment.

> "*Bhagavad-gītā* (5.17) further elucidates that when a learned man attains to absolute vision, he can observe every living being—whether a learned and gentle *brahmaṇa*, a cow, an elephant, a dog, or a dog-eater—with equanimity. A learned and gentle *brahmaṇa* is

the embodiment of nature's mode of goodness. Among the beasts, the cow is the embodiment of this same mode of goodness. The elephant and the lion are embodiments of the passionate mode of nature, while the dog and the *caṇḍāla* (dog-eater) are the embodiments of nature's mode of darkness, or ignorance. However, instead of focusing on the various external tabernacles of these living entities (their embodiments under various modes of nature), with his absolute vision the *karma-yogī* penetrates to the spirit which is embodied therein. And because this infinitesimal spirit emanates from the infinite Supreme Spirit, the *karma-yogī* in the highest state can observe everyone and everything with equanimity. Such a *karma-yogī* views everything in relation to the Absolute, and therefore he engages everything in the transcendental service of the Absolute. He observes all living entities as so many transcendental servitors of the absolute Godhead, Śrī Kṛṣṇa. His perfect spiritual vision cannot but penetrate the encagement of every material body, just as a red-hot iron cannot but burn everything that it contacts. Thus, the *karma-yogī* sets an example of transcendental character, by engaging everyone and everything in the transcendental service of the Personality of Godhead."

—*Message of Godhead* 2

Real love and affection for those who are near and dear is demonstrated by the action of giving Kṛṣṇa consciousness to family members.

"You can save your son, your disciple, your relative or anyone whom you love, with real affection. Give them Kṛṣṇa consciousness, and they'll be saved from death."
—Bhaktivedanta lecture, *Śrīmad Bhāgavatam* 1.8.47
Māyāpura 27/10/ 1974

Simple Living

While performing regular duties, *gṛhasthas* develop internal detachment from the material world by keeping their lives as simple as possible. In the meantime, to avoid disturbing the minds of their friends and relatives, they continue to play the part of attached householders.

"An intelligent man in human society should make his own program of activities very simple. If there are suggestions from his friends, children, parents, brothers or anyone else, he should externally agree, saying, 'Yes, that is all right,' but internally he should be determined not to create a cumbersome life in which the purpose of life will not be fulfilled."
—*Śrīmad Bhāgavatam* 7.14.6

Wise householders develop detachment by practising 'simple living and high thinking'. Instead of over-endeavouring for excessive economic development and sense enjoyment, they save time for cultivating spiritual knowledge.

"A wise man, however, learns from the *śāstras* and *guru* that we living entities are all eternal but are put into troublesome conditions because of associating with different modes under the laws of material nature. He therefore concludes that in the human form of life he should not endeavor for unnecessary necessities, but should live a very simple life, just maintaining body and soul together. Certainly one requires some means of livelihood, and according to one's *varṇa* and *āśrama* this means of livelihood is prescribed in the *śāstras*. One should be satisfied with this. Therefore, instead of hankering for more and more money, a sincere devotee of the Lord tries to invent some ways to earn his livelihood, and when he does so Kṛṣṇa helps him. Earning one's livelihood, therefore, is not a problem. The real problem is how to get free from the bondage of birth, death and old age. Attaining this freedom, and not inventing unnecessary necessities, is the basic principle of Vedic civilization. One should be satisfied with whatever means of life comes automatically. The modern materialistic civilization is just the opposite of the ideal civilization. Every day the so-called leaders of modern society invent something contributing to a cumbersome way of life that implicates people more and more in the cycle of birth, death, old age and disease."

—*Śrīmad Bhāgavatam* 7.14.5 Bhaktivedanta purport

In the modern world new gadgets are continually being invented to facilitate material enjoyment. To practise *yukta-vairāgya* is not to necessarily reject all the inventions of modern technology, but rather to accept whatever is favourable for devotional service to the Lord and reject whatever is unfavourable.

> "This devotional service means to accept favourable and reject unfavourable. This is called *śaraṇāgati*. Surrender means to accept favourable things, how I can make progress towards Kṛṣṇa; and *prātikūlya*, *pratikūla* means rejecting unfavourable things which are not very congenial for my progress in Kṛṣṇa consciousness."
>
> —Bhaktivedanta lecture, *Bhagavad-gītā* 18.67
> Ahmedabad 10/12/1972

A *gṛhastha* practises simple living and high thinking by collecting as much as necessary to maintain his family and to facilitate his service to the Lord and to his community.

> "Whether he is an impersonalist or a devotee, one who is actually interested in advancing spiritually should not mingle with those who are simply interested in maintaining the body by means of the so-called advancement of civilization. Those who are interested in spiritual life should not be attached to homely comforts in the company of wife, children, friends and so forth. Even if one is a *gṛhastha* and has to earn his livelihood, he should be satisfied by collecting only enough money to maintain body and soul together. One should not have more than that nor less than that. As indicated herein, a householder should endeavor to earn money for the execution of *bhakti-*

yoga (śravaṇaṁ kīrtanaṁ viṣṇoḥ smaraṇaṁ pāda-sevanam/ arcanaṁ vandanaṁ dāsyaṁ sakhyam ātma-nivedanam). A householder should lead such a life that he gets full opportunity to hear and chant. He should worship the Deity at home, observe festivals, invite friends in and give them *prasāda*. A householder should earn money for this purpose, not for sense gratification."

—*Śrīmad Bhāgavatam* 5.5.3 Bhaktivedanta purport

According to the *Upadeśāmṛta* of Rūpa Gosvāmī, to collect more than necessary and to over endeavour for mundane things that are difficult to obtain are two of the six activities that are unfavourable for progress in devotional service.

atyāhāraḥ prayāsaś ca
prajalpo niyamāgrahaḥ
jana-saṅgaś ca laulyaṁ ca
ṣaḍbhir bhaktir vinaśyati

"One's devotional service is spoiled when he becomes too entangled in the following six activities: (1) eating more than necessary or collecting more funds than required; (2) over endeavoring for mundane things that are very difficult to obtain; (3) talking unnecessarily about mundane subject matters; (4) practicing the scriptural rules and regulations only for the sake of following them and not for the sake of spiritual advancement, or rejecting the rules and regulations of the scriptures and working independently or whimsically; (5) associating with

> worldly-minded persons who are not interested in Kṛṣṇa consciousness; and (6) being greedy for mundane achievements."
>
> —*The Nectar of Instruction* 2

A householder who is serious about spiritual life, while dutifully maintaining his family, is not inclined to collect more than necessary.

> "Those who are interested in reviving Kṛṣṇa consciousness and increasing their love of Godhead do not like to do anything that is not related to Kṛṣṇa. They are not interested in mingling with people who are busy maintaining their bodies, eating, sleeping, mating and defending. They are not attached to their homes, although they may be householders. Nor are they attached to wives, children, friends or wealth. At the same time, they are not indifferent to the execution of their duties. Such people are interested in collecting only enough money to keep the body and soul together."
>
> —*Śrīmad Bhāgavatam* 5.5.3

A devotee of the Lord also avoids eating or sleeping more than necessary, and in this way saves time for devotional service.

> "Another feature of the devotee is *nirīhayā*, simple living. *Nirīhā* means 'gentle,' 'meek' or 'simple'. A devotee should not live very gorgeously and imitate a materialistic person. Plain living and high thinking are recommended for a devotee. He should accept only

so much as he needs to keep the material body fit for the execution of devotional service. He should not eat or sleep more than is required. Simply eating for living, and not living for eating, and sleeping only six to seven hours a day are principles to be followed by devotees."

—*Śrīmad Bhāgavatam* 4.22.24 Bhaktivedanta purport

A famous example of a spiritually advanced householder is Sudāmā, the *brāhmaṇa* friend of Lord Kṛṣṇa. He was not anxious to accumulate wealth, but simply depended on the Lord for his livelihood and surrendered to his destiny.

"Although the *brāhmaṇa* friend of Lord Kṛṣṇa was a householder, he was not busy accumulating wealth for very comfortable living; therefore he was satisfied by the income which automatically came to him according to his destiny. This is the sign of perfect knowledge. A man in perfect knowledge knows that one cannot be happier than he is destined to be. In this material world, everyone is destined to suffer a certain amount of distress and enjoy a certain amount of happiness. The amount of happiness and distress is already predestined for every living entity. No one can increase or decrease the happiness of the materialistic way of life. The *brāhmaṇa*, therefore, did not exert himself for more material happiness; instead, he used his time for advancement of Kṛṣṇa consciousness."

Kṛṣṇa the Supreme Personality of Godhead 80

One time Sudāmā and his wife were living in poverty and were becoming thin due to lack of sufficient food. Sudāmā's wife, being concerned for his welfare, requested him to approach Lord Kṛṣṇa in Dvārakā for help. Sudāmā very happily undertook the journey to visit the Lord, but he did not ask Kṛṣṇa for anything. The Lord was so moved by Sudāmā's love for Him and by his renunciation, that He bestowed great wealth on the poor *brāhmaṇa*. When Sudāmā returned home, he found that his humble hut had become transformed into a gorgeous palace. Rather than becoming bewildered by his newly acquired opulence, he accepted it as *prasādam* (God's mercy), and engaged it all in the service of the Lord.

> "The learned *brāhmaṇa* thus concluded that whatever opulences he had received from the Lord should be used not for his extravagant sense gratification but for the service of the Lord. The *brāhmaṇa* accepted his newly acquired opulence, but he did so in a spirit of renunciation, remaining unattached to sense gratification, and thus he lived very peacefully with his wife, enjoying all the facilities of opulence as the *prasādam* of the Lord. He enjoyed varieties of food by offering it to the Lord and then taking it as *prasādam*. Similarly, if by the grace of the Lord we get such opulences as material wealth, fame, power, education and beauty, it is our duty to consider that they are all gifts of the Lord and must be used for His service, not for our sense enjoyment. The learned *brāhmaṇa* remained in that position, and thus his love and

> affection for Lord Kṛṣṇa increased day after day; it did not deteriorate due to great opulence. Material opulence can be the cause of degradation and also the cause of elevation, according to the purposes for which it is used. If opulence is used for sense gratification it is the cause of degradation, and if used for the service of the Lord it is the cause of elevation."
>
> —*Kṛṣṇa the Supreme Personality of Godhead* 81

A Vaiṣṇava *gṛhastha* uses whatever wealth he receives to maintain himself and his family for the purpose of spiritual advancement rather than simply for material enjoyment.

> "Those who are faithful in hearing the topics of the Lord after receiving His mercy on the strength of their accumulated pious activities from many lifetimes are no longer attached to *karma*. They are called Vaiṣṇavas. Among them, those who are *gṛhasthas* enjoy whatever *artha* they obtain while practicing *dharma* for the purpose of liberation, not for the purpose of sense gratification; rather, this *artha* helps them purely maintain their lives in the favorable cultivation of Kṛṣṇa consciousness with the purpose of understanding the Absolute Truth. In this, the difference between *karma* and spiritual activities can be seen."
>
> —Bhaktivinoda Ṭhākura, *Śrī Bhaktyāloka* 11

Householders can also simplify their lives by growing their own food, as far as possible, thus reducing their dependence on others. Rural farm communities provide an ideal setting for self-sufficient living. Country life is conducive to the mode of goodness, while city life is more in the mode of passion.

> "It is by ignorance that people think that by opening factories they will be happy. Why should they open factories? There is no need. There is so much land, and one can produce one's own food grains and eat sumptuously without any factory. Milk is also available without a factory. The factory cannot produce milk or grains. The present scarcity of food in the world is largely due to such factories. When everyone is working in the city to produce nuts and bolts, who will produce food grains? Simple living and high thinking is the solution to economic problems. Therefore the Kṛṣṇa consciousness movement is engaging devotees in producing their own food and living self-sufficiently so that rascals may see how one can live very peacefully, eat the food grains one has grown oneself, drink milk, and chant Hare Kṛṣṇa."
>
> —*Teachings of Queen Kuntī* 18

Nowadays many householders live in urban settings and own neither a cow nor enough land to become self-sufficient. They are obliged to work hard for money to buy food and pay bills. Those who are blessed with gardens or allotments can at least reduce their food bills by growing fruits and vegetables, and fuel bills can be reduced by the use of natural free fuels such as wood. Householders can also reduce their expenses by shopping with restraint and cooking at home.

Modern stores and supermarkets are designed to entice the senses, inducing people to spend more than necessary. Those who shop like *yogīs* can protect themselves from being exploited by controlling the senses, buying no more than necessary, and selecting natural foods in the mode of goodness to offer to Kṛṣṇa. Money represents Lakṣmī-devī, the consort of the Supreme Lord, and should be carefully protected and engaged in His service. While household life is generally filled up with unending duties and obligations, when a householder becomes advanced in Kṛṣṇa consciousness, his material activities naturally become simplified as he gives priority to his spiritual life.

> "The innumerable obligations performed on behalf of wife and children constantly harass a householder, but as he becomes advanced in loving service to Kṛṣṇa, he is automatically elevated by the laws of nature to more enjoyable, spiritual occupations, and he somehow minimizes material duties."
> —*Śrīmad-Bhāgavatam* 10.20.34 purport by Hṛdayānanda Goswami

Vānaprastha-āśrama

As *gṛhasthas* mature and learn to simplify their lives, they are naturally preparing themselves to move on to the next stage of life, the *vānaprastha-āśrama*, when the time is right. This is the state of retirement from family life, ideally beginning at the age of around fifty years. *Vana* means forest, and the traditional practice of *vānaprastha* life is to give up material comforts and live in the forest.

"Therefore, I shall now give up all these desires and meditate upon the Supreme Personality of Godhead. Free from the dualities of mental concoction and free from false prestige, I shall wander in the forest with the animals."

—*Śrīmad Bhāgavatam* 9.19.19

Bhaktivedanta purport:

"To go to the forest and live there with the animals, meditating upon the Supreme Personality of Godhead, is the only means by which to give up lusty desires. Unless one gives up such desires, one's mind cannot be freed from material contamination. Therefore, if one is at all interested in being freed from the bondage of repeated birth, death, old age and disease, after a certain age one must go to the forest – *pañcāśordhvaṁ vanaṁ vrajet*. After fifty years of age, one should voluntarily give up family life and go to the forest."

The sacred forest of Vṛndāvana, where Kṛṣṇa performed His transcendental pastimes on earth, is an ideal place for devotees of Kṛṣṇa to practise *vānaprastha* life.

"The best forest is Vṛndāvana, where one need not live with the animals but can associate with the Supreme Personality of Godhead, who never leaves Vṛndāvana. Cultivating Kṛṣṇa consciousness in Vṛndāvana is the best means of being liberated from material bondage, for in Vṛndāvana one can automatically meditate upon Kṛṣṇa. Vṛndāvana has many temples, and in one or more of these temples one may see the form of the Supreme Lord as Rādhā-Kṛṣṇa or Kṛṣṇa-Balarāma and meditate upon this form. As expressed here by the words *brahmaṇy adhyāya*, one should concentrate one's mind upon the Supreme Lord, Parabrahman. This Parabrahman is Kṛṣṇa, as confirmed by Arjuna in *Bhagavad-gītā (paraṁ brahma paraṁ dhāma pavitraṁ paramaṁ bhavān)*. Kṛṣṇa and His abode, Vṛndāvana, are not different. Śrī Caitanya Mahāprabhu said, *ārādhyo bhagavān vrajeśa-tanayas tad-dhāma vṛndāvanam*. Vṛndāvana is as good as Kṛṣṇa. Therefore, if one somehow or other gets the opportunity to live in Vṛndāvana, and if one is not a pretender but simply lives in Vṛndāvana and concentrates his mind upon Kṛṣṇa, one is liberated from material bondage."

—*Śrīmad Bhāgavatam* 9.19.19 Bhaktivedanta purport

Vānaprasthas may also sometimes travel around, visiting various places of pilgrimage.

"This preparatory stage is called *vānaprastha-āśrama*, or retired life for travelling and visiting the holy places on the surface of the earth. In the holy places of India, like Vṛndāvana, Hardwar, Jagannātha Purī, and Prayāga, there are many great devotees, and there are still free kitchen houses for persons who desire to advance spiritually."

—*Śrīmad Bhāgavatam* 1.13.9 Bhaktivedanta purport

Wherever one chooses to spend the years of retirement, the main principle of *vānaprastha-āśrama* is to somehow or other develop detachment from family life and take full shelter of the Supreme Lord.

> "Going to the forest is compulsory for everyone. It is not a mental excursion upon which one person goes and another does not. Everyone should go to the forest at least as a *vānaprastha*. Forest-going means to take one-hundred-percent shelter of the Supreme Lord, as explained by Prahlāda Mahārāja in his talks with his father. *Sadā samudvigna-dhiyām* (*SB* 7.5.5). People who have accepted a temporary, material body are always full of anxieties. One should not, therefore, be very much affected by this material body, but should try to be freed. The preliminary process to become freed is to go to the forest or give up family relationships and exclusively engage in Kṛṣṇa consciousness. That is the purpose of going to the forest. Otherwise, the forest is only a place of monkeys and wild animals. To go to the forest does not mean to become a monkey or a ferocious animal. It means to accept exclusively the shelter of the Supreme Personality of Godhead and engage oneself in full service. One does not actually have to go to the forest. At the present moment this is not at all advisable for a man who has spent his life all along in big cities."
>
> —*Śrīmad Bhāgavatam* 3.24.41 Bhaktivedanta purport

The entrance into *vānaprastha-āśrama* is usually a gradual process of transition. During this stage a husband and wife may spend some time travelling and some time at home with their grown-up children.

> "This affection is a very hard knot for being bound up in this material world. Therefore, the Vedic civilisation enjoins that it is compulsory that the affection is cut off at a certain age, not that the affection should continue. If the affection continues, then there is no chance of becoming free from this material world. There is no chance. Therefore, *vānaprastha*. Affection for the wife is very, very strong. *Vānaprastha* means that the husband and wife give up the affection. Not give up, but go away from home, and they travel in the holy places just for purification, and then again, when drawn by family affection, they come back to the family. They remain again for one or two months, and then again they go away. There is no sex connection, but the wife remains as an assistant to the man to become accustomed to remaining aloof from the family. When he is well practised to remain aloof, then his wife is sent back to the family, to the care of the older children, and the man takes *sannyāsa*. This is compulsory. It is called 'civil suicide'. My *guru mahārāja* used to say, 'Commit civil suicide'."
>
> —Bhaktivedanta lecture, *Śrīmad Bhāgavatam* 1.8.41
> Māyāpura 21/10/74

To enter the *vānaprastha-āśrama* means to find a way to extricate oneself from *artha* and *kāma*, and to focus on *mokṣa*.

> "At the *vānaprastha* stage of retired life, or the stage midway between householder life and renounced life, one may keep his wife as an assistant without sex relations, but in the *sannyāsa* order of life one cannot keep his wife with him."
>
> —*Śrīmad Bhāgavatam* 3.24.40 Bhaktivedanta purport

Preaching and teaching are also suitable activities for *vānaprasthas*. In Vedic society a *vānaprastha brāhmaṇa* couple would often transform their forest *āśrama* into a *gurukula* for training *brahmacārī* students.

At the final stage of life, when a man takes *sannyāsa*, his wife also takes *sannyāsa*, not externally like him, but internally. As he renounces her association to focus on their spiritual future, she must also renounce his. By separating themselves from each other physically, they become even closer spiritually. The former wife of a *sannyāsī* traditionally remains with her grown-up sons for her protection. She lives a simple life, devoted to God, and becomes a spiritual role model for her family and community.

Five Kinds of Liberation

There are five different kinds of liberation described in the Vedic scriptures, as follows: 1) *sālokya* – to live on the same planet as the Lord; 2) *sārūpya* – to obtain the same bodily features as the Lord; 3) *sāmīpya* – to live in constant association with the Lord; 4) *sārṣṭi* – to achieve the same opulence as the Lord; and 5) *sāyujya* – to become one with the Lord. The last one, to become one with God, is aspired for by impersonalists and shunned by devotees.

> "A pure devotee does not like even to hear about *sāyujya-mukti*, which inspires him with fear and hatred. Indeed, the pure devotee would rather go to hell than merge into the effulgence of the Lord."
> —*Śrī Caitanya-caritāmṛta, Madhya-līlā* 6.268

Māyāvādīs, who negate the personal form of the Lord, aspire to merge with His Brahman effulgence and in this way become free from material suffering. This type of liberation is not eternal, however, since the soul is a person and naturally hankers for personal interaction.

> "O lotus-eyed Lord, although nondevotees who accept severe austerities and penances to achieve the highest position may think themselves liberated, their intelligence is impure. They fall down from their position of imagined superiority because they have no regard for Your lotus feet."
> —*Śrīmad Bhāgavatam* 10.2.32

Impersonal liberation, or merging with Brahman, is an attempt to attain relief from suffering by negating one's individual identity. Those who aim for this are deprived of the transcendental happiness that is derived from serving the Supreme Personality of Godhead.

> "There are two types of liberation – relief from extreme distress and attaining spiritual happiness. Those whose religious lives are regulated by dry knowledge

or impersonalism, for them relief from extreme distress is the prime goal. Those whose hearts are filled with pure knowledge ultimately search for transcendental happiness and do not remain bound in simply gaining relief from extreme distress. A Vaiṣṇava, whether a householder or a renunciant, is desirous of transcendental happiness. A householder Vaiṣṇava always works together with his wife with the aim of achieving transcendental happiness."

—Bhaktivinoda Ṭhākura, *Śrī Bhaktyāloka* 11

Apart from merging with Brahman, a devotee may sometimes accept one of the other four types of liberation, if it is favourable for devotional service.

"If there is a chance to serve the Supreme Personality of Godhead, a pure devotee sometimes accepts the *sālokya, sārūpya, sāmīpya* or *sārṣṭi* forms of liberation, but never *sāyujya*."

—*Śrī Caitanya-caritāmṛta, Madhya-līlā* 6.267

Those who become fully satisfied by serving the Lord no longer aspire for any kind of liberation. Nevertheless, the four types of liberation are awarded to them automatically.

"My devotees, who are always satisfied to be engaged in My loving service, are not interested even in the four principles of liberation (*sālokya, sārūpya, sāmīpya* and *sārṣṭi*), although these are automatically achieved by their service. What then is to be said of such perishable happiness as elevation to the higher planetary systems?"

—*Śrīmad Bhāgavatam* 9.4.67

Bhakti (Pure Devotional Service)

The perfection of the pursuance of *dharma, artha, kāma,* and *mokṣa* is to attain *bhakti*, pure devotional service to the Supreme Personality of Godhead.

> "The purpose of *dharma-artha-kāma-mokṣa* means to come to this platform of *bhakti*."
>
> —Bhaktivedanta lecture, *Śrīmad Bhāgavatam* 7.9.9
> Montreal 6/7/1968

Pure devotional service is so relishable that even the Supreme Lord derives more pleasure from serving His devotees than from receiving their service. For example, Lord Kṛṣṇa chose to become the chariot driver of His devotee Arjuna on the battlefield of Kurukṣetra. One who becomes liberated from material desires can taste the nectar of pure devotional service.

brahma-bhūtaḥ prasannātmā
na śocati na kāṅkṣati
samaḥ sarveṣu bhūteṣu
mad-bhaktiṁ labhate parām

> "One who is thus transcendentally situated at once realizes the Supreme Brahman and becomes fully joyful. He never laments or desires to have anything. He is equally disposed toward every living entity. In that state he attains pure devotional service unto Me."
>
> —*Bhagavad-gītā As It Is* 18.54

> "Without being on the platform of *mokṣa*, no one can enter into *bhakti*. It is a misconception that *bhakti* helps *mokṣa*. *Bhakti* begins when one is already liberated – *mokṣa*. *Brahma-bhūtaḥ prasannātmā*. Without Brahman realisation, *ahaṁ brahmāsmi*, there cannot be jubilation, *prasannātmā*. This is the sign. What is *prasannātmā*? *Na śocati na kāṅkṣati*. The material disease is that everyone is hankering after something that he hasn't got, and when he loses something, he's lamenting. These two businesses: *śocati kāṅkṣati*. So *brahma-bhūtaḥ prasannātmā*, when one is actually self-realised, *brahma-bhūtaḥ*, *na śocati na kāṅkṣati*. This is the symptom, and then *samaḥ sarveṣu bhūteṣu*. It is possible to see everyone equally. *Paṇḍitāḥ sama-darśinaḥ*. That is the liberated stage. When one has come to the liberated stage, from that platform he can begin *mad-bhaktiṁ labhate parām*. *Bhakti* means the activities of the liberated stage."
>
> —Bhaktivedanta lecture, *Śrīmad Bhāgavatam* 1.7.6
> Hyderabad 18/8/1976

While some householders may aspire for liberation or for elevation to the heavenly planets, those who are pure devotees of the Lord aspire only for devotional service.

> "Liberation may appear before me. The enduring kingdom of Lord Brahma may also appear before me. I do not care for them. I simply desire to serve Lord Kṛṣṇa, the leader of the cowherd boys."
>
> —Śrī Surottamācārya (*Padyāvalī* 84)

Those who are fully engaged in devotional service do not worry about liberation, but leave that in the hands of the Lord. For them liberation is automatically attained without any separate endeavour. This has been vividly portrayed in the following verse by Bilvamaṅgala Ṭhākura.

> "If I am engaged in devotional service unto You, my dear Lord, then very easily can I perceive Your presence everywhere. And as far as liberation is concerned, I think that liberation stands at my door with folded hands, waiting to serve me, and all material conveniences of *dharma* (religiosity), *artha* (economic development) and *kāma* (sense gratification) stand with her."
>
> —*Kṛṣṇa-karṇāmṛta* 107

One of the innumerable names of the Supreme Lord is Mukunda, 'the bestower of liberation'.

> "The words 'Kṛṣṇa! Kṛṣṇa!' are sufficient to purify the people's sins. If they have blissful service to Lord Mukunda, then the goddess of liberation bows before their lotus feet."
>
> —Śrī Sarvajña (*Padyāvalī* 12)

Householder men and women are engaged in many so-called 'material activities', but if they carry out their duties in Kṛṣṇa consciousness, they are considered to be already liberated.

īhā yasya harer dāsye
karmaṇā manasā girā

nikhilāsv apy avasthāsu
jīvan-muktaḥ sa ucyate

> "A person acting in the service of Kṛṣṇa with body, mind, intelligence and words is a liberated person even within the material world, although he may be engaged in many so-called material activities."
> —Rūpa Gosvāmī, *Bhakti-rasāmṛta-sindhu* 1.2.187

Since liberation is automatically included within pure devotional service, it can be understood that *bhakti* is higher than *mokṣa*. Even those who are already liberated become attracted to Kṛṣṇa.

ātmārāmāś ca munayo
nirgranthā apy urukrame
kurvanty ahaitukīṁ bhaktim
ittham-bhūta-guṇo hariḥ

> "All different varieties of *ātmārāmas* (those who take pleasure in *ātmā*, or spirit self), especially those established on the path of self-realization, though freed from all kinds of material bondage, desire to render unalloyed devotional service unto the Personality of Godhead. This means that the Lord possesses transcendental qualities and therefore can attract everyone, including liberated souls."
> —*Śrīmad Bhāgavatam* 1.7.10

For those who are engaged in pure devotional service, all other kinds of happiness are automatically supplied to them by the Lord, even without their asking.

"It is stated that as the personal attendants and maidservants of a queen follow the queen with all respect and obeisances, similarly the joys of religiousness, economic development, sense gratification and liberation follow the devotional service of the Lord. In other words, a pure devotee does not lack any kind of happiness derived from any source. He does not want anything but service to Kṛṣṇa, but even if he should have another desire, the Lord fulfills this without the devotee's asking."

—*The Nectar of Devotion* 1

Each devotee has his/her own eternal relationship with the Lord, flavoured by either neutrality, servitude, friendship, parental affection, or conjugal love.

"Direct devotional service is divided into five transcendental humors or flavors... as follows: neutrality, servitude, fraternity, paternity and conjugal love."

—*The Nectar of Devotion* 34

The nature of that spiritual relationship cannot be understood as long as we are subject to material influences. Devotees execute their devotional service in this world according to rules and regulations, as prescribed in *The Nectar of Devotion*, and under the guidance of a bona fide Vaiṣṇava *guru*. This is called *sādhana-bhakti*.

"When we wish to develop our innate capacity for devotional service, there are certain processes which, by our accepting and executing them, will cause that

> dormant capacity to be invoked. Such practice is called *sādhana-bhakti*."
>
> —*The Nectar of Devotion* 2

Only when a devotee has attained pure *bhakti*, free from all material contamination, will his eternal relationship with Kṛṣṇa eventually be revealed to him by the mercy of the *guru* and the holy name.

> "People generally believe that God is the father, and the son's business is to ask the father for whatever he needs. But that is really a lesser relationship. If you understand God perfectly, then there are intimate relationships also. Your intimate relationship will be revealed when you are perfectly liberated. Each and every living creature has a particular relationship with God, but we have, for now, forgotten. When that relationship is revealed in the process of devotional activities, or Kṛṣṇa consciousness, you will know that that is the perfection of your life."
>
> —*Kṛṣṇa Consciousness the Topmost Yoga System* 2

Pañcama-puruṣārtha (The Fifth Goal)

Beyond the four goals of human life, there is a fifth goal, which is transcendental to all of them and is the highest perfection of life. This goal can be attained only by the practice of devotional service.

> "It is clearly stated by Kapila Muni that *bhakti* activities, or activities in devotional service, are

> transcendental to *mukti*. This is called *pañcama-puruṣārtha*."
>
> —*Śrīmad Bhāgavatam* 3.25.34 Bhaktivedanta purport

The fifth goal is known as *prema*, or pure love of God. For those who have experienced even a small taste of this *prema*, the other four goals become insignificant.

> "Religiosity, economic development, sense gratification and liberation are known as the four goals of life, but before love of Godhead, the fifth and highest goal, these appear as insignificant as straw in the street."
>
> —*Śrī Caitanya-caritāmṛta, Ādi-līlā* 7.84

Śrī Caitanya Mahāprabhu is known as the most munificent incarnation of God because He appeared on earth to distribute *prema*, pure love for Kṛṣṇa.

namo mahā-vadānyāya
kṛṣṇa-prema-pradāya te
kṛṣṇāya kṛṣṇa-caitanya-
nāmne gaura-tviṣe namaḥ

> "O most munificent incarnation! You are Kṛṣṇa Himself appearing as Śrī Kṛṣṇa Caitanya Mahāprabhu. You have assumed the golden colour of Śrīmatī Rādhārāṇī, and You are widely distributing pure love of Kṛṣṇa. We offer our respectful obeisances unto You."
>
> —*Śrī Caitanya-caritāmṛta, Madhya-līlā* 19.53

Śrī Caitanya Mahāprabhu distributed Kṛṣṇa-*prema* by introducing the congregational chanting of the *mahā-mantra* (Hare Kṛṣṇa, Hare Kṛṣṇa, Kṛṣṇa Kṛṣṇa, Hare Hare; Hare Rāma, Hare Rāma, Rāma Rāma, Hare Hare) throughout the sub-continent of India. He was accompanied by His four principal associates, and together they are known as Pañca-tattva (the Absolute Truth in five features).

> "Śrī Caitanya Mahāprabhu is always accompanied by His plenary expansion Śrī Nityānanda Prabhu, His incarnation Śrī Advaita Prabhu, His internal potency Śrī Gadādhara Prabhu and His marginal potency Śrīvāsa Prabhu."
>
> —*Śrī Caitanya-caritāmṛta, Ādi-līlā* 7.4 Bhaktivedanta purport

The recommended process for achieving Kṛṣṇa-*prema* is to first take shelter of these merciful personalities by chanting the Pañca-tattva *mantra, śrī kṛṣṇa caitanya prabhu nityānanda śrī advaita gadādhara śrīvāsādi gaura bhakta vṛnda*, before chanting the Hare Kṛṣṇa *mahā-mantra*.

> "There are ten offences in the chanting of the Hare Kṛṣṇa *mahā-mantra*, but these are not considered in the chanting of the Pañca-tattva *mantra*, namely, *śrī kṛṣṇa caitanya prabhu nityānanda śrī advaita gadādhara śrīvāsādi gaura bhakta vṛnda*. Śrī Caitanya Mahāprabhu is known as *mahā-vadānyāvatāra*, the most magnanimous incarnation, for He does not consider the offences of the fallen souls. Thus to derive the full benefit of the chanting of the *mahā-mantra* (Hare Kṛṣṇa, Hare Kṛṣṇa, Kṛṣṇa Kṛṣṇa, Hare

> Hare; Hare Rāma, Hare Rāma, Rāma Rāma, Hare Hare), we must first take shelter of Śrī Caitanya Mahāprabhu, learn the Pañca-tattva *mahā-mantra*, and then chant the Hare Kṛṣṇa *mahā-mantra*. That will be very effective."
>
> —*Śrī Caitanya-caritāmṛta*, *Ādi-līlā* 7.4 Bhaktivedanta purport

Householders who pursue *artha* and *kāma* without caring for *dharma* and *mokṣa* are destined to take birth again and again in the material world, in various species of life, to enjoy and suffer the results of their fruitive activities.

> "Persons devoid of *ātma-tattva* do not inquire into the problems of life, being too attached to the fallible soldiers like the body, children and wife. Although sufficiently experienced, they still do not see their inevitable destruction."
>
> —*Śrīmad Bhāgavatam* 2.1.4

Those who pursue *varṇāśrama-dharma*, *artha*, and *kāma* with the aim of attaining heavenly planets for higher material enjoyment may reach their desired destination. However, this is a temporary situation and, once their pious credits are exhausted, they will return to planet Earth.

> "In the process of sacrifice, the living entity makes specific sacrifices to attain specific heavenly planets and consequently reaches them. When the merit of sacrifice is exhausted, the living entity descends to earth in the form of rain, then takes on the form of grains, and the grains are eaten by man and

> transformed into semen, which impregnates a woman, and thus the living entity once again attains the human form to perform sacrifice and so repeat the same cycle."
>
> —*Bhagavad-gītā As It Is* 8.3 purport

Those who have acquired some spiritual knowledge, *ātma-tattva*, and who pursue *dharma*, *artha*, *kāma* and *mokṣa* with the aim of attaining impersonal liberation may eventually attain that goal. However, this type of liberation is also not eternal, but is only a temporary negation of suffering.

> "When the materialist becomes frustrated in his attempts to enjoy himself in the limited material world, he may seek impersonal liberation by merging either with the Causal Ocean or with the impersonal *brahmajyoti* effulgence. However, as neither the Causal Ocean nor the impersonal *brahmajyoti* effulgence affords any superior substitute for association and engagement of the senses, the impersonalist will fall again into the limited material world to become entangled once more in the wheel of births and deaths, drawn on by the inextinguishable desire for sensual engagement."
>
> —*Śrīmad-Bhāgavatam* 2.2.31 Bhaktivedanta purport

Those householders who worship the Supreme Personality of Godhead in awe and reverence, and who pursue *dharma*, *artha*, *kāma* and *mokṣa* according to Vedic injunctions, with the aim of attaining any of the other four kinds of liberation, may also attain their goal by being promoted to the

Vaikuṇṭha planets. From there it is also possible to eventually become elevated to Kṛṣṇaloka.

> "Those who are already promoted to the Vaikuṇṭha planets and who possess the four kinds of liberation may also sometimes develop affection for Kṛṣṇa and become promoted to Kṛṣṇaloka. So those who are in the four liberated states may still be going through different stages of existence. In the beginning they may want the opulences of Kṛṣṇa, but at the mature stage the dormant love for Kṛṣṇa exhibited in Vṛndāvana becomes prominent in their hearts."
>
> —*The Nectar of Devotion* 4

And those who pursue *dharma, artha, kāma* and *mokṣa* according to the teachings of Śrī Caitanya Mahāprabhu, with the aim of attaining the fifth goal, pure love of Godhead, can procure that topmost treasure. Eventually they will reach the highest destination, Goloka Vṛndāvana, never to return again to the material world of birth and death.

> "Out of many kinds of devotees of the Supreme Personality of Godhead, the one who is attracted to the original form of the Lord, Kṛṣṇa in Vṛndāvana, is considered to be the foremost, first-class devotee. Such a devotee is never attracted by the opulences of Vaikuṇṭha, or even of Dvārakā, the royal city where Kṛṣṇa ruled. The conclusion of Śrī Rūpa Gosvāmī is that the devotees who are attracted by the pastimes of the Lord in Gokula, or Vṛndāvana, are the topmost devotees."
>
> —*The Nectar of Devotion* 4

By becoming deeply attracted to Kṛṣṇa's transcendental pastimes with His loving devotees in Vṛndāvana, a devotee becomes eligible to attain the highest destination.

janma karma ca me divyam
evaṁ yo vetti tattvataḥ
tyaktvā dehaṁ punar janma
naiti mām eti so 'rjuna

> "One who knows the transcendental nature of my appearance and activities does not, upon leaving the body, take his birth again in this material world, but attains my eternal abode, O Arjuna."
> —*Bhagavad-gītā As It Is* 4.9

This is the ultimate goal and resting place, the fulfilment of all desires, and the perfection of human life.

APPENDICES

Conclusion

As Vedic teachings explain, married couples who pursue their *dharma*, and pursue *artha* and *kāma* according to *dharma*, can live happily together and ultimately attain *mokṣa*. *Varṇāśrama-dharma* is all-encompassing and all-accomodating. It takes into account all the varieties of material conditioning that bind souls to the material world, and provides a way forward for every human being. Any difficulties that may be encountered in a marital relationship, due to our material conditioning, can be resolved by taking shelter of the divine teachings of the Vedic literatures.

The Vedic scriptures prescribe codes of *dharma* for all human beings, according to *varṇa* and *āśrama*, for their material and spiritual benefit. While these codes of behaviour were widely taught and practised in Vedic society, in modern society they have become neglected. Nevertheless, even more important than the details of *varṇāśrama-dharma* are the principles that they are meant to support. Rūpa Gosvāmī warns against the two faces of *niyamāgraha*. One is to neglect scriptural codes of conduct and the other is to follow them without understanding the principles behind them. (*The Nectar of Instruction* 2). If we learn to understand and practise the main principles of *sanātana-dharma*, or service to God, then the details of *varṇāśrama-dharma*, which are meant to support those principles, will gradually fall into place. All scriptural rules are servants to the mother of all instructions, which is to always remember God and never forget Him. For attaining this stage of perfection, the Lord offers us a gradual process. Kṛṣṇa tells Arjuna in *Bhagavad-gītā*:

> "My dear Arjuna, O winner of wealth, if you cannot fix your mind upon Me without deviation, then follow the regulative principles of *bhakti-yoga*. In this way develop a desire to attain Me. If you cannot practice the regulations of *bhakti-yoga*, then just try to work for Me, because by working for Me you will come to the perfect stage. If, however, you are unable to work in this consciousness of Me, then try to act giving up all results of your work and try to be self-situated. If you cannot take to this practice, then engage yourself in the cultivation of knowledge. Better than knowledge, however, is meditation, and better than meditation is renunciation of the fruits of action, for by such renunciation one can attain peace of mind."
>
> *Bhagavad-gītā As It Is* 12.9-12

Spiritual life begins with *jñāna-yoga*, the cultivation of spiritual knowledge, then *dhyāna-yoga*, meditation, then *karma-yoga*, renunciation of the fruits of action. People can begin to develop renunciation simply by giving in charity to the poor and needy. The next stage is to offer the results of work to God; the next is to follow the regulative principles of *bhakti-yoga*, devotional service; and the next is to fix the mind upon the Lord without deviation, which is the highest religious principle. Just as we can engage in any of these processes of *yoga*, according to our capacity, and make spiritual advancement, similarly we can follow any of the guiding principles for householders, as described in this book, according to what is possible for us, and reap the benefit. *Varṇāśrama-dharma* supports and nourishes the practice of *yoga*. The attainment of spiritual perfection may be a gradual process, but whatever advancement we make on the path is never lost.

> "In this endeavour there is no loss or diminution, and a little advancement on this path can protect one from the most dangerous type of fear."
>
> *Bhagavad-gītā As It Is* 2.40

The main principles prescribed by Śrī Caitanya Mahāprabhu for householders are simply to chant the holy names of the Lord and to serve Him and His devotees wherever possible. Couples who chant the holy names of the Lord with sincerity naturally develop a genuine mood of service towards the Lord and His devotees and, as a result, their relationships, both with God and with each other, become harmonious and loving.

HARE KṚṢṆA, HARE KṚṢṆA, KṚṢṆA KṚṢṆA, HARE HARE;
HARE RĀMA, HARE RĀMA, RĀMA RĀMA, HARE HARE.

Glossary

Ācārya—a spiritual master who teaches religious principles for all human beings by his own example.

Adhikārī—a qualified devotee; honourific suffix for a *gṛhastha.*

Advaita Prabhu—Advaitācārya, an incarnation of Lord Mahā-Viṣṇu, who appeared as one of the four principal associates of Lord Caitanya Mahāprabhu.

Ambarīṣa Mahārāja—a great devotee-king who perfectly executed all nine devotional practices (hearing, chanting, etc.)

Anusūyā—the wife of Atri Muni (one of the seven great sages born directly from Brahmā) and the mother of Lord Dattātreya.

Ānanda—transcendental spiritual bliss.

Ārati—a ceremony in which one greets and worships the Deity by offering Him various items such as incense, ghee lamp, camphor lamp, water, cloth, flowers, and fan, accompanied by bell-ringing and chanting.

Arcana—the procedures followed for worshipping the *arcā-vigraha*, the Deity in the temple.

Arci—the wife of King Pṛthu (the empowered incarnation of the Lord who demonstrated how to be an ideal ruler).

Artha—economic development.

Āryan—a follower of Vedic culture.

Āśrama—one of the four spiritual orders of life; a place where spiritual practices are executed.

Balarāma (Baladeva)—the first plenary expansion of the Supreme Personality of Godhead, Lord Kṛṣṇa. He appeared as the son of Rohiṇī and elder brother of Lord Kṛṣṇa.

Bhagavad-gītā—a seven-hundred verse record of a conversation between Lord Kṛṣṇa and His disciple, Arjuna, from the *Bhīṣma Parva* of the *Mahābhārata* of Vedavyāsa. It contains the essence of all Vedic knowledge.

Bhakti—pure loving devotion.

Bhakti-rasāmṛta-sindhu—one of the principal works on the science of *bhakti-yoga,* written in the sixteenth century by Śrīla Rūpa Gosvāmī, a confidential associate of Śrī Caitanya Mahāprabhu.

Bhakti-yoga—the process of engaging the senses in devotional service to the Supreme Personality of Godhead.

Bhaktisiddhānta Sarasvatī Ṭhākura—(1874-1937) the spiritual master of A.C. Bhaktivedanta Swami Prabhupāda and the son of Bhaktivinoda Ṭhākura, he founded the Gauḍīya Maṭha and established Lord Caitanya's teachings throughout India. He authored many erudite works on the science of *bhakti.*

Bhaktivedanta Swami Prabhupāda, A.C.—(1896-1977) disciple of Bhaktisiddhānta Sarasvatī and founder-*ācārya* of the International Society for Krishna Consciousness (ISKCON), Bhaktivedanta Swami Prabhupāda descends from the ancient line of spiritual masters known as the

Brahma-Madhva-Gauḍīya-*sampradāya*. He is the author of more than eighty books, including translations and summary studies of classical Vedic scriptures, together with detailed purports and commentaries. At the age of sixty-nine years, Śrīla Prabhupāda travelled from India to USA to introduce Kṛṣṇa consciousness to the Western world. In the last twelve years of his life, he circled the globe fourteen times on lecture tours and developed ISKCON into a thriving worldwide community of temples, farms, schools, and restaurants.

Bhaktivinoda Ṭhākura—(1838-1914) the father of Bhaktisiddhānta Sarasvatī, Bhaktivinoda Ṭhākura was a magistrate and a householder. He revived the mission of Caitanya Mahāprabhu in the nineteenth century and wrote approximately one hundred books.

Bhavabhūti—an eighth century scholar of India noted for his plays and poetry, written in Sanskrit.

Bilvamaṅgala Ṭhākura—a great devotee-author, whose works include the *Kṛṣṇa-karṇāmṛta*, the confidential pastimes of Lord Kṛṣṇa.

Brahmā—the first created living being and secondary creator of the material universe. Directed by Lord Viṣṇu, he creates all life forms in the universes. He also rules the mode of passion.

Brāhma-muhūrta—the auspicious period of the day just before dawn, from one and a half hours to fifty minutes before sunrise, which is especially favourable for spiritual practices.

Brahma-saṁhitā—an ancient Sanskrit scripture recording the prayers of Brahmā offered to the Supreme Lord Govinda, recovered from a temple in South India by Lord Caitanya.

Brahmacārī—a celibate student under the care of a spiritual master.

Brahman—the *vastu*, actual substance of the world: 1) Viṣṇu as the Supreme Soul (*paraṁ brahman*), 2) the individual self as the subordinate soul (*jīva-brahman*), and 3) matter as creative nature (*mahad-brahman*).

Brāhmaṇa—a member of the intellectual, priestly class; a person situated in goodness and knowledgeable of Brahman, the Absolute Truth.

Caitanya Mahāprabhu—(1486-1534) Lord Kṛṣṇa in the aspect of His own devotee. He appeared in Navadvīpa, West Bengal, and inaugurated the *yuga-dharma* of *saṅkīrtana* (congregational chanting of the holy names of the Lord) to revive pure love of God.

Caitanya-bhāgavata—one of the earliest biographies of Lord Caitanya, by Vṛndāvana dāsa Ṭhākura, in which he especially describes Caitanya Mahāprabhu's early pastimes.

Caitanya-caritāmṛta—the authorised biography of Caitanya Mahāprabhu written in the late sixteenth century by Kṛṣṇadāsa Kavirāja Gosvāmī.

Cāṇakya Paṇḍita—the *brāhmaṇa* advisor to King Candragupta, responsible for checking Alexander the Great's invasion of India. He is a famous author of books containing aphorisms on politics and morality.

Dāna—charity.

Dāsa—servant; term used as addition to the name of an initiated disciple, meaning servant of Kṛṣṇa.

Deity—a form of God as represented in stone, metal, wood or as a painted picture, through which He accepts the service of His devotees.

Demigods—universal controllers and residents of the higher planets; *jīvas* whom the *īśvara* empowers to represent Him in the management of the universe.

Devahūti—the daughter of Svāyambhuva Manu, wife of Kardama Muni, and mother of the Lord's incarnation as Kapiladeva.

Dharma—religious principles; one's natural occupation; the capacity to render service, which is the essential quality of a living being.

Dhruva Mahārāja—a great devotee who at the age of five performed severe austerities and propitiated the Supreme Personality of Godhead; ruler of the Pole Star.

Diti—wife of Kaśyapa Muni and mother of the demons Hiraṇyākṣa and Hiraṇyakaśipu.

Draupadī—the daughter of King Drupada and wife of the Pāṇḍavas.

Dvārakā—the island kingdom of Lord Kṛṣṇa; the capital city of the Yadus.

Ekādaśī—the eleventh day after both the full and new moon when abstinence from grains and beans is prescribed.

False ego—*ahaṅkāra* in Sanskrit, the soul's misidentification with matter.

Gadādhara Paṇḍita—a close associate of Śrī Caitanya Mahāprabhu, representing the internal energy of the Lord.

Gajendra—the king of the elephants. He was saved from a crocodile by Lord Viṣṇu and awarded liberation.

Gāndhārī—daughter of King Subala of Gāndhāra and wife of King Dhṛtarāṣṭra. When she found out that her future husband was blind, she voluntarily blindfolded herself for the rest of her life.

Garbhādhāna-saṁskāra—the Vedic ceremony of purification to be performed by parents before conceiving a child.

Gauḍiya Vaiṣṇava—a Vaiṣṇava who follows the teachings of Lord Caitanya.

Gauḍīya Vaiṣṇava *sampradāya*—the authorised Vaiṣṇava disciplic succession of bona fide spiritual masters coming through Śrīla Madhvācārya and Śrī Caitanya Mahāprabhu; the followers in that tradition.

Gaurakiśora dāsa Bābājī—(1838-1915) disciple of Bhaktivinoda Ṭhākura and initiating spiritual master of Bhaktisiddhānta Sarasvatī Ṭhākura. He was a great renunciate who spent most of his life in Vṛndāvana and Navadvīpa absorbed in chanting the Hare Kṛṣṇa *mahā-mantra*.

Gāyatrī—the mother of the *Vedas*.

Gāyatrī *mantra*—a sacred *mantra* that a *brāhmaṇa* chants silently three times a day at sunrise, noon and sunset, to attain the transcendental platform; the Vedic *mantra* that delivers one from material entanglement.

Godhead—the ultimate source of all energies.

Goloka Vṛndāvana —Kṛṣṇaloka; the highest planet in the spiritual world; Lord Kṛṣṇa's personal abode.

Gopāla Bhaṭṭa Gosvāmī—one of the Six Gosvāmīs of Vṛndāvana, who directly followed Śrī Caitanya Mahāprabhu and systematically presented His teachings. Gopāla Bhaṭṭa assisted Sanātana Gosvāmī in his writing.

Gopīs—cowherd girls; Kṛṣṇa's cowherd girlfriends, who are His most surrendered and confidential devotees.

Gosvāmī—a person who has his senses under full control; the title of a person in the renounced order of life, *sannyāsa*.

Govinda—name of the Supreme Lord Kṛṣṇa, 'One who gives pleasure to the land, the cows and the senses.'

Gṛhamedhi—materialistic householder.

Gṛhastha—one who marries and raises a family in God consciousness; regulated householder living according to the Vedic social system.

Guṇas—the three modes, or qualities, of material nature: goodness, passion, and ignorance.

Guru—spiritual master. Literally, this term means 'heavy'. The spiritual master is called *guru* because he is heavy with knowledge.

Gurukula—a school of Vedic learning where boys live as celibate students, guided by a spiritual master.

Hare Kṛṣṇa *mahā-mantra* —a sixteen-word prayer composed of the names Hare, Kṛṣṇa, and Rāma: Hare Kṛṣṇa, Hare Kṛṣṇa, Kṛṣṇa Kṛṣṇa, Hare Hare; Hare Rāma, Hare Rāma, Rāma Rāma, Hare Hare. Hare is the Lord's internal energy, His eternal consort, Śrīmatī Rādhārāṇī. Kṛṣṇa, 'the all-attractive,' and Rāma, 'the reservoir of all pleasure,' are names of God.

Haridāsa Ṭhākura—born in a Muslim family, he was a confidential associate of Caitanya Mahāprabhu. He used to chant 300,000 names of the Lord daily. Lord Caitanya made him *nāmācārya*, the topmost exemplary teacher of the chanting of the holy names.

Heavenly planets—the higher planets of the universe, residences of the demigods.

Hell—hellish planets within this universe meant for the punishment and rectification of the sinful.

Hindu—an adopted term for Indian people who follow Vedic culture.

Hinduism—This term is derived from the name of a river in present-day Pakistan, the Sindhu, Sind or Indus. Beginning around 1000 AD, invading armies from the Middle East called the place beyond the Sindhu river 'Hindustan' and the people who lived there the 'Hindus'. (Due to the invaders' language, the 's' was changed to 'h'.)

Hiraṇyakaśipu—a powerful demon who tormented his son, the great devotee Prahlāda Mahārāja, and was killed by the

Supreme Lord in His incarnation as Nṛsiṁhadeva (the half-man half-lion form).

Hiraṇyākṣa—the demoniac son of Kaśyapa and brother of Hiraṇyakaśipu, who was killed by Lord Varāha (the boar incarnation of the Lord).

Hṛṣīkeśa—a name of God meaning 'the master of the senses.'

ISKCON—abbreviation for the International Society for Krishna Consciousness; the Hare Krishna Movement; a worldwide non-sectarian movement dedicated to propagating the teachings of the *Vedas* for the benefit of mankind. ISKCON was founded in New York, 1966, by Śrīla A.C. Bhaktivedanta Swami Prabhupāda, who travelled by boat from Calcutta with just forty rupees and a trunk full of books

Īśopaniṣad—one of the 108 Vedic scriptures known as the *Upaniṣads*.

Japa—the soft recitation of the Lord's holy names as a private meditation, with the aid of 108 prayer beads.

Jīva (jīvātmā)—the living entity, who is an eternal soul, individual but part and parcel of the Supreme Lord.

Jñāna—knowledge.

Kali-yuga—the present age, known as 'the age of quarrel and hypocrisy'; the fourth and last age in the cycle of a *mahā-yuga*. It began 5,000 years ago and lasts for a total of 432,000 years.

Kāma—lust; the desire to gratify the bodily senses.

Kapila—an incarnation of God who appeared in Satya-yuga as the son of Devahūti and Kardama Muni and expounded the devotional *sāṅkhya* philosophy, the analysis of matter and spirit, as a means of cultivating devotional service to the Lord.

Kardama Muni—the father of Lord Kapila and one of the chief forefathers of the population of the universe.

Karma—work; activity; actions that incur reactions binding us to the material world.

Karma-yoga—action in devotional service; the path of God realisation through dedicating the fruits of one's work to God.

Kīrtana—glorification of the Supreme Lord; the narrating or singing of the holy names and glories of the Supreme Personality of Godhead.

Kṛṣṇa—the 'all-attractive'; the name of the original, two-armed form of the Supreme Lord, who is the source of all incarnations. The sublime youth who herds millions of cows in the forest of Vṛndāvana and dances with millions of cowherd girls (*gopīs*).

Kṛṣṇa the Supreme Personality of Godhead—a summary study by Bhaktivedanta Swami Prabhupāda of the *Tenth Canto* of *Śrīmad Bhāgavatam.*

Kṣatriya—a warrior who is inclined to fight and lead others; the administrative or protective occupation.

Kuntī—the mother of the Pāṇḍavas and aunt of Lord Kṛṣṇa.

Kuru—the founder of the dynasty in which the Pāṇḍavas, as well as their archrivals, the sons of Dhṛtarāṣṭra, took birth.

Kurukṣetra—a holy place due to the penances of King Kuru. Situated about ninety miles north of New Delhi, it was here that the great *Mahābhārata* war was fought and Lord Kṛṣṇa spoke the *Bhagavad-gītā* to Arjuna.

Lakṣmī—the goddess of fortune and eternal consort of the Supreme Lord Nārayaṇa.

Madana—Cupid; the demigod who incites lusty desires in the living beings.

Madana-mohana—a name of Kṛṣṇa meaning 'He who charms Cupid'.

Mahābhārata—an ancient, Sanskrit, epic history composed by Kṛṣṇa Dvaipāyana Vyāsadeva, the literary incarnation of Godhead, in 100,000 verses. *Mahabhārata* is a history of the earth from its creation to the great Kurukṣetra war.

Mahāprabhu—supreme master of all masters; Lord Caitanya.

Mahārāja—king, ruler; term of respect, also offered to a *sannyāsī*.

Mahātmā—'great soul'; broad-minded merciful person; great devotee of the Lord.

Mandodarī—the chief wife of the demon king Rāvaṇa.

Maṅgala-arati—the daily predawn worship ceremony honouring the Deity of the Supreme Lord.

Mantra—(*man*-'mind' + *tra*-'deliverance'); a pure sound vibration that delivers the mind from illusion and fear; a prayer or chant.

Manu—Svayambhuva Manu, a son of Brahmā and the

original father and lawgiver of the human race; also, a generic name for any of the fourteen universal rulers, also known as *manvantara-avatāras*, who appear in each day of Lord Brahmā.

Manu-saṁhitā—the scriptural lawbook for human society, written by Manu.

Māyā—'that which is not', unreality, deception, forgetfulness, material illusion; the external energy of the Supreme Lord, which deludes the living entities into forgetfulness of Him.

Māyāvāda—the impersonal philosophy propounded by Śaṅkarācārya, which proposes the unqualified oneness of God and the living entities (who are both conceived of as being ultimately formless) and the non-reality of manifest nature.

Modes of nature—the three *guṇas*, or modes of material nature: goodness (*sattva-guṇa*), passion (*rajo-guṇa*) and ignorance (*tamo-guṇa*). They make possible our mental, emotional and physical experiences of the universe.

Mokṣa—liberation from material bondage.

Muhūrta—a period of forty-eight minutes.

Mukunda—a name of Kṛṣṇa meaning 'the giver of liberation'.

Muni—a sage or self-realised soul.

Nārada Muni—a pure devotee of the Lord, one of the sons of Lord Brahmā, who travels throughout the universes in his eternal body, delivering the science of *bhakti*.

Nārāyaṇa—a name of the majestic four-armed form of the Supreme Personality of Godhead meaning 'He who is the source and goal of all living entities'.

Narottama dāsa Ṭhākura—a renowned Vaiṣṇava spiritual master in the disciplic succession from Śrī Caitanya Mahāprabhu, famous for his many compositions of devotional songs.

Navadvīpa—a holy place, ninety miles north of Calcutta, where Lord Caitanya appeared in the late 15th century.

Nectar of Devotion, The—summary study by Bhaktivedanta Swami Prabhupāda of Rūpa Gosvāmī's *Bhakti-rasāmṛta-sindhu*.

Nectar of Instruction, The—summary study by Bhaktivedanta Swami Prabhupāda of Rūpa Gosvāmī's *Upadeśāmṛta*.

Nityānanda Prabhu—the incarnation of Lord Balarāma (Kṛṣṇa's brother) who appeared as the principal associate of Śrī Caitanya Mahāprabhu.

Niyamāgraha—either rejecting rules and regulations (*niyama-agraha*) or following them fanatically without understanding the goal (*niyama-āgraha*).

Padma Purāṇa—one of the eighteen *Purāṇas*, or Vedic historical narratives, it consists of a conversation between Lord Śiva and his wife, Pārvatī.

Pañca-tattva—'five truths'; the Absolute Truth in five features; the Supreme Lord Caitanya Mahāprabhu, His expansion Nityānanda Prabhu, His incarnation Advaita

Prabhu, His energy Gadādhara Paṇḍita, and His devotee Śrīvāsa Ṭhākura.

Pāṇḍavas—the five sons of Pāṇḍu: Yudhiṣṭhira, Bhīma, Arjuna, Nakula, and Sahadeva. They were intimate friends of Lord Kṛṣṇa and inherited the leadership of the world upon their victory over the Kurus in the Battle of Kurukṣetra.

Paṇḍita—a learned scholar.

Pārvatī—Lord Śiva's consort, meaning daughter of the mountain. Satī was reborn as Pārvatī, the daughter of Himālaya, after consuming herself in mystic fire at Dakṣa's sacrificial arena.

Prabhu—master.

Prabhupāda—one who resides at the feet of the Supreme Master and at whose feet all masters sit.

Prahlāda Maharāja—a great devotee who was persecuted by his atheistic father, Hiraṇyakaśipu, and saved by the Lord in the form of Nṛsiṁhadeva.

Prajalpa—idle talk on mundane subjects.

Prasāda—'mercy'; vegetarian food that has been offered to God with love and devotion and becomes spiritualised and purifying, free from *karma.*

Prema—love, especially love of Kṛṣṇa; real love of God, the highest perfectional goal of life.

Priyavrata—son of Svāyambhuva Manu.

Pūjā—offering of worship.

Purāṇa—literally, very old.

Purāṇas—the eighteen major and eighteen minor ancient Vedic literatures that are histories of this and other planets.

Puruṣārtha—goals of human life.

Rādhārāṇī—Lord Kṛṣṇa's eternal consort, His merciful feminine counterpart. She appeared in Vṛndāvana as the daughter of King Vṛsabhānu and Kirtida-devī.

Rajo-guṇa—the material mode of passion.

Rāma—name of the Supreme Lord as the source of unlimited pleasure; incarnation of Lord Rāmacandra as a perfect, righteous king, who appeared in Ayodhyā in the Tretā-yuga.

Rāmāyaṇa—the epic poem by sage Vālmīki, which recounts the pastimes of Lord Rāmacandra.

Rāsa—mellow, or the sweet taste of a relationship, especially between the Lord and His devotees.

***Rāsa* dance**—Lord Kṛṣṇa's pleasure dance with the cowherd maidens of Vṛndāvana. It is a pure exchange of spiritual love between the Lord and His most confidential devotees.

Rāvaṇa—the powerful ten-headed demon king of Laṅkā who kidnapped Sītā-devī and was killed by her husband, the Supreme Lord in His form of Rāmacandra.

Ṛṣabhadeva—an incarnation of the Supreme Lord as a devotee king who, after instructing his sons in spiritual life, renounced His kingdom for a life of austerity.

Rukmiṇī—Lord Kṛṣṇa's principal queen in Dvārakā.

Rūpa Gosvāmī—chief of the six Gosvāmīs of Vṛndāvana, he extensively researched the scriptures and wrote books establishing the philosophy taught by Lord Caitanya on an unshakable foundation. He is known as the *rasācārya*, the 'teacher of devotional mellows'.

Śālagrāma-śilā—a Deity of the Supreme Lord in the form of a round sacred stone, found under the current of the Gandhaki river in the Himālayas.

Saṁhitās—supplementary Vedic literatures expressing the conclusions of self-realised authorities.

Sampradāya—a disciplic succession of spiritual masters, along with the followers in that tradition, through which spiritual knowledge is transmitted; school of thought.

Saṁskāra—Vedic reformatory rituals performed from the time of conception until death for purifying a human being.

Sanātana—eternal, having no beginning or end.

Sanātana-dharma—the eternal activity of the soul, or the eternal religion of the living being, to render service to the Supreme Lord.

Sanātana Gosvāmī—one of the Six Gosvāmīs of Vṛndāvana. He was the older brother of Rūpa Gosvāmī, who regarded Sanātana Gosvāmī as his spiritual master.

Saṅkīrtana—congregational chanting of the holy names of the Supreme Personality of Godhead, usually accompanied by hand cymbals (*karatālas*) and clay *mṛdaṅga* drums.

Sannyāsa—the renounced order, which is free from family relationships and in which all activities are completely dedicated to God. It is the order of ascetics who travel and preach for the benefit of all.

Sannyāsī—one in the *sannyāsa* (renounced) order.

Sanskrit—the ancient classical language in which the *Vedas* were written; also known as *devanāgarī*, the divine language of the demigods.

Śāstra—Vedic scriptures, the instructions of liberated souls, meant to guide the activities of human society. *Śās* means 'to regulate and direct' and *tra* means 'an instrument'.

Satī—the wife of Lord Śiva and daughter of Dakṣa, who self-immolated when her father insulted her husband.

Satī—chastity.

Sattva-guṇa—the material mode of goodness, predominated by Lord Viṣṇu.

Satyabhāmā—one of the principal queens of Lord Kṛṣṇa during His pastimes in the city of Dvārakā.

Śikṣā-guru—an instructing spiritual master.

Sītā—the chaste wife and beloved consort of Lord Rāmacandra.

Śiva—the demigod who is the superintendent of the mode of ignorance (*tamoguṇa*) and who takes charge of destroying the universe at the time of annihilation.

Śrī—Lakṣmīdevī, consort of Lord Viṣṇu; honourific prefix, used before the name of the Lord or an exalted personality.

Śrīla—title indicating possession of exceptional spiritual qualities.

Śrīmad Bhāgavatam—the foremost of the eighteen *Purāṇas*, also known as the *Bhāgavata Purāṇa*; a work of eighteen thousand verses compiled by sage Vyāsa as his natural commentary on the *Vedānta-sūtra*.

Srīvāsa Ṭhākura—the reincarnation of Nārada Muni in Lord Caitanya's pastimes; an intimate associate of Lord Caitanya. His home served as the birthplace of Lord Caitanya's *saṅkīrtana* movement.

Strī—woman.

Sudāmā Brāhmaṇa—a poor householder friend of Lord Kṛṣṇa who was given immeasurable riches by the Lord.

Śuddha-sattva—the spiritual platform of pure goodness.

Śūdra—a member of the labourer, artisan and servant class in the traditional Vedic social system.

Sunīti—the mother of Dhruva Mahārāja.

Supersoul—the localised aspect of the Supreme Lord residing in the heart of every living entity and in every atom. From Him come the living entity's knowledge, remembrance and forgetfulness. The Supersoul is the witness and permitter of *karma*.

Svadharma—specific duties of a particular body performed in accordance with religious principles in order to achieve liberation.

Svāyambhuva Manu—the Manu who appears first in Brahmā's day and who is the grandfather of Dhruva Mahārāja.

Tamo-guṇa—of the three modes of material nature, *tamo-guṇa* is the mode of ignorance, or darkness.

Tapasya—austerity; voluntary acceptance of hardship for spiritual benefit.

Tulasī—a pure devotee in the form of a plant, held sacred by the Vaiṣṇavas and very dear to Śrī Kṛṣṇa. Her leaves and *mañjarīs* (buds) are placed on offerings of food and water to Deities of the Supreme Lord, as well as on Their lotus feet. *Tulasī* wood is used to make neckbeads and chanting beads for devotees.

Upadeśāmṛta—'The Nectar of Instruction', a short Sanskrit work by Śrīla Rūpa Gosvāmī containing the essence of instructions on devotional service.

Upaniṣads—one hundred and eight Sanskrit treatises that embody the philosophy of the *Vedas*. The term *upaniṣad* literally means 'that which is learned by sitting close to the teacher'.

Vaikuṇṭha—literally 'the place with no anxiety', the spiritual world.

Vaiśya—member of the mercantile or agricultural class, according to the *varṇāśrama* social system.

Vairāgya—renunciation; detachment from matter.

Vaiṣṇava—a devotee of the Supreme Lord Viṣṇu, or Kṛṣṇa.

Vālmīki—author of the original *Rāmāyaṇa*, the epic history of the earthly pastimes of Lord Rāma and Sītādevī.

Vana—forest.

Vānaprastha—the third *āśrama*, retired life, in which a husband and wife travel together to holy places.

Varṇa—the four Vedic occupational divisions of society, distinguished by quality of work and situation within the modes of nature (*guṇas*).

Varṇāśrama-dharma—religious principles according to the four social and four spiritual orders established in the Vedic scriptures.

Vedānta-sūtra—Vyāsadeva's conclusive summary of Vedic philosophical knowledge, written in brief codes.

Vedas—the original *Veda*, divided by Śrīla Vyāsadeva into the four *Saṁhitās* (*Ṛg, Sāma, Atharva* and *Yajur*), and the 108 *Upaniṣads*, *Mahābhārata*, *Vedānta-sūtra*, etc. The word *veda* literally means 'knowledge', and in a wider sense refers to all literatures that are in harmony with the philosophical conclusions found in the original four Vedic *Saṁhitās* and *Upaniṣads*.

Vedic—based on the tenets of the *Vedas*.

Viṣṇu—literally 'the all-pervading God'; the Supreme Personality of Godhead in His four-armed form in Vaikuṇṭha; a plenary expansion of the original Supreme Personality of Godhead, Śrī Kṛṣṇa.

Vivāha-yajña—wedding sacrifice; marriage.

Vṛndāvana—Kṛṣṇa's eternal abode, where He fully manifests His quality of sweetness; the village on earth where He enacted His childhood pastimes.

Vyāsadeva—the literary incarnation of God and compiler of the original Vedic scriptures.

Yadu—one of the sons of King Yayāti; the founder of the Yadu dynasty.

Yajña—sacrifice.

Yāmunācārya—a great Vaiṣṇava spiritual master and author in the Śrī-*sampradāya* (one of the four bona-fide Vaiṣṇava *sampradāyas*.)

Yayāti—the king who was cursed by Śukrācārya to prematurely accept old age.

Yoga—'link'; a process of self-discipline meant for linking one's consciousness with the Supreme Lord.

Yogī—one who practises one of the authorised processes of *yoga*.

Yuga—the four ages of the universe, Satya-yuga, Treta-yuga, Dvāpara-yuga and Kali-yuga, which differ in length and rotate in a cycle.

Yukta-vairāgya—the process of renunciation by engaging everything in the service of the Supreme Lord.

Index

Bibliography

Bhaktisiddhānta Sarasvatī Gosvāmī. *Śrī Brahma-saṁhitā.* Madras: The Madras Law Journal Press, 1932

Bhaktivedanta Swami Prabhupāda, A.C.—
Beyond Illusion and Doubt. Mumbai: The Bhaktivedanta Book Trust, 1999

Bhagavad-gītā As It Is. Los Angeles: Bhaktivedanta Book Trust, 1983

Conversations with Śrīla Prabhupāda. Los Angeles: Bhaktivedanta Book Trust, 1988

KṚṢṆA The Supreme Personality of Godhead. Los Angeles: Bhaktivedanta Book Trust, 1972

Letters from Śrīla Prabhupāda. Los Angeles: The Vaisnava Institute, 1987

Śrīmad Bhāgavatam. Bombay: Bhaktivedanta Book Trust, 1987

Śrī Īśopaniṣad. Los Angeles: ISKCON Books, 1969

Śrī Caitanya-caritāmṛta. Los Angeles: Bhaktivedanta Book Trust, 1973

Songs of the Vaiṣṇava Ācāryas. Mumbai: The Bhaktivedanta Book Trust, 1991

Teachings of Queen Kuntī. Los Angeles: Bhaktivedanta Book Trust, 1978

The Bhaktivedanta Vedabase. Windows 98 XP Pro version. The Bhaktivedanta Book Trust International, Inc., 2003

The Nectar of Devotion. Los Angeles: Bhaktivedanta Book Trust, 1970

The Nectar of Instruction. Los Angeles: Bhaktivedanta Book Trust, 1975

The Quest for Enlightenment. Los Angeles: Bhaktivedanta Book Trust, 1997

Bhaktivinoda Ṭhākura—
Śrī Bhaktyāloka. Vrindaban: Vrajaraj Press, 1996

Sri Harinama Cintamani. Bombay: Bhaktivedanta Books, 1990

Buhler, George. *The Laws of Manu*. Delhi: Banarsidass, (Reprint from Oxford University's 1886 edition) 1984

Chandrasekharan, K. & V.H Brahmasri Subrahmanya Sastri. *Sanskrit Literature*. Bombay: The International Book House Ltd., 1951

Dutt, Romesh. *Indian Poetry*. London: J.M. Dent & Co., 1905

Ganguli, Kisari Mohan. *The Mahabharata of Krishna-Dwaipayana Vyasa* (1883-96). Delhi: Munshiram Manoharlal Publishers Pvt. Ltd., 2004

Gopāla Bhaṭṭa Gosvāmī. *Sat-kriyā-sāra-dīpika.* Mayapur: Bhaktivedanta Academy, 1997

Goswami, Chimmanlal. *Śrīmad Vālmīki-Rāmāyaṇa.* Gorakhpur: Gita Press, 1969

Hridayānanda dāsa Goswami and Gopīparāṇadhana dāsa Adhikārī. *Śrīmad Bhāgavatam (Tenth Canto* and *Eleventh Canto).* Los Angeles: Bhaktivedanta Book Trust, 1988

Karṇāmṛta dāsa Adhikārī. *Bābājī Mahārāja.* Washington: New Jaipur Press, 1990

Knapp, Stephen. *Death of the Aryan Invasion Theory.* www.stephen-knapp.com

Patita Pāvana dāsa Adhikārī and Pt. V. Badaryana Murthy. *Śrī Cāṇakya Nīti-śāstra.* Unpublished manuscript

Rūpa Gosvāmī. *Padyāvalī.* Vrindaban: Rasabihari Lal & Sons, 2007

Rūpa Vilāsa dāsa Adhikārī. A *Ray of Viṣṇu.* Mumbai: Sri Sri Sitaram Seva Trust, 1998

Swami Krishnapada. *Spiritual Warrior II.* Washington: Hari-Nama Press, 1998

Guide to Sanskrit Pronunciation

The *devanāgarī* alphabet consists of forty-eight characters, including thirteen vowels and thirty-five consonants.

Vowels. The short vowel **a** is pronounced like the **u** in b**u**t, long **ā** like the **a** in f**a**r, short **i** as in p**i**n, long **ī** as in p**i**que, short **u** as in p**u**ll, long **ū** as in r**u**le. The vowel **ṛ** is pronounced like the **ri** in **ri**m. The vowel **e** is pronounced as in th**ey**, **ai** as in **ai**sle, **o** as in g**o**, **au** as in h**ow**. The *anusvāra* **ṁ**, which is a pure nasal, is pronounced like the **n** in the French word *bo***n**. The *visarga* **ḥ**, which is a strong aspirate, is pronounced as a final **h** sound. At the end of a couplet **aḥ** is pronounced like **aha**, and **iḥ** like **ihi**.

Consonants. The guttural consonants, **k, kh, g, gh,** and **ṅ,** are pronounced from the throat; **k** as in **k**ite, **kh** as in Ec**kh**art, **g** as in **g**ive, **gh** as in di**g h**ard, **ṅ** as in si**ng**. The palatal consonants, **c, ch, j, jh, and ṇ,** are pronounced from the palate with the middle of the tongue; **c** as in **ch**air, **ch** as in staun**ch h**eart, **j** as in **j**oy, **jh** as in he**dgeh**og, **ñ** as in ca**ny**on. The cerebral consonants, **ṭ, ṭh, ḍ, ḍh,** and **ṇ,** are pronounced with the tip of the tongue turned up and drawn back against the dome of the palate; **ṭ** as in **t**ub, **ṭh** as in ligh**t h**eart, **ḍ** as in **d**ove, **ḍh** as in re**d h**ot, and **ṇ** as in **n**ut. The dental consonants, **t, th, d, dh,** and **n**, are pronounced in the same manner as the cerebrals but with the forepart of the tongue against the teeth. The labial consonants, **p, ph, b, bh,** and **m,** are pronounced with the lips; **p** as in **p**ine, **ph** as in u**ph**ill, **b** as in **b**ird, **bh** as in ru**b h**ard, **m** as in **m**other. The semivowels, **y, r, l,** and **v,** are pronounced as in **y**es, **r**un, **l**ight, and **v**ine respectively. The sibilants, **ś, ṣ, and s**, are pronounced, respectively, as in the German word *sprechen* and the English words **sh**ine and **s**un. The letter **h** is pronounced as in **h**ome.

About the Author

Born in Leicestershire, England, in 1953, Jagannātheśvarī devī dāsī (Jane E. Grappa, nee Thomas) graduated from Essex University in 1975 with a BA in Literature. In the same year she travelled to India where she met her spiritual master, Śrīla A.C. Bhaktivedanta Swami Prabhupāda. Jagannātheśvarī studied Vedic philosophy and practised *bhakti-yoga* for fifteen years in ISKCON temples of India, UK, and South Africa. In 1985 she produced a 500-page Souvenir Book to commemorate the opening of the landmark Temple of Understanding in Durban, South Africa. As project Head of Public Relations and Publications, she worked together with local media and Durban Publicity Association to inscribe the temple on the tourist map, as well as editing a monthly newspaper, initiating the 'Food for Life' feeding programme in South Africa, and securing local government permissions for the *Rathayātrā* Festival of the Chariots to be staged as an annual event on Durban beachfront. In 1989 she returned to England where she subsequently married Viśvambhara dāsa (Raffaele Grappa), settled in Hertfordshire and raised two sons, Daujī and Gaurāṅga Kṛpa. Viśvambhara is the UK Minister for BBT Book Distribution and a member of the ISKCON UK Board of Directors. Jagannātheśvarī publishes articles and provides matrimonial services through her website:

www.krishnamarriage.com.

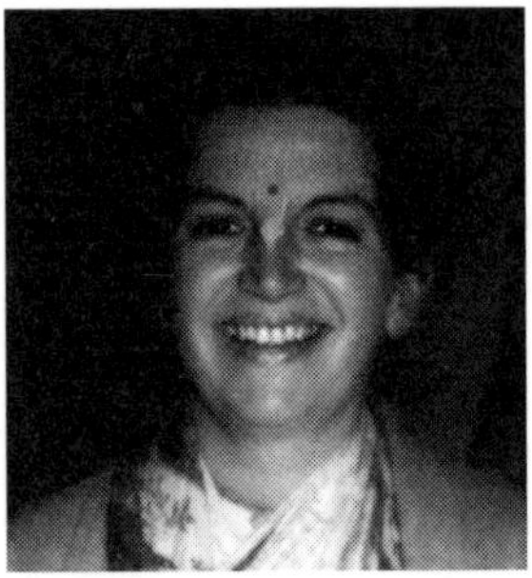

